THE
HASHEESH EATER

THE
HASHEESH EATER

BEING PASSAGES FROM THE

LIFE OF A PYTHAGOREAN

BY FITZ HUGH LUDLOW

"Weave a circle round him thrice,
And close your eyes with holy dread,
For he on honey-dew hath fed,
And drunk the milk of Paradise."

-- Kubla Kahn.

Preface

I like prefaces as little as my readers can. If this so proverbially unnoticed part of the book catch any eye, the glance that it gives will of course travel no farther to find my apology for making this preface a short one. There is but one thought for which I wish to find place here. I am deeply aware that, if the succeeding pages are read at all, it will be by those who have already learned to love De Quincey. Not that I dare for a moment to compare the manner of my narrative with that most wondrous, most inspired Dreamer's; but in the experience of his life and my own there is a single common characteristic which happens to be the very one for whose sake men open any such book. The path of De Quincey led beyond all the boundaries of the ordinary life into a world of intense lights and shadows -- a realm in which all the range of average thought found its conditions surpassed, if not violated. My own career, however far its recital may fall short of the Opium Eater's, and notwithstanding it was not coincident and but seldom parallel with his, still ran through lands as glorious, as unfrequented, as weird as his own, and takes those who would follow it out of the trodden highways of mind. In the most candid and indulgent reader who has come to my story from the perusal of the Confessions, I forsee that there will exist an inevitable tendency to compare the two, to seek resemblances, and perhaps, if such be found, to ascribe them to my at least unconscious imitation of the great, the elder author. How much to my disparagement this would be, my natural desire for the success of this book makes unpleasant to represent even to myself.

If it be possible to forestall such a state of things, let me aim at it by a few brief representations of the manner in which this work has been written.

Frankly do I say that I admire De Quincey to such a degree that, were not imitation base and he inimitable, I know no master of style in whose footsteps I should more earnestly seek to tread; but, in the first place, as this book asserts, it is a resumé of experiences which, so far from being fiction, have received at my hands a delineation unsatisfactory to myself from its very inadequacy. The fact of my speaking truths, so far as they can be spoken, out of my actual memory, must shield me, if the assertion be received by any but one who has tasted my cup of Awakening, from the imputation of being a copyist of incidents.

In the second place, to copy style, study, care, and frequent references to the proposed model are indispensable. Very well; not one of the pages which make this book has ever been rewritten. It has been printed from the first draft, and that, through necessities of other occupation, illness, and care, compelled to be thrown off, though on its author's part unwillingly, currente calamo. Moreover, out of particular jealousy against the risk of burlesquing the inimitable, I have refrained from looking at the Confessions from the beginning to the end of my undertaking

My memory, however, tells me that occasionally there are actual resemblances both in incident and method. As an incident-resemblance, I instance the perception, in both experiences, of the inerasible character of the mind's memorial inscriptions -- as De Quincey grandly has it -- the Palimpsest characteristic of memory. Acknowledging the resemblance, I only say that we both saw the same thing. The state of insight which he attained through opium, I reached by the way of hasheesh. Almost through the very same symbols as De Quincey, a hasheesh-maenad friend of mine also saw it, as this book relates, and the vision is accessible to all of the same temperament and degree of exaltation. For a place, New York for instance, a stranger accounts, not by saying that any one of the many who testify to its existence copied from one another, but by acknowledging "there is such a place." So do I account for the fact by saying "there is such a fact."

As a resemblance in method, by which I mean mechanical arrangement, I am aware only of this, viz., that I divide my narrative into use and abandonment of hasheesh, and speculations upon the phenomena after abandonment, which latter, for the sake of anticipating the charge, I say might perhaps be compared as to its order with Suspiria but the most perfect Zoilus among hypercritics would be aware that in this arrangement I follow Nature, who begins, goes on, and finishes, and reflects the past in her progress, so that I should seem no copyist on that score.

But, at any rate, if influenced by the memory of the great Visionary's method in any sense (and it is true that I might have made my course more dissimilar by neglecting the order of time), I feel that the influence must necessarily have been beneficial to my own efforts.

As the bard who would sing of heroes follows the blind old harper of Ionia along that immortal corridor of resounding song which first made Greece imperishable, and tells his battles in the Epic, not the Elegy, so must every man hereafter, who opens the mysteries of that great soul within him, speak, so far as he can, down the channels through which Thomas de Quincey has spoken, nor out of vain perversity refuse to use a passage which the one grand pioneer has made free to all.

If in any way, therefore, except servilely, I seem to have followed De Quincey, I am proud of it. If there be any man who does not feel the grace which the mantle of that true poet's influence confers upon every thinker and scholar who loves truth, beauty, and the music of the English tongue, I ask that he will transfer unto me his share thereof, and at once the Preface and the Prayer of

THE HASHEESH EATER

The Son of Pythagoras

are ended.

CONTENTS

Introduction

The singular energy and scope of imagination which characterize all Oriental tales, and especially that great typical representative of the species, the Arabian Nights, were my ceaseless marvel from earliest childhood. The book of Arabian and Turkish story has very few thoughtful readers among the nations of the West, who can rest contented with admiring its bold flights into unknown regions of imagery, and close the mystic pages that have enchanted them without an inquiry as to the influences which have turned the human mind into such rare channels of thought. Sooner or later comes the question of the producing causes, and it is in the power of few -- very few of us -- to answer that question aright.

We try to imitate Eastern narrative, but in vain. Our minds can find no clew to its strange, untrodden by-ways of speculation; our highest soarings are still in an atmosphere which feels heavy with the reek and damp of ordinary life. We fail to account for those storm-wrapped peaks of sublimity which hover over the path of Oriental story, or those beauties which, like rivers of Paradise, make music beside it. We are all of us taught to say, "The children of the East live under a sunnier sky than their Western brethren: they are the repositors of centuries of tradition; their semi-civilized imagination is unbound by the fetters of logic and the schools." But the Ionians once answered all these conditions, yet Homer sang no Eblis, no superhuman journey on the wings of genii through infinitudes of rosy ether. At one period of their history, France, Germany and England abounded in all the characteristics of the untutored Old-world mind, yet when did an echo of Oriental music ring from the lute of minstrel, minnesinger, or trouvére? The difference can not be accounted for by climate, religion, or manners. It is not the supernatural in Arabian story which is inexplicable, but the peculiar phase of the supernatural both in beauty and terror.

I say inexplicable, because to me, in common with all around me, it bore this character for years. In later days, I believe, and now with all due modesty assert, I unlocked the secret, not by a hypothesis, not by processes of reasoning, but by journeying through those self-same fields of weird experience which are dinted by the sandals of the glorious old dreamers of the East. Standing on the same mounts of vision where they stood, listening to the same gurgling melody that broke from their enchanted fountains, yes, plunging into their rayless caverns of sorcery, and imprisoned with their genie in the unutterable silence of the fathomless sea, have I dearly bought the right to come to men with the chart of my wanderings in my hands, and unfold to them the foundations of the fabric of Oriental story.

The secret lies in the use of hasheesh. A very few words will suffice to tell what hasheesh is. In northern latitudes the hemp plant (Cannabis Sativa) grows almost entirely to fibre, becoming, in virtue of this quality, the great resource for mats and cordage. Under a southern sun this same plant loses its fibrous texture, but secretes, in quantities equal to one third of its bulk, an opaque and greenish resin. Between the northern and the southern hemp there is no difference, except the effect of diversity of climate upon the same vegetable essence; yet naturalists, misled by the much greater extent of gummy secretion in the latter, have distinguished it from its brother of the colder soil by the name Cannabis Indica. The resin of the Cannabis Indica is hasheesh. From time immemorial it has been known among all the nations of the East as possessing powerful stimulant and narcotic properties; throughout Turkey, Persia, Nepaul, and India it is used at this day among all classes of society as an habitual indulgence. The forms in which it is employed are various. Sometimes it appears in the state in which it exudes from the mature stalk, as a crude resin; sometimes it is manufactured into a conserve with clarified butter, honey, and spices; sometimes a decoction is made of the flowering tops in water or arrack. Under either of these forms the method of administration is by swallowing. Again, the dried plant is smoked in pipes or chewed, as tobacco among ourselves.

Used in whatever preparation, hasheesh is characterized by the most remarkable phenomena, both physical and spiritual. A series of experiments made with it by men of eminent attainments in the medical profession, principally at Calcutta, and during the last ten years, prove it to be capable of inducing all the ordinary symptoms of catalepsy, or even of trance.

However, from the fact of its so extensive daily use as a pleasurable stimulus in the countries where experiments with it have been made, it has doubtless lost interest in the field of scientific research, and has come to be regarded as only one more means among the multitude which mankind in all latitudes are seeking for the production of a sensual intoxication. Now and then a traveler, passing by the bazar where it was exposed for sale, moved by curiosity, has bought some form of the hemp, and made the trial of its effects upon himself; but the results of the experiment were dignified with no further notice than a page or a chapter in the note-book of his journeyings, and the hasheesh phenomena, with an exclamation of wonder, were thenceforward dismissed from his own and the public mind. Very few even of the permanently domesticated foreign residents in the countries of the East have ever adopted this indulgence as a habit, and of those few I am not aware of any who have communicated their experience to the world, or treated it as a subject possessing scientific interest.

My own personal acquaintance with this drug, covering as it did a considerable extent of time, and almost every possible variety of phenomena, both physical and psychological, proper to its operation, not only empowers, but for a long time has been impelling me to give it a publicity which may being it in contact with a larger number of minds interested in such researches than it could otherwise hope to meet. As a key to some of the most singular manifestations of the Oriental mind, as a narrative interesting to the attentive student of the human soul and body, and the mysterious network of interacting influences which connect them, I therefore venture to present this experience to the investigation of general readers, accompanying it with the sincere disavowal of all fiction in my story, and the assurance that whatever traits of the marvelous may appear in its gradual development are inherent in the truth as I shall simply delineate it. I am aware that, without this disavowal, much -- nay, even most that I shall say, will be taken "cum grano salis." I desire it, therefore, to be distinctly understood at the outset that my narrative is one of unexaggerated fact, its occurrences being recorded precisely as they impressed themselves upon me, without one additional stroke of the pencil of an after-fancy thrown in to heighten the tone or harmonize the effect. Whatever of the wonderful may appear in these pages belongs to the subject and not to the manner.

The progress of my narration will be in the order of time. I shall begin with my first experiment of the use of hasheesh, an experiment made simply from the promptings of curiosity; it will then be my endeavor to detail the gradual change of my motive for its employment from the desire of research to the fascinated longing for its weird and immeasurable ecstasy; I shall relate how that ecstasy by degrees became daily more and more flecked with shadows of immeasurable pain, but still, in this dual existence, assumed a character increasingly apocalyptic of utterly unpreconceived provinces of mental action. In the next succeeding stage of my experience, torture, save at rare intervals, will have swallowed up happiness altogether, without abating in the least the fascination of the habit. In the next and final one will be beheld my instantaneous abandonment of the indulgence, the cause which led to it, and the discipline of suffering which attended the self-denial.

The aim of this relation is not merely æsthetic nor scientific: though throughout it there be no stopping to moralize, it is my earnest desire that it may teem with suggestions of a lesson without which humanity can learn nothing in the schools. It is this: the soul withers and sinks from its growth toward the true end of its being beneath the dominance of any sensual indulgence. The chain of its bondage may for a long time continue to be golden -- many a day may pass before the fetters gall -- yet all the while there is going on a slow and insidious consumption of its native strength, and when at last captivity becomes a pain, it may awake to discover in inconceivable terror that the very forces of disenthralment have perished out of its reach.

16

I. The Night Entrance

About the shop of my friend Anderson the apothecary there always existed a peculiar fascination, which early marked it out as my favorite lounging-place. In the very atmosphere of the establishment, loaded as it was with a composite smell of all things curative and preventive, there was an aromatic invitation to scientific musing, which could not have met with a readier acceptance had it spoken in the breath of frankincense. The very gallipots grew gradually to possess a charm for me as they sat calmly ranged upon their oaken shelves, looking like a convention of unostentatious philanthropists, whose silent bosoms teemed with every variety of renovation for the human race. A little sanctum at the inner end of the shop, walled off with red curtains from the profane gaze of the unsanative, contained two chairs for the doctor and myself, and a library where all the masters of physic were grouped, through their sheep and paper representatives, in more friendliness of contact than has ever been known to characterize a consultation of like spirits under any other circumstances. Within the limits of four square feet, Pereira and Christison condensed all their stores of wisdom and research, and Dunglison and Brathwaite sat cheek by jowl beside them. There stood the Dispensatory, with the air of a business-like office, wherein all the specifics of the materia medica had been brought together for a scientific conversazione, but, becoming enamored of each other's society, had resolved to stay, overcrowded though they might be, and make an indefinite sitting of it. In a modest niche, set apart like a vestibule from the apartments of the medical gentlemen, lay a shallow case, which disclosed, on the lifting of a cover, the neatly-ordered rank of tweezers, probe, and lancet, which constituted my friend's claim to the confidence of the plethoric community; for although unblessed with metropolitan fame, he was still no

"Cromwell guiltless of his country's blood."

17

Here many an hour have I sat buried in the statistics of human life or the history of the make-shifts for its preservation. Here the details of surgical or medical experiment have held me in as complete engrossment as the positions and crises of romance; and here especially, with a disregard to my own safety which would have done credit to Quintus Curitus, have I made upon myself the trial of the effects of every strange drug and chemical which the laboratory could produce. Now with the chloroform bottle beneath my nose have I set myself careering upon the wings of a thrilling and accelerating life, until I had just enough power remaining to restore the liquid to its place upon the shelf, and sink back into the enjoyment of the delicious apathy which lasted through the few succeeding moments. Now ether was substituted for chloroform, and the difference of their phenomena noted, and now some other exhilarant, in the form of an opiate or stimulant, was the instrument of my experiments, until I had run through the whole gamut of queer agents within my reach.

In all these experiences research and not indulgence was my object, so that I never became the victim of any habit in the prosecution of my headlong investigations. When the circuit of all the accessible tests was completed, I ceased experimenting, and sat down like a pharmaceutical Alexander, with no more drug-worlds to conquer.

One morning, in the spring of 185-, I dropped in upon the doctor for my accustomed lounge.

"Have you seen," said he, "my new acquisitions?"

I looked toward the shelves in the direction of which he pointed, and saw, added since my last visit, a row of comely pasteboard cylinders inclosing vials of the various extracts prepared by Tilden & Co. Arranged in order according to their size, they confronted me, as pretty a little rank of medicinal sharp-shooters as could gratify the eye of an amateur. I approached the shelves, that I might take them in review.

A rapid glance showed most of them to be old acquaintances." Conium, taraxacum, rhubarb -- ha! what is this? Cannabis Indica?" "That," answered the doctor, looking with a parental fondness upon his new treasure, "is a preparation of the East Indian hemp, a powerful agent in cases of lock- jaw." On the strength of this introduction, I took down the little archer, and, removing his outer verdant coat, began the further prosecution of his acquaintance. To pull out a broad and shallow cork was the work of an instant, and it revealed to me an olive-brown extract, of the consistency of pitch, and a decided aromatic odor. Drawing out a small portion upon the point of my penknife, I was just going to put it to my tongue, when "Hold on!" cried the doctor; "do you want to kill yourself? That stuff is deadly poison." "Indeed!" I replied; "no, I can not say that I have any settled determination of that kind;" and with that I replaced the cork, and restored the extract, with all its appurtenances, to the shelf.

The remainder of my morning's visit in the sanctum was spent in consulting the Dispensatory under the title "Cannabis Indica." The sum of my discoveries there may be found, with much additional information, in that invaluable popular work, Johnston's Chemistry of Common Life. This being universally accessible, I will allude no further to the result of that morning's researches than to mention the three following conclusions to which I came.

First, the doctor was both right and wrong; right, inasmuch as a sufficiently large dose of the drug, if it could be retained in the stomach, would produce death, like any other narcotic, and the ultimate effect of its habitual use had always proved highly injurious to mind and body; wrong, since moderate doses of it were never immediately deadly, and many millions of people daily employed it as an indulgence similarly to opium. Second, it was the hasheesh referred to by Eastern travelers, and the subject of a most graphic chapter from the pen of Bayard Taylor, which months before had moved me powerfully to curiosity and admiration. Third, I would add it to the list of my former experiments.

In pursuance of this last determination, I waited till my friend was out of sight, that I might not terrify him by that which he considered a suicidal venture, and then quietly uncapping my little archer a second time, removed from his store of offensive armor a pill sufficient to balance the ten grain weight of the sanctorial scales. This, upon the authority of Pereira and the Dispensatory, I swallowed without a tremor as to the danger of the result.

Making all due allowance for the fact that I had not taken my hasheesh bolus fasting, I ought to experience its effects with the next four hours. That time elapsed without bringing the shadow of a phenomenon. It was plain that my dose had been insufficient.

For the sake of observing the most conservative prudence, I suffered several days to go by without a repetition of the experiment, and then, keeping the matter equally secret, I administered to myself a pill of fifteen grains. This second was equally ineffectual with the first.

Gradually, by five grains at a time, I increased the dose to thirty grains, which I took one evening half an hour after tea. I had now almost come to the conclusion that I was absolutely unsusceptible of the hasheesh influence. Without any expectation that this last experiment would be more successful than the former ones, and indeed with no realization of the manner in which the drug affected those who did make the experiment successfully, I went to pass the evening at the house of an intimate friend. In music and conversation the time passed pleasantly. The clock struck ten, reminding me that three hours had elapsed since the dose was taken, and as yet not an unusual symptom had appeared. I was provoked to think that this trial was as fruitless as its predecessors.

Ha! what means this sudden thrill? A shock, as of some unimagined vital force, shoots without warning through my entire frame, leaping to my fingers' ends, piercing my brain, startling me till I almost spring from my chair.

I could not doubt it. I was in the power of the hasheesh influence. My first emotion was one of uncontrollable terror -- a sense of getting something which I had not bargained for. That moment I would have given all I had or hoped to have to be as I was three hours before.

No pain any where -- not a twinge in any fibre -- yet a cloud of unutterable strangeness was settling upon me, and wrapping me impenetrably in from all that was natural or familiar. Endeared faces, well known to me of old, surrounded me, yet they were not with me in my loneliness. I had entered upon a tremendous life which they could not share. If the disembodied ever return to hover over the hearth-stone which once had a seat for them, they look upon their friends as I then looked upon mine. A nearness of place, with an infinite distance of state, a connection which had no possible sympathies for the wants of that hour of revelation, an isolation none the less perfect for seeming companionship.

Still I spoke, a question was put to me, and I answered it; I even laughed at a bon mot. Yet it was not my voice which spoke; perhaps one which I once had far away in another time and another place. For a while I knew nothing that was going on externally, and then the remembrance of the last remark which had been made returned slowly and indistinctly, as some trait of a dream will return after many days, puzzling us to say here we have been conscious of it before.

A fitful wind all the evening had been sighing down the chimney; it now grew into the steady hum of a vast wheel in accelerating motion. For a while this hum seemed to resound through all space. I was stunned by it -- I was absorbed in it. Slowly the revolution of the wheel came to a stop, and its monotonous din was changed for the reverberating peal of a grand cathedral organ. The ebb and flow of its inconceivably solemn tone filled me with a grief that was more than human. I sympathized with the dirge-like cadence as spirit sympathizes with spirit. And then, in the full conviction that all I heard and felt was real, I looked out of my isolation to see the effect of the music on my friends. Ah! we were in separate worlds indeed. Not a trace of appreciation on any face.

Perhaps I was acting strangely. Suddenly a pair of busy hands, which had been running neck and neck all the evening with a nimble little crochet- needle over a race-ground of pink and blue silk, stopped at their goal, and their owner looked at me steadfastly. Ah! I was found out -- I had betrayed myself. In terror I waited, expecting every instant to hear the word "hasheesh." No, the lady only asked me some question connected with the previous conversation. As mechanically as an automaton I began to reply. As I heard once more the alien and unreal tones of my own voice, I became convinced that it was some one else who spoke, and in another world. I sat and listened; still the voice kept speaking. Now for the first time I experienced that vast change which hasheesh makes in all measurements of time. The first word of the reply occupied a period sufficient for the action of a drama; the last left me in complete ignorance of any point far enough back in the past to date the commencement of the sentence. Its enunciation might have occupied years. I was not in the same life which had held me when I heard it begun.

And now, with time, space expanded also. At my friend's house one particular arm-chair was always reserved for me. I was sitting in it at a distance of hardly three feet from the centre-table around which the members of the family were grouped. Rapidly that distance widened. The whole atmosphere seemed ductile, and spun endlessly out into great spaces surrounding me on every side. We were in a vast hall, of which my friends and I occupied opposite extremities. The ceiling and the wall ran upward with a gliding motion, as if vivified by a sudden force of resistless growth.

Oh! I could not bear it. I should soon be left alone in the midst of an infinity of space. And now more and more every moment increased the conviction that I was watched. I did not know then, as I learned afterward, that suspicion of all earthly things and persons was the characteristic of the hasheesh delirium.

In the midst of my complicated hallucination, I could perceive that I had a dual existence. One portion of me was whirled unresistingly along the track of this tremendous experience, the other sat looking down from a height upon its double, observing, reasoning, and serenely weighing all the phenomena. This calmer being suffered with the other by sympathy, but did not lose its self-possession. Presently it warned me that I must go home, lest the growing effect of the hasheesh should incite me to some act which might frighten my friends. I acknowledged the force of this remark very much as if it had been made by another person, and rose to take my leave. I advanced toward the centre-table. With every step its distance increased. I nerved myself for a long pedestrian journey. Still the lights, the faces, the furniture receded. At last, almost unconsciously, I reached them. It would be tedious to attempt to convey the idea of the time which my leave-taking consumed, and the attempt, at least with all minds that have not passed through the same experience, would be as impossible as tedious. At last I was in the street.

Beyond me the view stretched endlessly away. It was an unconverging vista, whose nearest lamps seemed separated from me by leagues. I was doomed to pass through a merciless stretch of space. A soul just disenthralled, setting out for his flight beyond the farthest visible star, could not be more overwhelmed with his newly acquired conception of the sublimity of distance than I was at that moment. Solemnly I began by infinite journey. Before long I walked in entire unconsciousness of all around me. I dwelt in a marvelous inner world. I existed by turns in different places and various states of being. Now I swept my gondola through the moonlit lagoons of Venice. Now Alp on Alp towered above my view, and the glory of the coming sun flashed purple light upon the topmost icy pinnacle. Now in the primeval silence of some unexplored tropical forest I spread my feathery leaves, a giant fern, and swayed and nodded in the spice-gales over a river whose waves at once sent up clouds of music and perfume. My soul changed to a vegetable essence, thrilled with a strange and unimagined ecstasy. The palace of Al Haroun could not have brought me back to humanity.

I will not detail all the transmutations of that walk. Ever and anon I returned from my dreams into consciousness, as some well-known house seemed to leap out into my path, awaking me with a shock. The whole way homeward was a series of such awakings and relapses into abstraction and delirium until I reached the corner of the street in which I lived.

Here a new phenomenon manifested itself. I had just awaked for perhaps the twentieth time, and my eyes were wide open. I recognized all surrounding objects, and began calculating the distance home. Suddenly, out of a blank wall at my side a muffled figure stepped into the path before me. His hair, white as snow, hung in tangled elf-locks on his shoulders, where he carried also a heavy burden, like unto the well-filled sack of sins which Bunyan places on the back of his pilgrim. Not liking his manner, I stepped aside, intending to pass around him and go on my way. This change of our relative positions allowed the blaze of a neighboring street-lamp to fall full on his face, which had hitherto been totally obscured. Horror unspeakable! I shall never, till the day I die, forget that face. Every lineament was stamped with the records of a life black with damning crime; it glared upon me with a ferocious wickedness and a stony despair which only he may feel who is entering on the retribution of the unpardonable sin. He might have sat to a demon painter as the ideal of Shelly's Cenci. I seemed to grow blasphemous in looking at him, and, in an agony of fear, began to run away. He detained me with a bony hand, which pierced my wrist like talons, and, slowly taking down the burden from his own shoulders, laid it upon mine. I threw it off and pushed him away. Silently he returned and restored the weight. Again I repulsed him, this time crying out, "Man, what do you mean?" In a voice which impressed me with the sense of wickedness as his face had done, he replied, "You shall bear my burden with me," and a third time laid it on my shoulders. For the last time I hurled it aside, and, with all my force, dashed him from me. He reeled backward and fell, and before he could recover his disadvantage I had put a long distance between us.

Through the excitement of my struggle with this phantasm the effects of the hasheesh had increased mightily. I was bursting with an uncontrollable life; I strode with the thews of a giant. Hotter and faster came my breath; I seemed to pant like some tremendous engine. An electric energy whirled me resistlessly onward; I feared for myself lest it should burst its fleshly walls, and glance on, leaving a wrecked frame-work behind it.

At last I entered my own house. During my absence a family connection had arrived from abroad, and stood ready to receive my greeting. Partly restored to consciousness by the naturalness of home-faces and the powerful light of a chandelier which shed its blaze through the room, I saw the necessity of vigilance against betraying my condition, and with an intense effort suppressing all I felt, I approached my friend, and said all that is usual on such occasions. Yet recent as I was from my conflict with the supernatural, I cast a stealthy look about me, that I might learn from the faces of the others if, after all, I was shaking hands with a phantom, and making inquiries about the health of a family of hallucinations. Growing assured as I perceived no symptoms of astonishment, I finished the salutation and sat down.

It soon required all my resolution to keep the secret which I had determined to hold inviolable. My sensations began to be terrific -- not from any pain that I felt, but from the tremendous mystery of all around me and within me. By an appalling introversion, all the operations of vitality which, in our ordinary state, go on unconsciously, came vividly into my experience. Through every thinnest corporeal tissue and minutest vein I could trace the circulation of the blood along each inch of its progress. I knew when every valve opened and when it shut; every sense was preternaturally awakened; the room was full of a great glory. The beating of my heart was so clearly audible that I wondered to find it unnoticed by those who were sitting by my side. Lo, now, that heart became a great fountain, whose jet played upward with loud vibrations, and, striking upon the roof of my skull as on a gigantic dome, fell back with a splash and echo into its reservoir. Faster and faster came the pulsations, until at last I heard them no more, and the stream became one continuously pouring flood, whose roar resounded through all my frame. I gave myself up for lost, since judgment, which still sat unimpaired above my perverted senses, argued that congestion must take place in a few moments, and close the drama with my death. But my clutch would not yet relax from hope. The thought struck me, Might not this rapidity of circulation be, after all, imaginary? I determined to find out.

Going to my own room, I took out my watch, and placed my hand upon my heart. The very effort which I made to ascertain the reality gradually brought perception back to its natural state. In the intensity of my observations, I began to perceive that the circulation was not as rapid as I had thought. From a pulseless flow it gradually came to be apprehended as a hurrying succession of intense throbs, then less swift and less intense, till finally, on comparing it with the second-hand, I found that about 90 a minute was its average rapidity. Greatly comforted, I desisted from the experiment. Almost instantly the hallucination returned. Again I dreaded apoplexy, congestion, hemorrhage, a multiplicity of nameless deaths, and drew my picture as I might be found on the morrow, stark and cold, by those whose agony would be redoubled by the mystery of my end. I reasoned with myself; I bathed my forehead -- it did no good. There was one resource left:I would go to a physician.

With this resolve, I left my room and went to the head of the staircase. The family had all retired for the night, and the gas was turned off from the burner in the hall below. I looked down the stairs: the depth was fathomless; it was a journey of years to reach the bottom! The dim light of the sky shone through the narrow panes at the sides of the front door, and seemed a demon-lamp in the middle darkness of the abyss. I never could get down! I sat me down despairingly upon the topmost step.

Suddenly a sublime thought possessed me. If the distance is infinite, I am immortal. It shall be tried. I commenced the descent, wearily, wearily down through my league-long, year-long journey. To record my impressions in that journey would be to repeat what I have said of the time of hasheesh. Now stopping to rest as a traveler would turn aside at a wayside inn, now toiling down through the lonely darkness, I came by-and-by to the end, and passed out into the street.

II. Under the Shadow of Esculapius

On reaching the porch of the physician's house, I rang the bell, but immediately forgot whom to ask for. No wonder; I was on the steps of a palace in Milan -- no (and I laughed at myself for the blunder), I was on the staircase of the Tower of London. So I should not be puzzled through my ignorance of Italian. But whom to ask for? This question recalled me to the real bearings of the place, but did not suggest its requisite answer. Whom shall I ask for? I began setting the most cunning traps of hypothesis to catch the solution of the difficulty. I looked at the surrounding houses; of whom had I been accustomed to think as living next door to them? This did not bring it. Whose daughter had I seen going to school from this house but the very day before? Her name was Julia -- Julia -- and I thought of every combination which had been made with this name from Julia Domna down to Giulia Grisi. Ah! now I had it -- Julia H.; and her father naturally bore the same name. During this intellectual rummage I had rung the bell half a dozen times, under the impression that I was kept waiting a small eternity. When the servant opened the door she panted as if she had run for her life. I was shown up stairs to Dr. H.'s room, where he had thrown himself down to rest after a tedious operation. Locking the door after me with an air of determined secrecy, which must have conveyed to him pleasant little suggestions of a design upon his life, I approached his bedside.

"I am about to reveal to you," I commenced, "something which I would not for my life allow to come into other ears. Do you pledge me your eternal silence?"

"I do; what is the matter?"

"I have been taking hasheesh -- Cannabis Indica, and I fear that I am going to die."

"How much did you take?"

"Thirty grains."

"Let me feel your pulse." He placed his finger on my wrist and counted slowly, while I stood waiting to hear my death- warrant. "Very regular," shortly spoke the doctor; "triflingly accelerated. Do you feel any pain?" "None at all." "Nothing the matter with you; go home and go to bed." "But -- is there -- is there -- no -- danger of -- apoplexy?" "Bah!" said the doctor; and, having delivered himself of this very Abernethy-like opinion of my case, he lay down again. My hand was on the knob, when he stopped me with, "Wait a minute; I'll give you a powder to carry with you, and if you get frightened again after you leave me, you can take it as a sedative. Step out on the landing, if you please, and call my servant."

I did so, and my voice seemed to reverberate like thunder from every recess in the whole building. I was terrified at the noise I had made. I learned in after days that this impression is only one of the many due to the intense susceptibility of the sensorium as produced by hasheesh. At one time, having asked a friend to check me if I talked loudly or immoderately while in a state of fantasia among persons from whom I wished to conceal my state, I caught myself shouting and singing from very ecstasy, and reproached him with a neglect of his friendly office. I could not believe him when he assured me that I had not uttered an audible word. The intensity of the inward emotion had affected the external through the internal ear.

I returned and stood at the foot of the doctor's bed. All was perfect silence in the room, and had been perfect darkness also but for the small lamp which I held in my hand to light the preparation of the powder when it should come. And now a still sublimer mystery began to enwrap me. I stood in a remote chamber at the top of a colossal building, and the whole fabric beneath me was steadily growing into the air. Higher than the topmost pinnacle of Bel's Babylonish temple -- higher than Ararat -- on, on forever into the lonely dome of God's infinite universe we towered ceaselessly. The years flew on; I heard the musical rush of their wings in the abyss outside of me, and from cycle to cycle, from life to life I careered, a mote in eternity and space. Suddenly emerging from the orbit of my transmigrations, I was again at the foot of the doctor's bed, and thrilled with wonder to find that we were both unchanged by the measureless lapse of time. The servant had not come.

"Shall I call her again?" "Why, you have this moment called her." "Doctor," I replied solemnly, and in language that would have seemed bombastic enough to any one who did not realize what I felt, "I will not believe you are deceiving me, but to me it appears as if sufficient time has elapsed since then for all the Pyramids to have crumbled back to dust." "Ha! ha! you are very funny to-night," said the doctor; "but here she comes, and I will send her for something which will comfort you on that score, and reestablish the Pyramids in your confidence." He gave the girl his orders, and she went out again.

The thought struck me that I would compare my time with other people's. I looked at my watch, found that its minute-hand stood at the quarter mark past eleven, and, returning it to my pocket, abandoned myself to my reflections.

Presently I saw myself a gnome imprisoned by a most weird enchanter, whose part I assigned to the doctor before me, in the Domdaniel caverns, "under the roots of the ocean." Here, until the dissolution of all things, was I doomed to hold the lamp that lit that abysmal darkness, while my heart, like a giant clock, ticked solemnly the remaining years of time. Now, this hallucination departing, I heard in the solitude of the night outside the sound of a wondrous heaving sea. Its waves in sublime cadence, rolled forward till they met the foundations of the building; they smote them with a might which made the very topstone quiver, and then fell back, with hiss and hollow murmur, into the broad bosom whence they had arisen. Now through the street, with measured tread, an armed host passed by. The heavy beat of their footfall and the griding of their brazen corslet-rings alone broke the silence, for among them all there was no more speech nor music than in a battalion of the dead. It was the army of the ages going by into eternity. A godlike sublimity swallowed up my soul. I was overwhelmed in a fathomless barathrum of time, but I leaned on God, and was immortal through all changes.

And now, in another life, I remembered that far back in the cycles I had looked at my watch to measure the time through which I passed. The impulse seized me to look again. The minute-hand stood half way between fifteen and sixteen minutes past eleven. The watch must have stopped; I held it to my ear; no, it was still going. I had traveled through all that immeasurable chain of dreams in thirty seconds. "My God!" I cried, "I am in eternity." In the presence of that first sublime revelation of the soul's own time, and her capacity for an infinite life, I stood trembling with breathless awe. Till I die, that moment of unveiling will stand in clear relief from all the rest of my existence. I hold it still in unimpaired remembrance as one of the unutterable sanctities of my being. The years of all my earthly life to come can never be as long as those thirty seconds.

Finally the servant reappeared. I received my powder and went home. There was a light in one of the upper windows, and I hailed it with unspeakable joy, for it relieved me from a fear which I could not conquer, that while I had been gone all familiar things had passed away from earth. I was hardly safe in my room before I doubted having ever been out of it. "I have experienced some wonderful dream," said I, "as I lay here after coming from the parlor." If I had not been out, I reasoned that I would have no powder in my pocket. The powder was there, and it steadied me a little to find that I was not utterly hallucinated on every point. Leaving the light burning, I set out to travel to my bed, which gently invited me in the distance. Reaching it after a sufficient walk, I threw myself down.

III. The Kingdom of the Dream

The moment that I closed my eyes a vision of celestial glory burst upon me. I stood on the silver strand of a translucent, boundless lake, across whose bosom I seemed to have been just transported. A short way up the beach, a temple, modeled like the Parthenon, lifted its spotless and gleaming columns of alabaster sublimely into a rosy air -- like the Parthenon, yet as much excelling it as the godlike ideal of architecture must transcend the ideal realized by man. Unblemished in its purity of whiteness, faultless in the unbroken symmetry of every line and angle, its pediment was draped in odorous clouds, whose tints outshone the rainbow. It was the work of an unearthly builder, and my soul stood before it in a trance of ecstasy. Its folded doors were resplendent with the glory of a multitude of eyes of glass, which were inlaid throughout the marble surfaces at the corners of diamond figures from the floor of the porch to the topmost moulding. One of these eyes was golden, like the midday sun, another emerald, another sapphire, and thus onward through the whole gamut of hues, all of them set in such collocations as to form most exquisite harmonies, and whirling upon their axes with the rapidity of thought. At the mere vestibule of the temple I could have sat and drunk in ecstasy forever; but lo! I am yet more blessed. On silent hinges the doors swing open, and I pass in.

I did not seem to be in the interior of a temple. I beheld myself as truly in the open air as if I had never passed the portals, for whichever way I looked there were no walls, no roof, no pavement. An atmosphere of fathomless and soul- satisfying serenity surrounded and transfused me. I stood upon the bank of a crystal stream, whose waters, as they slid on, discoursed notes of music which tinkled on the ear like the tones of some exquisite bell-glass. The same impression which such tones produce, of music refined to its ultimate ethereal spirit and borne from a far distance, characterized every ripple of those translucent waves. The gently sloping banks of the stream were luxuriant with a velvety cushioning of grass and moss, so living green that the eye and the soul reposed on them at the same time and drank in peace. Through this amaranthine herbage strayed the gnarled, fantastic roots of giant cedars of Lebanon, from whose primeval trunks great branches spread above me, and interlocking, wove a roof of impenetrable shadow; and wandering down the still avenues below those grand arboreal arches went glorious bards, whose snowy beards fell on their breasts beneath countenances of ineffable benignity and nobleness.

They were all clad in flowing robes, like God's high- priests, and each one held in his hand a lyre of unearthly workmanship. Presently one stops midway down a shady walk, and, baring his right arm, begins a prelude. While his celestial chords were trembling up into their sublime fullness, another strikes his strings, and now they blend upon my ravished ear in such a symphony as was never heard elsewhere, and I shall never hear again out of the Great Presence. A moment more, and three are playing in harmony; now the fourth joins the glorious rapture of his music to their own, and in the completeness of the chord my soul is swallowed up. I can bear no more. But yes, I am sustained, for suddenly the whole throng break forth in a chorus, upon whose wings I am lifted out of the riven walls of sense, and music and spirit thrill in immediate communion. Forever rid of the intervention of pulsing air and vibrating nerve, my soul dilates with the swell of that transcendent harmony, and interprets from it arcana of a meaning which words can never tell. I am borne aloft upon the glory of sound. I float in a trance among the burning choir of the seraphim. But, as I am melting through the purification of that sublime ecstasy into oneness with the Deity himself, one by one those pealing lyrics faint away, and as the last throb dies down along the measureless ether, visionless arms swiftly as lightning carry me far into the profound, and set me down before another portal. Its leaves, like the first, are of spotless marble, but ungemmed with wheeling eyes of burning color.

Before entering on the record of this new vision I will make a digression, for the purpose of introducing two laws of the hasheesh operation, which, as explicatory, deserve a place here. First, after the completion of any one fantasia has arrived, there almost invariably succeeds a shifting of the action to some other stage entirely different in its surroundings. In this transition the general character of the emotion may remain unchanged. I may be happy in Paradise and happy at the sources of the Nile, but seldom, either in Paradise or on the Nile, twice in succession. I may writhe in Etna and burn unquenchably in Gehenna, but almost never, in the course of the same delirium, shall Etna or Gehenna witness my torture a second time.

Second, after the full storm of a vision of intense sublimity has blown past the hasheesh-eater, his next vision is generally of a quiet, relaxing, and recreating nature. He comes down from his clouds or up from his abyss into a middle ground of gentle shadow, where he may rest his eyes from the splendor of the seraphim or the flames of fiends. There is a wise philosophy in this arrangement, for otherwise the soul would soon burn out in the excess of its own oxygen. Many a time, it seems to me, has my own thus been saved from extinction.

This next vision illustrated both, but especially the latter of these laws. The temple-doors opened noiselessly before me, but it was no scene of sublimity which thus broke in upon my eyes. I stood in a large apartment, which resembled the Senate-chamber at Washington more than any thing else to which I can compare it. Its roof was vaulted, and at the side opposite the entrance the floor rose into a dais surmounted by a large arm-chair. The body of the house was occupied by similar chairs disposed in ares; the heavy paneling of the walls was adorned with grotesque frescoes of every imaginable bird, beast, and monster, which, by some hidden law of life and motion, were forever changing, like the figures of the kaleidoscope. Now the walls bristled with hippogriffs; now, from wainscot to ceiling, toucans and maccataws swung and nodded from their perches amid emerald palms; now Centaurs and Lapithae clashed in ferocious tumult, while crater and cyathus were crushed beneath ringing hoof and heel. But my attention was quickly distracted from the frescoes by the sight of a most witchly congress, which filled all the chairs of that broad chamber. On the dais sat an old crone, whose commanding position first engaged my attention to her personal appearance, and, upon rather impolite scrutiny, I beheld that she was the product of an art held in preeminent favor among persons of her age and sex. She was knit of purple yarn! In faultless order the stitches ran along her face; in every pucker of her reentrant mouth, in every wrinkle of her brow, she was a yarny counterfeit of the grandam of actual life, and by some skillful process of stuffing her nose had received its due peak and her chin its projection. The occupants of the seats below were all but reproductions of their president, and both she and they were constantly swaying from side to side, forward and back, to the music of some invisible instruments, whose tone and style were most intensely and ludicrously Ethiopian. Not a word was spoken by any of the woolly conclave, but with untiring industry they were all knitting, knitting, knitting ceaselessly, as if their lives depended on it. I looked to see the objects of their manufacture. They were knitting old women like themselves! One of the sisterhood had nearly brought her double to completion; earnestly another was engaged in rounding out an eyeball; another was fastening the gathers at the corners of a mouth; another was setting up stitches for an old woman in petto.

With marvelous rapidity this work went on; ever and anon some completed crone sprang from the needles which had just achieved her, and, instantly vivified, took up the instruments of reproduction, and fell to work as assiduously as if she had been a member of the congress since the world began. "Here," I cried, "here, at last, do I realize the meaning of endless progression!" and, though the dome echoed with my peals of laughter, I saw no motion of astonishment in the stitches of a single face, but, as for dear life, the manufacture of old women went on unobstructed by the involuntary rudeness of the stranger.

An irresistible desire to aid in the work possessed me; I was half determined to snatch up a quartette of needles and join the sisterhood. My nose began to be ruffled with stitches, and the next moment I had been a partner in their yarny destinies but for a hand which pulled me backward through the door, and shut the congress forever from my view.

For a season I abode in an utter void of sight and sound, but I waited patiently in the assurance that some new changes of magnificence were preparing for me. I was not disappointed. Suddenly, at a far distance, three intense luminous points stood on the triple wall of darkness, and through each of them shot twin attenuated rays of magic light and music. Without being able to perceive any thing of my immediate surroundings, I still felt that I was noiselessly drifting toward those radiant and vocal points. With every moment they grew larger, the light and the harmony came clearer, and before long I could distinguish plainly three colossal arches rising from the bosom of a waveless water. The mid arch towered highest; the two on either side were equal to each other. Presently I beheld that they formed the portals of an enormous cavern, whose dome rose above me into such sublimity that its cope was hidden from my eyes in wreaths of cloud. On each side of me ran a wall of gnarled and rugged rock, from whose jutting points, as high as the eye could reach, depended stalactites of every imagined form and tinge of beauty, while below me, in the semblance of an ebon pavement, from the reflection of its overshadowing crags, lay a level lake, whose exquisite transparency wanted but the smile of the sun to make it glow like a floor of adamant. On this lake I lay in a little boat divinely carved from pearl after the similitude of Triton's shelly shallop; its rudder and its oarage were my own unconscious will, and, without the labors of especial volition, I floated as I list with a furrowless keel swiftly toward the central giant arch. With every moment that brought me nearer to my exit, the harmony that poured through it developed into a grander volume and an intenser beauty.

And now I passed out.

Claude Lorraine, freed from the limitations of sense, and gifted with an infinite canvas, may, for aught I know, be upon some halcyon island of the universe painting such a view as now sailed into my vision. Fitting employment would it be for his immortality were his pencil dipped into the very fountains of the light. Many a time in the course of my life have I yearned for the possession of some grand old master's soul and culture in the presence of revelations of Nature's loveliness which I dared not trust to memory; before this vision, as now in the remembrance of it, that longing became a heartfelt pain. Yet after all, it was well; the mortal limner would have fainted his task. Alas! how does the material in which we must embody the spiritual cramp and resist its execution! Standing before windows where the invisible spirit of the frost had traced his exquisite algae, his palms and his ferns, have I said to myself, with a sigh, Ah! Nature alone, of all artists, is gifted to work out her ideals!

Shall I be so presumptuous as to attempt in words that which would beggar the palette and the pencil of old-time disciples of the beautiful? I will, if it be only to satisfy a deep longing.

From the arches of my cavern I had emerged upon a horizonless sea. Through all the infinitudes around me I looked out, and met no boundaries of space. Often in after times have I beheld the heavens and the earth stretching out in parallel lines forever, but this was the first time I had ever stood un-"ringed by the azure world," and I exulted in all the sublimity of the new conception. The whole atmosphere was one measureless suffusion of golden motes, which throbbed continually in cadence, and showered radiance and harmony at the same time. With ecstasy vision spread her wings for a flight against which material laws locked no barrier, and every moment grew more and more entranced at further and fuller glimpses of a beauty which floated like incense from the pavement of that eternal sea. With ecstasy the spiritual ear gathered in continually some more distant and unimaginable tone, and grouped the growing harmonics into one sublime chant of benediction. With ecstasy the whole soul drank in revelations from every province, and cried out, "Oh, awful loveliness!" And now out of my shallop I was borne away into the full light of the mid firmament; now seated on some toppling peak of a cloud- mountain, whose yawning rifts disclosed far down the mines of reserved lightning; now bathed in my ethereal travel by the rivers of the rainbow, which, side by side, coursed through the valleys of heaven; now dwelling for a season in the environment of unbroken sunlight, yet bearing it like the eagle with undazzled eye; now crowned with a coronal of prismatic beads of dew. Through whatever region or circumstances I passed, one characteristic of the vision remained unchanged: peace -- everywhere godlike peace, the sum of all conceivable desires satisfied.

Slowly I floated down to earth again. There Oriental gardens waited to receive me. From fountain to fountain I danced in graceful mazes with inimitable houris, whose foreheads were bound with fillets of jasmine. I pelted with figs the rare exotic birds, whose gold and crimson wings went flashing from branch to branch, or wheedled them to me with Arabic phrases of endearment. Through avenues of palm I walked arm-in-arm with Hafiz, and heard the hours flow singing through the channels of his matchless poetry. In gay kiosques I quaffed my sherbet, and in the luxury of lawlessness kissed away by drops that other juice which is contraband unto the faithful. And now beneath citron shadows I laid me down to sleep. When I awoke it was morning -- actually morning, and not a hasheesh hallucination. The first emotion that I felt upon opening my eyes was happiness to find things again wearing a natural air. Yes; although the last experience of which I had been conscious had seemed to satisfy every human want, physical or spiritual, I smiled on the four plain white walls of my bed-chamber, and hailed their familiar unostentatiousness with a pleasure which had no wish to transfer itself to arabesque or rainbows. It was like returning home from an eternity spent in loneliness among the palaces of strangers. Well may I say an eternity, for during the whole day I could not rid myself of the feeling that I was separated from the preceding one by an immeasurable lapse of time. In face, I never got wholly rid of it.

I rose that I might test my reinstated powers, and see if the restoration was complete. Yes, I felt not one trace of bodily weariness nor mental depression. Every function had returned to its normal state, with the one exception mentioned; memory could not efface the traces of my having passed through a great mystery. I recalled the events of the past night, and was pleased to think that I had betrayed myself to no one but Dr. H. I was satisfied with my experiment.

Ah! would that I had been satisfied! Yet history must go on.

IV. Cashmere and Cathay by Twilight

"You will never take it again, will you?"

"Oh no, I never expect to; I am satisfied with my one successful experiment."

It was the fair lady of the crochet-needle who asked me the question as, a few days after my first practical acquaintance with hasheesh, I have her the recital contained in the preceding pages. In my answer I spoke truly; I did suppose that I never should repeat my experiment. The glimpse which I had gained in that single night of revelation of hitherto unconceived modes and uncharted fields of spiritual being seemed enough to store the treasure-house of grand memories for a lifetime. Unutterably more, doubtless, still remained unveiled, but it contented me to say,

"In Nature's infinite book of secrecy
A little I can read,"
when that little swept a view whose faintest lineament outshone all the characters upon the scroll of daily existence. No, I never should take it again.

I did not know myself; I did not know hasheesh. There are temperaments, no doubt, upon which this drug produces, as a reactory result, physical and mental depression. With me, this was never the case. Opium and liquors fix themselves as a habit by becoming necessary to supply that nervous waste which they in the first place occasioned. The lassitude which succeeds their exaltation demands a renewed indulgence, and accordingly every gratification of the appetite is parent to the next. But no such element entered into the causes which attached me to hasheesh. I speak confidently, yet without exaggeration, when I say that I have spent many an hour in torture such as was never known by Cranmer at the stake, or Gaudentio di Lucca in the Inquisition, yet out of the depths of such experience I have always come without a trace of its effect in diminished strength or buoyancy.

Had the first experiment been followed by depression, I had probably never repeated it. At any rate, unstrung muscles and an enervated mind could have been resisted much more effectually when they pleaded for renewed indulgence than the form which the fascination actually took. For days I was even unusually strong; all the forces of life were in a state of pleasurable activity, but the memory of the wondrous glories which I had beheld wooed me continually like an irresistible sorceress. I could not shut my eyes for midday musing without beholding in that world, half dark, half light, beneath the eyelids, a steady procession of delicious images which the severest will could not banish nor dim. Now through an immense and serene sky floated luxurious argosies of clouds, continually changing form and tint through an infinite cycle of mutations.

Now, suddenly emerging from some deep embowerment of woods, I stood upon the banks of a broad river that curved far off into dreamy distance, and glided noiselessly past its jutting headlands, reflecting a light which was not of the sun nor of the moon, but midway between them, and here and there thrilling with subdued prismatic rays. Temples and gardens, fountains and vistas stretched continually through my waking or sleeping imagination, and mingled themselves with all I heard, or read, or saw. On the pages of Gibbon the palaces and lawns of Nicomedia were illustrated with a hasheesh tint and a hasheesh reality; and journeying with old Dan Chaucer, I drank in a delicious landscape of revery along all the road to Canterbury. The music of my vision was still heard in echo; as the bells of Bow of old time called to Whittington, so did it call to me -- "Turn again, turn again." And I turned.

Censure me not harshly, ye who have never known what fascination there is in the ecstasy of beauty; there are baser attractions than those which invited me. Perhaps ye yourselves have turned from the first simple-mindedness of life to be led by the power of a more sordid wooing. The hope of being one day able to sleep lazily in a literally golden sun, the lazzaroni of fortune; of securing a patient hearing for some influential and patriotic whisper in the ear of the "mobilium turba Quiritium;" of draining any cup which drugs the soul and leaves the body to rifle it of its prerogative -- each and all of these are lower fascination than that to which I yielded.

40

And ye better, wiser, and therefore gentler ones, who decry not another's weakness because it is not your own, who are free from all bondage, be it of the sordid or the beautiful, be kindly in your judgement. Wherein I was wrong I was invited as by a mother's voice, and the blandishments which lulled me were full of such spiritual sweetness as we hear only twice in a lifetime -- once at its opening, once at its close; the first time in the cradle-hymn that lulls innocence to slumber, the last in that music of attendant angels through which the soul begins to float upward in its euthanasia toward the restoration of primeval purity and peace. I yielded to no sensual gratification. The motives for the hasheesh-indulgence were of the most exalted ideal nature, for of this nature are all its ecstasies and its revelations -- yes, and a thousand-fold more terrible, for this very reason, its unutterable pangs. I yielded, moreover, without realizing to what. Within a circle of one hundred miles' radius there was not a living soul who knew or could warn me of my danger. Finally, I yielded without knowing that I yielded, for I ascribed my next indulgence to a desire of research.

One day, about the hour of noon, a little more than a week after my first experiment, I rolled twenty grains of hasheesh into a pill and swallowed it, saying as I did so, "Here is the final test for the sake of science." The afternoon lay before me unoccupied by any especial appointment, and, after dining, I threw myself down upon a lounge to await the result of the dose. The day was soft and hazy, and its influence lay so nepenthe-like upon my eyelids, that before long, without knowing it, I fell asleep. It was tea-time when I awoke, and I had not experienced any visions. A friend of mine joined me at the table, and when we pushed back our chairs, he proposed that we should take a walk. Every thing above, below, around us united in the invitation. It was one of those evenings when the universal sense of balminess makes all outdoors as homelike and delicious as the cheeriest winter fireside can be, with its enlivenment of ruddy blaze, and its charm of sheltered privacy. The very soul seems turned inside out for an airing, and we are almost ashamed of ourselves for ever preferring rafters to the sky, and fleeing from the presence of Nature to find a home.

Through all the streets that ran toward the west the sun was sending a thrill of light from his good-by place on the horizon, and the pavements were a mosaic of dancing leaf- shadows and golden polygons, forever shifting as the trees quivered over us in the gentlest of southern winds. Arm- in-arm with Dan, I strolled down the checkered avenue, and more and more luxuriant grew the sunset as we came gradually out of the environment of houses and breathed the air of the open country. The suburbs of P----- are very beautiful. If the stranger knows it and remarks it, it is not because he is smitten with the mere novelty of his view. There are few landscapes which will bear so frequent beholding -- few whose admirers so soon and lastingly become their lovers. Were there any jealousy in my love for that, my own home- scenery, I know no season which would ever have given me more pangs for fear of a rival than the one of which I speak, for the earth and sky were fair around us, even with a human fascination. Of my companion let me say that which any man of varying moods will realize to be one of the highest eulogies that can be passed upon a friend. Dan was one of those choice spirits whom you are always glad to have beside you, whatever may be your feeling. He belonged to that rare and sensitive order of beings who can never become uncongenial to one who has once been in sympathy with them. How many a time, most valued and longed-for one, have I tested this in thee! How often, in this very intuitive perception of our accordance, have I felt the proof that friendship is as inborn a principle in hearts as the quality of their harmony in tones of a chord.

There is a road running south from the suburbs of P----- which in many respects affords one of the most delightful walks which can be imagined. On the one hand, for a long distance, a terraced embankment rises luxuriantly green through all the days of summer, and crowned with picturesque rusurban cottages. On the other, a broad table-land stretches away to the abrupt banks of the Hudson, dotted over all its surface with clumps of healthful trees and embowered villas. Here and there, through the fringes of shade which skirt the brink, delicious views of the river break upon the eye, with a background of mountains, still unsubdued by labor, rising in primeval freshness from the other side. Under the tutelar protection of their evening shadows the farther water lay, at the season of which I speak, like a divine child asleep, watched by an eternal nurse.

Along this road we traveled arm-in-arm, so filled and overcome with the beauty of the view that we read each other's feelings and went silently. Perhaps we had come half a mile from the town when, without the smallest premonition, I was smitten by the hasheesh thrill as by a thunderbolt. Though I had felt it but once in a life before, its sign was as unmistakable as the most familiar thing of daily life. I have often been asked to explain the nature of this thrill, and have as often tried to do it, but no analogue exists which will represent it perfectly, hardly even approximately. The nearest resemblance to the feeling is that contained in our idea of the instantaneous separation of soul and body. Very few in the world have ever known before absolute death what state accompanies this separation, yet we all of us have an idea more or less distinct of that which it must be when it arrives. Even on this vague conception I throw myself for the sake of being understood with more confidence than I would dare to give to the most thorough description that I could elaborate.

The road along which we walked began slowly to lengthen. The hill over which it disappeared, at the distance of half a mile from me, soon came to be perceived as the boundary of the continent itself. But for the infinite loveliness of the sky, and waters, and fields, I should have been as greatly terrified with the increasing mystery of my state as I had been at the commencement of my first experience. But a most beautiful sunset was dying in the west, the river was tinged by it, the very zenith clouds were bathed in it, and the world beneath seemed to be floating in a dream of rosy tranquility. My awakened perceptions drank in this beauty until all sense of fear was banished, and every vein ran flooded with the very wine of delight. Mystery enwrapped me still, but it was the mystery of one who walks in Paradise for the first time.

Could I keep it from Dan? No, not for moment. I had no remembrance of having taken hasheesh. The past was the property of another life, and I supposed that all the world was reveling in the same ecstasy as myself. I case off all restraint; I leaped into the air; I clapped my hands, and shouted for joy. An involuntary exclamation raised the mustache of the poet beside me. "What in the world," he cried, "is the matter with you?" I could only answer, "Bliss! bliss! unimagined bliss!" In an instant he saw all, for he knew my former experience, and as quickly formed the resolution of humoring me to the utmost in all my vagaries.

I glowed like a new-born soul. The well-known landscape lost all of its familiarity, and I was setting out upon a journey of years through heavenly territories, which it had been the longing of my previous lifetime to behold. "My dear friend," I said, "we are about to realize all our youthful dreams of travel. Together you and I will wander on foot at our will through strange and beauteous countries; our life spreads before us henceforward unoccupied by cares, and the riches of all nature stretch onward through the immense domain we see in exultant expectancy to become the fool for our thought and the fountains of our delight. To think that we should have been spared until this day -- spared to each other, spared for such glorious scenes! My friend, we shall travel together, linked soul to soul, and gaining ecstasy by impartition. At night, beneath the shade of zephyr-fanned mimosas, we shall lay ourselves down to sleep on the banks of primeval Asian rivers, and Bulbul shall sing us to sleep with his most delicious madrigals. When the first auroral tinges are glassed back from the peaks of Himmaleh, we will arise, and, bathing ourselves in rock-o'ershadowed fountains, will start again upon our immortal way. Sleep shall repeat the echoes of the day to another and unfatigued inner sense of dreams, and awaking shall bear repetition of birth into newer and still more enchanting life. On! on!"

"I will go," said my friend, "with delight." Not a shadow of incredulousness or inappreciation passed over his face, and, drawing his arm still closer through my own, I hastened onward, as delighted with his consent as I was thoroughly convinced of the reality of the presence of grand old Asia.

The peculiar time of hasheesh, already so frequently mentioned, added one more rapturous element to my enjoyment. Through leagues of travel the shadows did not deepen around us, but the same unutterable sunset peace and beauty transfused the earth unchangeably. In watching the glories of the west at sunset in our ordinary state, they pass away from us so soon that they dying lustres have become to us almost the synonym for transition and decay. The golden masses become ruddy, the ruddy fall away to purple, the purple speedily grow black, and all this transmutation occupies no longer time than we may lean our foreheads, unfatigued, against a window-pane. In my present state of enlarged perception, Time had no kaleidoscope for me; nothing grew faint, nothing shifted, nothing changed except my ecstasy, which heightened through interminable degrees to behold the same rose-radiance lighting us up along all our immense journey. I might style my present chapter "Notes of Travel through the Champaigns of perpetual Sunset."

From the road along which we traveled another leads back into P-----, across a more precipitous hill than any we had already ascended. Into this second road we turned. Yet, from the absence of all familiar appearances in the world around me, I did not suppose that we were returning to the town, but merely that we were continuing our journey through a new and less frequented by-path. Presently we struck a plank walk, and began mounting the hill of which I have spoken.

The moment that the planks began to resound beneath our feet I realized in what part of Asia we were journeying. We were on the great wall of China. Below us stretched into grand distances the plains of Thibet. Multitudinous were the flocks that covered them; countless groups of goats and goatherds were dispersed over the landscape as far as the eye could reach. The banks of innumerable streams were dotted with picturesque tents, and every minutest detail of the view in all respects harmonized with the idea of Asiatic life. Beyond Thibet, as with clairvoyant eyes, I looked straight through and over Hindoo Koosh, and beheld Cashmere sleeping in grand shadows. The fountains of the Punjaub were unveiled, and among their spicy outflowings there gamboled, in Old-world freshness of heart, children of a primitive race whom prodigal nature had put beyond the necessity of labor. Through greenest valleys roved pairs of Oriental lovers, while above them flashed golden light from the fruit that hung in a Vallambrosa of citron-branches. Distance did not dim either scenery or countenances; every living thing was audible and visible in its rejoicing through leagues of light and shadow stretched between us. Again I leaped into the air and shouted for joy.

Along the road that skirted the outside of my Chinese wall a carriage came, drawn by a span of richly-caparisoned white horses. In it a young man and a maiden were sitting, and as they drew nearer they bowed to myself and my fellow-traveler. "Who are those?" asked Dan. "An eminent mandarin of the interior," I replied, "of the order of the Blue Button, and by name Fuh-chieng, who, with his sister, at this season every year takes the tour of the provinces, dispensing justice and examining into the state of the public works. Verily, an estimable youth. Having known him during the summer we spent together at Pekin, I feel constrained to speak with him." With a choice compliment on my lips, worded in the most courtly Chinese with which I as conversant, I was about to rush up the carriage and make my kow-tow, when my friend, grasping my arm, entreated me to desist, begging to know whether I were not aware that, since the year 580 B.C., when Ching-Chong was assassinated in his palanquin, it had been a criminal offense to approach within ten paces of a mandarin on his travels. "My dearest friend," I replied, "you have saved me! I am astonished at your knowledge of Chinese law, this title of which had entirely escaped my mind. With thankfulness I yield to your suggestion, and will suffer the young man to pass on." It was well that I did so, as my acquaintances in the carriage might otherwise have been terrified beyond measure by the singularity, if not by the sublimity of the dialect in which I should have addressed them.

46

It is possible for a man of imaginative mind, by mere suggestions of rich veins of thought, to lead a companion in the hasheesh state through visions of incomparable delight. This fact Dan had discovered in the good grace with which I instantly received his advice as to the mandarin. In our journeying we came to a tall gate-post of granite, which stood at the entrance to a lawn in front of one of the suburban residences of which I have spoken. Making his manner Oriental, to suit our supposed surroundings, he said to me, "Seest thou that tower that rises into the rosy air?" In an instant I beheld the tower with such conviction of reality that I did not even think of it as a metamorphose from something else. From the battlements flaunted yellow flags gorgeous with crimson dragons, and over each corner of the turret glared a rampant hippogriff, flaming, from his forked tongue even to his anomalous tail, with scales of dazzling gold. There was revelry within; its ecstasy worded in Shemitic monosyllables, and accompanied by the mellifluous flights of gong and tom-tom. We passed on through Asia.

We now reached the summit of the hill. The broadest scope of vision which was possible was now ours. My ecstasy became so great that I seemed to cast off all shackles of flesh. The lover of beauty who should, for the first time, drink in the richness of this exalted view through the channels of the soul which are ordinarily opened, might well burst forth into singing were not reverence the stronger feeling. But when, with me, that flow of loveliness broke in through doors in the spiritual nature to which no open sesame had ever before been granted, I felt, I cried out, "Why need we, in our journey, touch the earth at all? Let us sweep through air above this expanse of beauty, and read it like the birds."

I was about to fly heavenward, chanting a triumphant hymn, when I turned and looked at Dan. He was standing sorrowfully, without means of flight. I was filled with contrition. "Dear brother of my pilgrimage," I said, "did I speak of tempting the air, forgetful that thou wast not like unto myself? Forgive me -- I will not leave thee; yet, oh that thou couldst also fly! through what abysses of sublimity would we float!" Restoring myself to contentment with the airy tread of feet which hardly seemed to touch the ground, and my wish to oblivion, I again took his arm, and we voyaged as before.

Now we went singing, and I question whether Mozart ever rejoiced in his own musical creations as I did in that symphony we sang together. The tune and the words were extemporaneous, yet, by a close sympathy, he sang an accordant base to my air, and I heard delicious echoes thrown back from the dome of heaven. We sang the primal simplicity of Asia, the cradle of the nations, the grand expectancy of the younger continents, looking eastward to their mysterious mother for the gift of races still treasured in her womb. On our paean were borne the praises of the golden days of Foh and the serene prophecies of Confucius; we spoke of the rivers that for numberless centuries bore down to the eternal ocean no freight but the sere leaves of uninhabited wildernesses, whose shadows they glassed, and of fountains upon whose face no smile had rested save that of Hesper and the rising sun. I lived in what we sang: our music seemed a wondrous epic, whose pages we illustrated, not with pictures, but with living groups; the ancient days were restored before my eyes and to my ears, and I exulted in the perception with such conviction of reality that I ascribed it to no power of my own, but knew it as an exterior and universal fact.

This will be realized, perhaps, by very few who read my recital. The word for every strange phenomenon with all the world is "only imagination." Truly, this was imagination; but to me, with eyes and ears wide open in the daylight, an imagination as real as the soberest fact.

It will be remembered that the hasheesh states of ecstasy always alternate with less intense conditions, in which the prevailing phenomena are those of mirth or tranquility. In accordance with this law, in the present instance, Dan, to whom I had told my former experience, was not surprised to hear me break forth at the final cadence of our song into a peal of unextinguishable laughter, but begged to know what was its cause, that he might laugh too. I could only cry out that my right leg was a tin case filled with stair-rods, and as I limped along, keeping that member perfectly rigid, both from fear of cracking the metal and the difficulty of bending it, I heard he rattle of the brazen contents shaken from side to side with feelings of the most supreme absurdity possible to the human soul. Presently the leg was restored to its former state, but in the interim its mate had grown to a size which would have made it a very respectable trotter for Brian Borru or one of the Titans. Elevated some few hundred feet into the firmament, I was compelled to hop upon my giant pedestal in a way very ungraceful in a world where two legs were the fashion, and eminently disagreeable to the slighted member, which sought in vain to reach the earth with struggles amusing from their very insignificance. This ludicrous affliction being gradually removed, I went on my way quietly until we again began to be surrounded by the houses of the town.

Here the phenomenon of the dual existence once more presented itself. One part of me awoke, while the other continued in perfect hallucination. The awakened portion felt the necessity of keeping in side streets on the way home, lest some untimely burst of ecstasy should startle more frequented thoroughfares. I mentioned this to Dan, who drew me into a quiet lane, by the side of which we sat down together to rest on a broad stone. By this time the sunset had nearly faded, while my attention was directed to other things, and its regency of all the beauties of the sky was replaced by that of the full moon, now at the zenith. A broad and clearly-defined halo surrounded her, and refracted her rays in such a manner as to shower them from its edge in a prismatic fringe. That vision of loveliness was the only possible one which could have recompensed me for the loss of my sunset. I gazed heavenward, as one fascinated by mystical eyes. And now the broad luminous belt began to be peopled with myriads of shining ones from the realm of Faery who plunged into the translucent lake of ether as into a sea, and dashing back its silvery spray from their breasts, swam to the moon and ascended its gleaming beach.

Between this moon-island and the shore of halo now growing multitudes endlessly passed and repassed, and I could hear, tinkling down through the vacant spaces, the thrill of their gnome-laughter. I could have kept that stony seat all night, and looked speechlessly into heaven, unmoved though an armed host had passed by me on the earth, but unconsciously I closed my eyes, and was in a moment whirling on through a visionary dance, like that in which I had been borne as soon as I lay down at the time of my first experiment. Temples and gardens, pyramids and unearthly rivers, began to float along before the windows of my sense, when Dan, looking around, saw that I would become unconscious, and aroused me. Again we walked on.

And now that unutterable thirst which characterizes hasheesh came upon me. I could have lain me down and lapped dew from the grass. I must drink, wheresoever, howsoever. We soon reached home -- soon, because it was not five squares off from where we sat down, yet ages, from the thirst which consumed me and the expansion of time in which I lived. I came into the house as one would approach a fountain in the desert, with a wild bound of exultation, and gazed with miserly eyes at the draught which my friend poured out for me until the glass was brimming. I clutched it -- I put it to my lips. Ha! a surprise! It was not water, but the most delicious metheglin in which ever bard of the Cymridrank the health of Howell Dda. It danced and sparkled like some liquid metempsychosis of amber; it gleamed with the spiritual fire of a thousand chrysolites. To sight, to taste it was metheglin, such as never mantled in the cups of Valhalla.

The remainder of the evening I spent in a delirium which, unlike all that had preceded it, was one of unutterable calm. Not the heavy sleep of a debauch, not the voluntary musing of the visionary, but a clarifying of all thought, and the lowing in of the richest influences from the world around me, without the toil of selecting them. I looked at the stars, and felt kindred with them; I spoke to them, and they answered me. I dwelt in an inner communion with heaven -- a communion where every language is understood, rather where all speak the same language, and deeply did I realize a voice which seemed to say, as in my waking dreams I had faintly

Πολλαὶ μὲν θνητοῖς γλῶτται, μια δἀθὐνατοισιν.
heard in murmur upon earth,

50

V. The Hour and the Power of Darkness

It may perhaps be not altogether a fanciful classification to divide every man's life into two periods, the locomotive and the static. Restless fluidity always characterizes the childish mind in its healthy state, exemplifying itself in the thousand wayward freaks, hair-breadth experiments, and unanswerable questions which keep the elder portions of a family in continual oscillation between mirth and terror. There is not always a thorough solidification of the mental nature, even when the great boy has learned what to do with his hands, and how to occupy his station at maturer tea-parties with becoming dignity and resignation. No longer, to be sure, does he gratify experimental tendencies by taking the eight-day clock to pieces to look at its machinery; no longer does he nonplus grave aunts and grandmothers with questions upon the causes of his own origination, but the same dynamic propensities exist expanded into a larger and more self-conscious sphere. His restlessness of limb has now become the desire of travel, his investigation into the petty matters of household economy has grown into a thirst for research whose field is the world and whose instruments are the highest faculties of induction.

With some men this state remains unchanged through a long life, but to most of us there comes, sooner or later, a period when the longing for change dies out, and a fixed place and an unalterable condition become the great central ideas of existence. We look back with a wonder that is almost incredulousness upon the time when a ride by railway was the dream of weeks preceding, and try in vain to realize the supernatural freshness which the earth put on when for the first time we discovered that we were near-sighted, and looked through some friend's spectacles. Motion, except for the rare purpose of recreation, becomes an annoyance to us beyond a circumscribed territory, and we have emerged into the static condition of life before we are aware.

Much earlier than the usual period did this become the case with me. A feeble childhood soon exhausted its superfluous activities, and into books, ill health, and musing I settled down when I should have been playing cricket, hunting, or riding. The younger thirst for adventure was quenched by rapid degrees as I found it possible to ascend Chimborazo with Humboldt lying on a sofa, or chase harte-beests with Cumming over muffins and coffee. The only exceptions to this state of imaginative indolence were the hours spent in rowing or sailing upon the most glorious river of the world, and the consciousness that the Hudson rolled at my own door only contributed to settle the conviction that there was no need of going abroad to find beauties in which the soul might wrap itself as in a garment of delight. Even at these seasons exercise was not so much the aim as musing. Many a time, with the handles of my sculls thrust under the side-girders, and the blades turned full to the wind, have I sat and drifted for hours through mountain-shadows, and past glimpses of light that flooded the woody gorges, with a sense of dreamy ecstasy which all the novelties of a new world could never have supplied.

Oh, most noble river, what hast thou not been to me? In childhood thy ripples were the playmates of my perpetual leisure, dancing up the sandy stretches of thy brink, and telling laughing tales of life's beamy spray and sunshine. In after years, the grand prophet of a wider life, thine ebb sang chants to the imperial ocean, into whose pearly palaces thou wast hastening, and thy flood brought up the resounding history of the infinite surges whence thou hadst returned. It is not thine to come stealing from unnamed fountains of mystery, nor to crown thy sublime mountains with the ruined battlements of a departed age; but more than Nile hath. God glorified thee, and Nature hath hallowed thy walls with her own armorial bearings till thou art more reverend than Rhine. On thy guarding peaks Antiquity sits enthroned, asking no register in the crumbling monuments of man, but bearing her original sceptre from the hand of Him who first founded her domain beside thy immortal flow.

Gradually the Hudson came to supply all my spiritual wants. Were I sad, I found sympathy in the almost human murmurs of his waters, as, stretched upon the edge of some rocky headland, I heard them go beating into the narrow caves beneath me, and return sighing, as if defrauded of a hiding-place and a home. Were I merry, the white-caps danced and laughed about my prancing boat, and the wind whistled rollicking glees against my stays. In weariness, I leaped into the stream; his cool hand upbore and caressed me till I returned braced for thought, and renewed as by a plunge into El Dorado. In the Hudson I found a wealth which satisfied all wishes, and my supreme hope was that on his banks I might pass all my life. Thus supplied with beauty, consolation, dreams, all things, every day I became more and more careless of the world beyond, and in my frame grew even hyperstatic.

It was in this state that hasheesh found me. After the walk which I last recorded, the former passion for travel returned with powerful intensity. I had now a way of gratifying it which comported both with indolence and economy. The whole East, from Greece to farthest China, lay within the compass of a township; no outlay was necessary for the journey. For the humble sum of six cents I might purchase an excursion ticket over all the earth; ships and dromedaries, tents and hospices were all contained in a box of Tilden's extract. Hasheesh I called the "drug of travel," and I had only to direct my thoughts strongly toward a particular part of the world previously to swallowing my bolus to make my whole fantasia in the strongest possible degree topographical. Or, when the delirium was at its height, let any one suggest to me, however faintly, mountain, wilderness, or market-place, and straightway I was in it, drinking in the novelty of my surroundings in all the ecstasy of a discoverer. I swam up against the current of all time; I walked through Luxor and Palmyra as they were of old; on Babylon the bittern had not built her nest, and I gazed on the unbroken columns of the Parthenon.

Soon after my pedestrian journey through Asia I changed my residence for a while, and went to live in the town of Schenectady. It was here that the remainder of my hasheesh-life was passed, and here, for many days, did I drain alternately cups of superhuman joy and superhuman misery. At Union College, of which I was a resident, I had a few friends to whom I communicated my acquaintance with the wondrous drug which was now becoming a habit with me. Some of them were surprised, some warned me, and as the will most of them be introduced into the narrative which I am writing, I now mention them thus particularly, lest it may be thought strange that, in an ordinary town of small size, there should be found by one man a sufficient number of congenial persons to vary the dramatis personae of a story as mine will be varied.

Having exhausted the supply of hasheesh which I had originally obtained from the shelves of my old lounging-place at the shop of the doctor, I procured a small jar of a preparation of the same drug by another chemist, which, I was told, was much weaker than the former. Late in the evening I took about fifty grains of the new preparation, arguing that this amount was a rational equivalent for the thirty which had before been my maximum dose.

It is impossible, however, to base any calculation of the energy of hasheesh upon such a comparison. The vital forces upon which this most magical stimulant operates are too delicate, to recondite to be treated like material parts in a piece of mechanism whose power of resistance can be definitely expressed by an equation. There are certain nerves, no doubt, which the anatomist and the physician will find affected by the cannabine influence -- certain functions over which its essence appears to hold peculiar regency; but we must have proceeded much farther in the science which treats of the connection between matter and mind, must know much more of those imponderable forces which, more delicate than electricity and more mysterious than the magnetic fluid, weave the delicate interacting network that joins our human duality, before we can treat that part of us affected by hasheesh as a constant in any calculation.

There are two facts which I have verified as universal by repeated experiment, which fall into their place here as aptly as they can in the course of my narrative: 1st. At two different times, when body and mind are apparently in precisely analogous states, when all circumstances, exterior and interior, do not differ tangibly in the smallest respect, the same dose of the same preparation of hasheesh will frequently produce diametrically opposite effects. Still further, I have taken at one time a pill of thirty grains, which hardly gave a perceptible phenomenon, and at another, when my dose had been but half that quantity, I have suffered the agonies of a martyr, or rejoiced in a perfect phrensy. So exceedingly variable are its results, that, long before I abandoned the indulgence, I took each successive bolus with the consciousness that I was daring an uncertainty as tremendous as the equipoise between hell and heaven. Yet the fascination employed Hope as its advocate, and won the suit. 2d. If, during the ecstasy of hasheesh delirium, another dose, however small -- yes, though it be no larger than half a pea -- be employed to prolong the condition, such agony will inevitably ensue as will make the soul shudder at its own possibility of endurance without annihilation. By repeated experiments, which now occupy the most horrible place upon my catalogue of horrible remembrances, have I proved that, among all the variable phenomena of hasheesh, this alone stands unvarying. The use of it directly after any other stimulus will produce consequences as appalling.

But to return from my digression. It was perhaps eight o'clock in the evening when I took the dose of fifty grains. I did not retire until near midnight, and as no effects had then manifested themselves, I supposed that the preparation was even weaker than my ratio gave it credit for being, and, without any expectation of result, lay down to sleep. Previously, however, I extinguished my light. To say this may seem trivial, but it is as important a matter as any which it is possible to notice. The most direful suggestions of the bottomless pit may flow in upon the hasheesh-eater through the very medium of darkness. The blowing out of a candle can set an unfathomed barathrum wide agape beneath the flower-wreathed table of his feast, and convert his palace of sorcery into a Golgotha. Light is a necessity to him, even when sleeping; it must tinge his visions, or they assume a hue as sombre as the banks of Styx.

I do not know how long a time had passed since midnight, when I awoke suddenly to find myself in a realm of the most perfect clarity of view, yet terrible with an infinitude of demoniac shadows. Perhaps, I thought, I am still dreaming; but no effort could arouse me from my vision, and I realized that I was wide awake. Yet it was an awakening which, for torture, had no parallel in all the stupendous domain of sleeping incubus. Beside my bed in the centre of the room stood a bier, from whose corners drooped the folds of a heavy pall; outstretched upon it lay in state a most fearful corpse, whose livid face was distorted with the pangs of assassination. The traces of a great agony were frozen into fixedness in the tense position of every muscle, and the nails of the dead man's fingers pierced his palms with the desperate clinch of one who has yielded not without agonizing resistance. Two tapers at his head, two at his feet, with their tall and unsnuffed wicks, made the ghastliness of the bier more luminously unearthly, and a smothered laugh of derision from some invisible watcher ever and anon mocked the corpse, as if triumphant demons were exulting over their prey. I pressed my hands upon my eyeballs till they ached, in intensity of desire to shut out the spectacle; I buried my head in the pillow, that I might not hear that awful laugh of diabolic sarcasm

But -- oh horror immeasurable! I beheld the walls of the room slowly gliding together, the ceiling coming down, the floor ascending, as of the lonely captive saw them, whose cell was doomed to be his coffin. Nearer and nearer am I borne toward the corpse. I shrunk back from the edge of the bed; I cowered in most abject fear. I tried to cry out, but speech was paralyzed. The walls came closer and closer together. Presently my hand lay on the dead man's forehead. I made my arm as straight and rigid as a bar of iron; but of what avail was human strength against the contraction of that cruel masonry? Slowly my elbow bent with the ponderous pressure; nearer grew the ceiling -- I fell into the fearful embrace of death. I was pent I was stifled in the breathless niche, which was all of space still left to me. The stony eyes stared up into my own, and again the maddening peal of fiendish laughter rang close beside my ear. Now I was touched on all sides by the walls of the terrible press; there came a heavy crush, and I felt all sense blotted out in darkness.

I awaked at last; the corpse was gone, but I had taken his place upon the bier. In the same attitude which he had kept I lay motionless, conscious, although in darkness, that I wore upon my face the counterpart of his look of agony. The room had grown into a gigantic hall, whose roof was framed of iron arches; the pavement, the walls, the cornice were all of iron. The spiritual essence of the metal seemed to be a combination of cruelty and despair. It's massive hardness spoke a language which it is impossible to embody in words, but any one who has watched the relentless sweep of some great engine crank, and realized its capacity for murder, will catch a glimpse, even in the memory, of the thrill which seemed to say, "This iron is a tearless fiend," of the unutterable meaning I saw in those colossal beams and buttresses. I suffered from the vision of that iron as from the presence of a giant assassin.

But my senses opened slowly to the perception of still worse presences. By my side there gradually emerged from the sulphureous twilight which bathed the room the most horrible form which the soul could look upon unshattered -- a fiend also of iron, white hot and dazzling with the glory of the nether penetralia. A face that was the ferreous incarnation of all imaginations of malice and irony looked on me with a glare, withering from its intense heat, but still more from the unconceived degree of inner wickedness which it symbolized. I realized whose laughter I had heard, and instantly I heard it again. Beside him another demon, his very twin, was rocking a tremendous cradle framed of bars of iron like all things else, and candescent with as fierce a heat as the fiend's.

And now, in a chant of the most terrific blasphemy which it is possible to imagine, or rather of blasphemy so fearful that no human thought has ever conceived of it, both the demons broke forth, until I grew intensely wicked merely by hearing it. I still remember the meaning of the song, although there is no language yet coined which will convey it, and far be it from me even to suggest its nature, lest I should seem to perpetuate in any degree such profanity as beyond the abodes of the lost no lips are capable of uttering. Every note of the music itself accorded with the thought as symbol represents essence, and with its clangor mixed the maddening creak of the forever-oscillating cradle, until I felt driven into a ferocious despair. Suddenly the nearest fiend, snatching up a pitchfork (also of white-hot iron), thrust it into my writhing side, and hurled me shrieking into the fiery cradle. I sought in my torture to scale the bars; they slipped from my grasp and under my feet like the smoothest icicles. Through increasing grades of agony I lay unconsumed, tossing from side to side with the rocking of the dreadful engine, and still above me pealed the chant of blasphemy, and the eyes of demoniac sarcasm smiled at me in mockery of a mother's gaze upon her child.

"Let us sing him," said one of the fiends to the other, "the lullaby of Hell." The blasphemy now changed into an awful word-picturing of eternity, unveiling what it was, and dwelling with raptures of malice upon its infinitude, its sublimity of growing pain, and its privation of all fixed points which might mark it into divisions. By emblems common to all language rather than by any vocal words, did they sing this frightful apocalypse, yet the very emblems had a sound a distinct as tongue could give them. This was one, and the only one of their representatives that I can remember. Slowly they began, "To-day is father of to-morrow, to-morrow hath a son that shall beget the day succeeding." With increasing rapidity they sang in this way, day by day, the genealogy of a thousand years, and I traced on the successive generations, without a break in one link, until the rush of their procession reached a rapidity so awful as fully to typify eternity itself; and still I fled on through that burning genesis of cycles. I feel that I do not convey my meaning, but may no one else ever understand it better!

Withered like a leaf in the breath of an oven, after millions of years I felt myself tossed upon the iron floor. The fiends had departed, the cradle was gone. I stood alone, staring into immense and empty spaces. Presently I found that I was in a colossal square, as of some European city, alone at the time of evening twilight, and surrounded by houses hundreds of stories high. I was bitterly athirst. I ran to the middle of the square, and reached it after an infinity of travel. There was a fountain carved in iron, every jet inimitably sculptured in mockery of water, yet dry as the ashes of a furnace. "I shall perish with thirst," I cried. "Yet one more trial. There must be people in all these immense houses. Doubtless they love the dying traveler, and will give him to drink. Good friends! water! water!" A horribly deafening din poured on me from the four sides of the square. Every sash of all the hundred stories of every house in that colossal quadrangle flew up as by one spring. Awakened by my call, at every window stood a terrific maniac. Sublimely in the air above me, in front, beside me, on either hand, and behind my back, a wilderness of insane faces gnashed at me, glared, gibbered, howled, laughed horribly, hissed and cursed. At the unbearable sight I myself became insane, and, leaping up and down, mimicked them all, and drank their demented spirit.

A hand seized my arm -- a voice called my name. The square grew lighter -- it changed -- it slowly took a familiar aspect, and gradually I became aware that my room-mate was standing before me with a lighted lamp. I sank back into his arms, crying "Water! water, Robert! For the love of heaven, water!" He passed across the room to the wash-stand, leaving me upon the bed, where I afterward found he had replaced me on being awakened by hearing me leap frantically up and down upon the floor. In going for the water, he seemed to be traveling over a desert plain to some far-off spring, and I hailed him on his return with the pitcher and the glass as one greets his friend restored after a long journey. No glass for me! I snatched the pitcher, and drank a Niagara of refreshment with every draught. I reveled in the ecstasy of a drinker of the rivers of Al Ferdoos.

Hasheesh always brings with it an awakening of perception which magnifies the smallest sensation till it occupies immense boundaries. The hasheesh-eater who drinks during his highest state of exaltation almost invariably supposes that he is swallowing interminable floods, and imagines his throat an abyss which is becoming gorged by the sea. Repeatedly, as in an agony of thirst I have clutched some small vessel of water and tipped it at my lips, I have felt such a realization of an overwhelming torrent that, with my throat still charred, I have put the water away, lest I should be drowned by the flow.

With the relighting of the lamp my terrors ceased. The room was still immense, yet the iron of its structure, in the alembic of that heavenly light, had been transmuted into silver and gold. Beamy spars, chased by some unearthly graver, supported the roof above me, and a mellow glory transfused me, shed from sunny panels that covered the walls. Out of this hall of grammarye I suddenly passed through a crystal gate, and found myself again in the world outside. Through a valley carpeted with roses I marched proudly at the head of a grand army, and the most triumphant music pealed from all my legions. In the symphony joined many an unutterable instrument, bugles and ophicleides, harps and cymbals, whose wondrous peals seemed to say, "We are self-conscious; we exult like human souls". There were roses every where -- roses under foot, roses festooning the lattices at our sides, roses showering a prodigal flush of beauty from the arches of an arbor overhead. Down the valley I gained glimpses of dreamy lawns basking in a Claude Lorraine sunlight. Over them multitudes of rosy children came leaping to throw garlands on my victorious road, and singing paeans to me with the voices of cherubs. Nations that my sword had saved ran bounding through the flowery walls of my avenue to cry "Our hero -- our savior," and prostrate themselves at my feet. I grew colossal in a delirium of pride. I felt myself the centre of all the world's immortal glory. As once before the ecstasy of music had borne me from the body, so now I floated out of it in the intensity of my triumph. As the last cord was dissolved, I saw all the attendant splendors of my march fade away, and became once more conscious of my room restored to its natural state.

Not a single hallucination remained. Surrounding objects resumed their wonted look, yet a wonderful surprise broke in upon me. In the course of my delirium, the soul, I plainly discovered, had indeed departed from the body. I was that soul utterly divorced from the corporeal nature, disjoined, clarified, purified. From the air in which I hovered I looked down upon my former receptacle. Animal life, with all its processes, still continued to go on; the chest heaved with the regular rise and fall of breathing, the temples throbbed, and the cheek flushed. I scrutinized the body with wonderment; it seemed no more to concern me than that of another being. I do not remember, in the course of the whole experience I have had of hasheesh, a more singular emotion that I felt at that moment. The spirit discerned itself as possessed of all the human capacities, intellect, susceptibility, and will - - saw itself complete in every respect; yet, like a grand motor, it had abandoned the machine which it once energized, and in perfect independence stood apart. In the prerogative of my spiritual nature I was restrained by no objects of a denser class. To myself I was visible and tangible, yet I knew that no material eyes could see me. Through the walls of the room I was able to pass and repass, and through the ceiling to behold the start unobscured. This was neither hallucination nor dream. The sight of my reason was preternaturally intense, and I remembered that this was one of the states which frequently occur to men immediately before their death has become apparent to lookers-on, and also in the more remarkable conditions of trance. That such a state is possible is incontestably proved by many cases on record in which it has fallen under the observation of students most eminent in physico-psychical science.

A voice of command called on me to return into the body, saying in the midst of my exultation over what I thought was my final disenfranchisement from the corporeal, "The time is not yet." I returned, and again felt the animal nature joined to me by its mysterious threads of conduction. Once more soul and body were one.

VI. The Mysteries of the
Life-sign Gemini

In this vision the conception of our human duality was presented to me in a manner more striking than ever before. Hitherto it had been more a suggestion than a proof; now it appeared in the light of an intuition. A wonderful field of questions is opened by such an experience, and I am constrained to sketch a few of them as they have occurred to myself.

1st. Are the animal and spiritual conjoint parts of the same life, or two different lives which intensely interact, yet are not altogether dependent upon each other for their continuance?

That the soul is dependent upon aught that we call material for the preservation of its highest functions, very few men will feel disposed to assert. Yet we are all exceedingly loth to concede that the animal has a distinct life of its own, which, for some time after the dissolution of the ties which bind it to the spiritual, might continue to throb on unimpaired. Your critic, who aims altogether at uses comprehended in bread, meat, and broad-cloth, may ask, "If it be so, of what practical utility would it be to discover it?" A sufficient answer lies in the fact that men would know one more truth. A truth tested and established may lie for centuries, mildewed and rusted, in the armory of knowledge, until some great soul comes along, draws it out of the rubbish, buckles it on, rushes into the conflict, and with it pries open the portals of one more promised land of blessing for the human race. Gunpowder is a truth; wise men sneer at the monk's obstreperous plaything. The years float calmly on; that plaything strikes the cliffs of Dover, and as they go toppling down to leave a highway for the nations, contemned truth vindicates her uses with a triumphant voice of thunder.

But there is also a tangible utility in this discovery of an independent animal life (supposing it to be made) which arises out of the fact that we should thus possess much higher notions of the spiritual than we have at present. In the desire to make the body entirely dependent on the soul for all its processes, we have linked the two in so close a marriage that the soul itself has become materialized by contact in our conceptions. What we call spirit is, after all, when its vague and variable boundaries are somewhat accurately drawn, nothing but an exceedingly rarefied mist, capable, to be sure, of self-conscious phenomena, but nevertheless subject to most of the conditions of matter. We grant, indeed, that after death the interior eyes may see without the mediation of our present lens and retina, but scout the idea that those eyes, in this world, ever employ a power which, after a few years, they shall keep in constant activity forever. Now, if we can more definitely mark the line between the spiritual and the animal as between two independent lives hinged on each other, yet not interpenetrating, we shall have done much to glorify the soul and reinstate it in its proper reverence.

Not to assert the separate of the animal life as proven, let us look at some singular phenomena which, by such an hypothesis, would be explained, and (as it seems to me) by such a one only.

1st. In surgical operations performed while the patient lay under the influence of an anæsthetic, as chloroform or ether, I have witnessed contortions of the whole muscular system, and heard outcries so fearful that it was impossible to persuade the lookers-on that the application of the instrument was not causing the severest agony. Upon one occasion I myself stood by a man who was to suffer a difficult dental operation, and with my own hands administered chloroform to him. All the usual symptoms of complete anæsthesia ensuing, I signaled the dentist to begin his work. The moment that the instrument came into successful operation, the patient uttered a harrowing cry of pain and struggled convulsively, at the same time entreating the operator to stop. I was persuaded, from former cases of a similar nature, that the man had no consciousness of pain, and so advised the dentist. From motives of humanity, however, the latter desisted when his work was but partly accomplished, and, having extracted a single tooth instead of the several which were to be drawn, permitted the seeming sufferer to return to his natural state. He presently awoke, as from a dream; and on being asked whether he endured great torture, he laughed at the idea, denying that he had even been aware of the application of the forceps, although fully self-conscious internally during the whole effect of the anæsthetic.

I believe I am only stating one of many cases which fall under the almost daily observation of men of wide experience in the surgical profession. Although far from being an expert myself, I have been an eye-witness to two such instances.

Now what is it, or who is it that is suffering tortures so great that the face, the lips, the limbs must give vent to them in such intensity of expression? The soul has been all the time lying in a delicious calm of meditation, or gliding through a succession of strange images, whose order was not once broken by the thrill of pain. It frequently remembers its visions, and can repeat them coherently; it would certainly have recollected, if it had ever known them, some traits of an experience so utterly discordant as suffering.

An inference directly suggests itself. Where all the outer phenomena of torture have been witnessed, the anæsthetic has not so much affected the body as the ties which unite it with the soul. A temporary disjunction has taken place between the two, and the animal nature has been suffering while the spiritual, completely insulated, was left to its own free activity.

2d. I believe it is gradually becoming conceded that the agonies which universal belief once attached to the idea of death are rather imaginary than real. Yet the hour of dissolution is almost invariably accompanied by groans and contortions, which tell tales of the bitter pang felt somewhere in the depths of that mysterious being which is becoming disjoined. While the dying man, if still fully conscious, frequently asserts that he is in ecstasy beyond compare, tense muscles and writhing limbs are telling another story. What is it that is suffering?

3d. There have been instances of the trance state which throw an additional light upon this question, or involve it in deeper mystery, according to the mental temperament of the man who considers them. It is needless to quote the case of Tennant in our own country, and many cataleptic and hypnotic states which have fallen under private notice, when an argument à fortiori may be drawn from the remarkable phenomena which but a few years ago transpired under the eye-witness of many eminent men of the medical and other professions in India*. So important a field of inquiry did these phenomena seem to open, that Dr. Braid, of Edinburgh, a physician of considerable fame, made it the groundwork of a book, condensed, yet valuable for its research, upon the trance condition, and the scientific mind throughout Great Britain took a lively interest in the subject. A fakeer presented himself at one of the Company's stations, and proffered the singular request that he might be buried alive. Though not much astonished at any possible petition coming from one of an order of men so wildly fanatic as those who infest India with their monstrous devotions and insatiable alms-begging, the servants of the Company still treated him as insane, and answered his request with corresponding neglect. Still, the fakeer insisted upon their compliance, asserting that he possessed the power of separating soul and body at will, and was able to live without air or food for the space of thirty days. Upon his producing native witnesses who fully corroborated his statement, he obtained a more deferential attention to his demand. As his reason for asking sepulture, he stated the desire for a more complete abstraction of soul than he could attain above ground and among the things of sense, positively assuring his questioners that this abstraction, as he had tested by repeated experiments, was in no danger of proving fatal to the body.

At last, then, his petition was granted. By an effort of will he threw himself into the ecstatic or trance state, and when the vital processes had become absolutely imperceptible, and he lay to all appearance dead, he was closely wrapped in a winding-sheet, and, for fear of imposition, buried in a tightly-masoned tomb. The opening was then filled with earth, and the mound thus raised above him thickly sown with barley. A Mohammedan guard (the last in the world which would be likely to connive at the cheat of a disciple of Brahm) was stationed about the grave night and day. The barley grew up undisturbed till the month was accomplished, and, at the expiration of that time, hundreds of people thronged to be present at the disentombing of the fakeer. Among them were grave men, men of calm and scientific minds, and many utterly incredulous of the possibility that human life could have been sustained from inner sources through so long a period. Every test was thus present which could make evidence of any fact conclusive beyond doubt.

The body of the fakeer was found unaltered by decay, yet shriveled to a mummy. Means of restoration were used very similar to those employed in bringing a cataleptic patient to consciousness. Presently the seemingly dead man began to breathe, his color returned, and before the close of the day, as the nutriment which was given him was assimilated, all his functions were in their ordinary activity.

A more complete separation of the animal and spiritual probably never existed without death, yet the two lives, through the whole period of sepulture, were sustained apart without the slightest consciousness in the soul that the body was growing emaciated, convulsed, and juiceless. Many of the eye-witnesses to this wonderful experiment are living to the present day.

Upon the theory of these independent existences it may be asked, "How is death possible at all to the animal?" We reply, In most cases, doubt-less, the animal dies first, and the spiritual deserts it afterward; but, wherever the spiritual is the more powerfully agonized of the two, in the very shock of its exertions to depart it may bear the animal away with it, which, not being immortal, has no possible residence outside of the body, but instantly perishes. Yet when, as by the gentle disentanglement of patient fingers, the ligaments of the corporeal life are unwound from about the soul, the latter, undestroyed, may still remain through its allotted day of endurance. If this be more than mere visionary conjecture, it accounts for the unchanged appearance of bodies disentombed after a hundred years, and the relics unconsumed by time, which, in the world's reaction from hyper-credulity, we have so long been apt to classify with the other legends of the Vita Sanctorum.

2. Another question suggested by the experience of my own duality is this: If the two existences are independent, may not the fact account for that blind feeling which almost every man has experienced, that he has lived previously to his present form in other and entirely different states? The idea of the metempsychosis was never, indeed, made the central one of any system of philosophy until the time of Pythagoras. He was the first of whom we have historic mention to scale off from the original gem the laminae of grosser Egyptian and Indian fable, which covered it like a later deposit (and he had reasons for doing so, which we think will be proved, to a strong probability at least, in a future portion of this narrative); yet, after all, metempsychosis, as a fact, has been dimly felt by universal humanity, and even at the present day presents itself at times so strongly to many a mind as almost to carry the conviction of an intuition.

But, upon our hypothesis, can the idea be accounted for? Let us see.

Except in the prerogative of the peculiar quality of that life which animates it, the body has no more claims to reverence than the same number of pounds of alkali, water, iron, and other chemicals composing it, in any other form.

But for the energizing, vital element of the particular rank in the scale of vitality which energizes man, he would be worthy of quite as much consideration were he sealed up in carboys, poured into pitchers, blown into bladders, and tied up in brown paper parcels. His body has not the faintest stamp of originality. As bovine muscle he existed long ago in the food which nourished his parents; still farther back he was eaten by an ox in the form of some succulent weed of the pasture, and that very weed educed him from the soil through microscopic tubes by capillary attraction. Wash this soil, and he will be deposited in the form of a precipitate; yet after all this investigation of his material genealogy, we have only arrived at the same result which could be attained by any skillful chemist who would undergo the labor of taking him to pieces in his present state, and subject him to adequate tests. The man of visionary mind may sit down before one solitary cabbage, and find food for his thought, if not for his palate, in the reflection, "Truly thou mightest have been my brother."

Now, without the least shadow of a wish to prove matter self-conscious, may we not hold it possible that the particles entering into our corporeal composition still preserve some subtle properties (not memory, be it understood) of the other bodies through which they have passed, which, being felt by our own animal nature, are suggested by it to the spiritual as a ground for the idea of metempsychosis? The body will then be that part of us which has really transmigrated, while the soul is original.

The idea that the soul has ever transmigrated leads us into painful, disgusting, irrational, and irreligious conclusions. But grant that, in the animal life, a blind perception exists of peculiar qualities in the corporeal particles, arising out of former conditions through which they have passed, and we can then see how it may be possible for the spiritual to sympathize with the animal to such a degree as to etherealize these perceptions into a dreamy echo of its own former being. The problem, therefore, stands thus: Both for the sake of right and reason we must utterly disown the idea of spiritual metempsychosis. How, then, can we explain the fact of its universality among the race? We offer our hypothesis.

VII. The Night of Apotheosis

It may be thought strange that, after that experience of infinite agony which I have last related, I should ever take hasheesh again. "Surely," it will be said, "another experiment with the drug would be a daring venture into the realms of insanity and death. The gentlest name that could be applied to it is foolhardiness."

The morning immediately succeeding my night of horror found me as vigorous and buoyant as I ever was in my life. No pain, no feeling of lassitude remained, and on my face there was not the faintest record of the tortures through which I had passed. In the midst of the very astonishment with which I noted this fact, I felt assured that I had done myself no injury. Yet, mentally, I had the conception of being older by many years than on the night previous; all past experiences in life seemed separated from me by a measureless gulf of duration, and when the demon faces or hellish songs of my vision flashed up into memory, I shuddered and turned my head as if they were close at hand. Quietly I made a resolve that I would experiment with the drug of sorcery no more, for I dreaded another plunge into the abyss of terror as I dreaded hell itself.

Slowly passed away from my mind the image of my sufferings. The elastic force of thought threw off the weight of all direful remembrances, and whenever I recalled my last night of vision it was only to dwell with tenderness upon the roses of my valley, and exult in the echo of the paeans which had glorified my march. So beautiful did such memories make the inner world, that I wearied of the outer till it became utterly distasteful, like a heavy tragedy seen for the fortieth time. I tried in vain to detect in the landscape that ever-welling freshness of life which hasheesh unveils; trees were meaningless wood, the clouds a vapory sham. I thirsted for insight, adventure, strange surprises, and mystical discoveries. I took hasheesh again.

I was sitting at the tea-table when the thrill smote me. I had handed my cup to Miss M'Ilvaine to be replenished for the first time, and she was about restoring it to me brimming with that draught "which cheers but not inebriates." I should be loth to calculate the arc through which her hand appeared to me to travel on its way to the side of my plate. The wall grew populous with dancing satyrs; Chinese mandarins nodded idiotically in all the corners, and I felt strongly the necessity of leaving the table before I betrayed myself.

I rose and hurried from the room. A friend of mine, thinking that I had been taken suddenly ill, immediately followed me. The look of wild delight with which I greeted him would have revealed my secret, even had I not spontaneously imparted it to him.

In the first stages of his singular life, the hasheesh- eater finds so much that is strange, beautiful, or appalling, that he can restrain neither his outbursts of enthusiasm nor of pain. He is big with infinite arcana, which he feels he must disclose or perish. Gradually self-control becomes with him more of a possibility, and finally it is stereotyped into a habit. In my earlier experience I found it beyond my power, even with the most agonizing efforts, to keep back the wonders which I saw, and accordingly, the moment that I found my brain expanding into the hasheesh-dome, I made it my wont to rush from the presence of all who ought not to share my secret. When many days had taught me lessons of self-retention, I sat frequently for hours charred in demoniac flames, or lifted into the seventh heaven of ecstasy, with a throng around me who could not have gained the faintest intimation from my manner of the processes which were going on within.

When Sam joined me I was on the eve of another journey through vast territories. I say "Sam," for I shall take the liberty of calling all my friends by those familiar names which imbody to me all that is loving, genial, and belonging to idiosyncrasy in my remembrance of them. Doubtless such a practice is discordant with courtly style in the most eminent degree. It would be much more polite to say Villiers where I meant Joe, and Cholmondeley instead of Harry; for in this way I should much more readily and thoroughly conciliate those minds which, enervated by the spicy feasts of high-life literature, are unable to find the least sapidity in the vocabulary of daily affections.

Southey, discoursing of the Doctor, has made that mirror of true-heartedness, as well as true courtesy, remark (I quote from memory), that among the most painful, though quiet and unnoticed losses which a man sustains in his passage from the infant to the gray-beard, is the gradual divestment of his right to be called by the name which he heard in the nursery and on the play-ground. "Now," saith Daniel Dove, with a gentle sigh, "even my wife speaks of me as 'the Doctor.'" most genial men have felt the same thing with sorrow as the "toga virilis" slowly wrapped them closer and closer into the reserve of middle life, hiding those earlier insignia of frankness and good-fellowship which no longer give them a claim to be hailed with affectionate intimacy, yet which every true man will still bear with lively remembrance upon his heart of hearts.

I have always entertained a deep grudge against the cold and courtly Cicero for that unworthy sneer launched at the friendship between Catiline and Tongilius, "Quem amare in prætexta coeperat." It was in the style of Cicero, indeed, yet not in the style of the truly noble man, nor of one who holds in fitting reverence the bond of our earlier humanities. It seems impossible to conceive how any one dignified with the better and deeper feelings of our nature should become aware, with any other sentiment than pain, that he is surviving the days when a more intimate confidence and unworldly simplicity gave genial friends a right to address him and treat him as a brother.

I shall therefore, without any apology, unless this digression may be styled so, call all the nearer and dearer companions of my youth by those names which sound as the sweetest echoes of the Past in the chambers of my memory, since the strings with which they vibrate in unison can not too long be kept thrilling in any heart that would not neglect all music beyond that with which the march of our dusty life in the exterior keeps step.

I have said that when Sam joined me I was once more filled with the phrensy of travel. I besought him to go with me, painting in the most glowing tints the treasures which such a gigantic tour as I had laid out would add to his acquaintance with the grand Kosmos. He consented to become my compagnon de voyage for a few hundred miles, at any rate, and directly we set out. Our way led through a broad meadow, at that season beautifully green, and before my gaze it grew into a tremendous Asiatic plateau thronged with innumerable Tartars. As if assembling for a foray, they rushed past me in mad haste, their oblique eyes snapping with a ferocious light, and plumes of horse-hair streaming from their tufted caps. It is not possible to convey to a mind in its ordinary state the effect produced by beholding a field which one has been accustomed to see vacant suddenly bristling with weird and foreign forms, which by perfect distinctness of outline equal in reality, while they surpass in impressiveness the most usual objects of daily sight.

Sam was a man unexcelled by any of his age that I have ever met for the breadth of his historic, geographical, and political knowledge. Mention a fact in the Saracen annals, and straightway he would give you its date, and run its parallel of chronological latitude through all the empires and dynastics of the world. The name of the most inconsiderable place suggested to him every thing of note that had ever been transacted in its neighborhood, and on the factious efforts of an Athenian demagogue he would build you in an instant the intricate fabric of all the coups d' état, revolutions, and strokes of diplomacy up to the present day. It is not to be wondered at, such being the case, that some incongruous remark of my own, which confounded two utterly distinct tribes of Tartary, should grate on his historic taste to such a degree as to force from him a mild correction.

"It is impossible," said Sam, "that the tribe of which you speak should occupy this territory through whose boundaries you inform me we are traveling."

The instantaneous thrill of pain which this slight contradiction darted through me can not be imagined by any one who does not know the intense sensitiveness of the hasheesh state. In a tone of deepest reproach I said, "Alas! my friends, I see you do not sympathize with me. Let us travel apart."

So saying, I wandered from his side and walked alone, feeling hurt in the very centre of my pride and self- respect. But Sam, who now saw that he must humor my hallucination, followed me, and appeasing my indignation upon the delicate subject of the Ukraine Tartars, took my arm, and we walked together as before.

With all the delicious ecstasy of a traveler who looks for the first time upon the gorgeous piles of mediaeval architecture, I saw far in the distant east a palace rise sublimely above its emerald terraces. We walked for hours and through leagues, yet it grew no nearer, and I enjoyed the luxury of anticipation indefinitely prolonged, yet growing sweeter by delay. The wind came to me freighted with spicy odors; it whispered of dalliance with citron blossoms, and reeled in playful circles; new-flown from its deep draught among the vines of Muscat. In my ears it sang promises of immortal youth, and added its own wings to my already superhuman lightness.

What mattered it that my far-off battlements were the walls of college, my mighty plain a field, and my wind of balm but an ordinary sunset breeze? To me all joys were real -- yes, even with a reality which utterly surpasses the hardest facts of the ordinary world.

Hasheesh is indeed an accursed drug, and the soul at last pays a most bitter price for all its ecstasies; moreover, the use of it is not the proper means of gaining any insight, yet who shall say that at that season of exaltation I did not know things as they are more truly than ever in the ordinary state? Let us not assert that the half-careless and uninterested way in which we generally look on nature is the normal mode of the soul's power of vision. There is a fathomless meaning, an intensity of delight in all our surroundings, which our eyes must be unsealed to see. In the jubilance of hasheesh, we have only arrived by an improper pathway at the secret of that infinity of beauty which shall be beheld in heaven and earth when the veil of the corporeal drops off, and we know as we are known. Then from the muddy waters of our life, defiled by the centuries of degeneracy through which they have flowed, we shall ascend to the old-time original fount, and grow rapturous with its apocalyptic draught.

But for this reflection I had never abandoned hasheesh. Yet through all the long agonies which attended its abjurement, I consoled myself with the knowledge that the infinite glories of the past should beam on me again. I had caught a glimpse through the chinks of my earthly prison of the immeasurable sky which should one day overarch me with an unconceived sublimity of view, and resound in my ear with unutterable music. Then I stayed myself upon the hope, and grew into calm endurance.

We may depend upon it, we have not read the world within or the world without. Some mystic wind, like that of hasheesh, now and then just flutters the leaves of those shut books as it passes by, and the gleam of the divine characters for an instant ravishes us. As from children too young to bear them, they are kept against that day when, grown into perfect men, the props, and helps, and screens of the earthly shall be removed from us, and "the books shall be opened."

Presently we reached the doors of college. I do not remember whether I have yet mentioned that in the hasheesh state an occasional awaking occurs, perhaps as often as twice in an hour (though I have no way of judging accurately, from the singular properties of the hasheesh time), when the mind returns for an exceedingly brief space to perfect consciousness, and views all objects in their familiar light. Such an awaking occurred to me as we drew near the steps of the building, and I took advantage of it to request Sam that he would conduct me to the room of another friend of mine, if he were unable to remain longer with me himself. He answered that he was obliged to leave me, and accordingly led me to the place I had mentioned. The hasheesh fantasia having returned directly after I had made my request, I might never have been able to find it alone.

Repeatedly have I wandered past doors and houses which, in my ordinary condition, were as well known as my own, and have at last given up the search for them in utter hopelessness, recognizing not the faintest familiar trace in their aspect. Certainly, a hasheesh eater should never be alone.

I found Sidney in his room: in his charge Sam left me, after apprising him of my state, and I easily persuaded him to go with me on my travels. Back of the buildings a very large domain of woods and fields extends toward the east. From the door of one of the entries a continuous path leads to the further extent of these grounds, and into this path we struck. The evening shadows were deepening, yet the woods had not yet become so sombre as to wear that terrible air of mystery which, among them, in my after hasheesh-life, oppressed me to an unbearable degree, even in the daylight. Our way skirted the banks of a little stream, which, tinkling over its rocky bed, makes music through all those shades from boundary to boundary. Coming to a convenient place, we crossed it on broad stepping- stones a pebble's throw from a low waterfall, which, higher up the bed, was now swolen by recent rains. An instantaneous dart of exultation shot through me. Could it be possible? Yes, true, beyond doubt! I clapped my hands and cried, "The Nile! the Nile! the eternal Nile!" Lo, now I was Bruce, and beside me walked Clapperton. "Companion of my journey," I exclaimed, "see you yonder cataract? Above it lie the sources. Out of that gleaming chasm which you behold toward the east, this mystery-veiled river has poured his floods since God first awakened the years. I drink in the ecstasy of his material fount now for the second time. Through lonely pilgrimages I toiled, foot-sore, in the desert; my life hung, many a night of sleeplessness and many a day of famine, upon the mood of ferocious men; I did all things, I suffered all things; and one day, at even, the sources broke upon me. Oh, that unshared view was glory enough for a lifetime!" "But why," asked Clapperton, "has the world never known this discovery of yours? In all my wanderings (and, as you are aware, they have been only exceeded by your own), I have never heard of your visit to this fountain before."

"I died in the desert on my way homeward. As I felt the unmistakable signs of death come upon me, I gathered strength to trace upon a small piece of paper a few words, simply stating the fact of the discovery, and the bearings of the sources. This I committed to my guide, extorting from him a reluctant promise never to part with it until he had carried it to my friends at Alexandria."

"Why reluctant?"

"Because he declared that it was sacrilege to unveil the forehead of the Nile, and that he dreaded some fearful recompense for his impiety."

"Where is that paper now? Did he fulfill his promise?"

"No. He carried the writing as far as Alexandria, and there, being overcome by the terrors of his superstition, burned it, and forever deprived me of the triumph of my labors. Yet with you, Clapperton -- you, who so well know my toils -- I rejoice as if the world were applauding me. Glory, glory in the highest, that I behold again -- that I behold with you -- the Nile, the eternal Nile!"

My eyes ran tears of ecstasy. I clasped Clapperton to my bosom in speechless joy. I heard the river in its upper caverns hymning such invitations as float down to the seer, entranced, from the lips of angels. Bruce revisiting earth felt such exultation as can only be excelled by that of Bruce first freed from earth.

Leaving the banks of the Nile, we struck deeper into the dense shade of pines and chestnuts, which, to my sense, were spice-trees of the African wilderness. On a stile over which our way led sat two students repeating Shakspeare to each other. To avoid their beholding my rejoicing, Sid gently took me into another path, yet we came near enough to hear one sentence:

"With this, farewell; I'm on my way to Padua."
(Not exactly Shakspeare, but they meant it to be, and I was not in a mood to cavil.)
In an instant, like the shifting of a scene, all the thoughts and images of Africa vanished. Italy, the glad, the sunny, took its place, and the wood grew dense with palaces and fountains. In a broad piazza we sauntered up and down, transfused with a dreamy summer languor, or strolled from portico to portico, on all sides surrounded by the most beautiful creations of Art.

At first I had a dim conception of the unreality of this vision, for I saw its groundwork in certain material things, remembered as once existing in other forms. For instance, I sometimes perceived the development of an arch in its transition state from two curved branches which locked over us, and now and then a new column grew up gradually from the vacant light-spaces between two trunks of trees. But in a very short time, of course, much shorter than I supposed, every suspicion of the imaginary utterly vanished from my mind, and I no more doubted our being in some fair Italian city than I doubted my own existence.

The effect of the hasheesh increased, as it always does, with the excitement of the visions and the exercise of walking. I began to be lifted into that tremendous pride which is so often a characteristic of the fantasia. My powers became superhuman; my knowledge covered the universe; my scope of sight was infinite. I was invested with a grand mission to humanity, and slowly it dawned upon me that I was the Christ, come in the power and radiance of his millennial descent, and bearing to the world the restoration of perfect peace. I spoke, and it was done: with a single sentence I regenerated the Creation. A smile of exultation beamed from the awakened earth. I could hear her low music of rejoicing as she perceived that the fullness of the times with which, for centuries, she had travailed in woe, had at length been brought forth. All men once more lived in love to God and their neighbor, and, secure in an eternal compact, began marching on harmoniously to the sublime end of spiritual greatness. The nature of all beasts grew mild; the satyr walked down from his mountain fastness, and led his young fearlessly into the presence of his old foe, the leopard; the kite and the dove imped their wings upon the same branch; out of the depths of the jungle the tiger stepped forth and gently drew near to fawn upon his king. The terrible lustre of his eyes was dissolved into the serene light of love, and as I caressed his spotted hide, he returned the kindness with a thankful purr.

My mission being accomplished, we passed on. Returning o the college, a most singular phenomenon presented itself. The faces of all that I met were metamorphosed into appearances which symbolized some inner attribute, or some speciality of manners and habits. One of my friends was an admirable whist-player, noted for his accurate observance and employment of the times and seasons for returning leads, finessing, and crying privilege. His face was changed to a fan-like display of cards, which winked at me with a quiet and balmy air of exultation, as in the consciousness of being

"Quite irresistible,
Like a man with eight trumps in his hand at a whist-table."
Another, famous for his studently habits, a great reader, and fond of research, looked at me for a moment, and his visage immediately turned into a book-case bristling with encyclopaedias. I stretched forth my hand to take one from its shelf, and, by a sudden outcry, became aware that I had performed that amiable office known among mortals as pulling one's nose.

But this vision of the ludicrous was soon dissipated by the return of the former ecstasy of pride. Now braced for its exaltation by the few moments of jocose refreshment, I towered into all the sublimity of self-adulation. Pacing the floor, which, for my display, had been changed into that of the Senate, as Webster revivified, I rolled a thunder-cloud of colossal argument over the head of a mythical opponent, and brought all time to the witness-stand with testimony against the direful results of some intemperate measure.

And now, the hallucination changing, I was exhaustlessly rich, and as exhaustlessly benevolent. Through long avenues I walked between kneeling files of poor, and scattered handfuls of gold into their bosoms. "Be comfortable, be opulent, be luxurious," I cried; and as the metallic rain dripped from my thrilling fingers, again the plaudits of my march poured in upon me, and the famine-stricken shouted, "Our savior!" I rejoiced in the measureless pride of bounteousness.

Awaking on the morrow after a succession of vague and delicious dreams, I had not yet returned to the perfectly natural state. I now began to experience a law of hasheesh which developed its effects more and more through all the future months of its use. With the progress of the hasheesh life, the effect of every successive indulgence grows more perduring until the hitherto isolated experiences become tangent to each other; then the links of the delirium intersect, and at last so blend that the chain has become a continuous band, now resting with joyous lightness as a chaplet, and now mightily pressing in upon the soul like the glowing hoop of iron which holds martyrs to the stake. The final months of this spell-bound existence, be it terminated by mental annihilation or by a return into the quiet and mingled facts of humanity, are passed in one unbroken yet checkered dream.

In the morning the ludicrous side of the hasheesh sphere alone was turned toward me. I was whirled through the progress of an infinite number of strange transmutations. Now, as a powerful saw in some mill of a northern lumber region, I darted up and down at the imperative instigation of an overshot wheel, and on either side of me the planks flew off in the unmost completeness of manufacture. Now changed to a bottle of soda-water, I ran hither and thither with intricate and rapid involutions, pursued by an army of publicans, who, with awl in hand, were trying to break the wires which kept in my vital effervescence. Weak with laughter, for I was strangely reckless of the peril which my life sustained, I sat down to rest, having distanced the whole troop of my persecutors. Suddenly the sentiment of an intense mortification overcame me. "Is it possible," I soliloquized, "that thou, the descendant of an ancient and glorious line, canst be so utterly dishonored as to merge thy being in one of society's grossest and basest potables? Child worthy of a better destiny, I will implore the gods for thee, that in heir condescension they may elevate thee to some more spiritual essence." No sooner said than done. My neck grew longer, my head was night-capped with snowy kid, ethereal odors of delight streamed through my brain, and, exultant with apotheosis, I beheld by patent of nobility stamped on my crystal breast in these golden characters:

EAU DE COLOGNE.
JEAN MARIA DE FARINA.

A lordly hippopotamus, I wandered in from the wilderness, and with my fore- foot knocked at the door of a friend of mine celebrated for wasting the midnight burning-fluid in the pursuit of classical and mathematical researches. "Tidings!" I cried; "tidings from the interior of Africa!" With a look of astonishment and half terror, for he had never seen me in the hasheesh state before, the lover of books opened unto me, and I passed in.

An unceremonious hippopotamus, I sat down, with the most incongruous disregard of the breadth of beam proper to my species, in the nearest chair, without explanation or apology. A poetical hippopotamus, I soared into a sublime description of equatorial crags, medio-terrene lakes, and marshy jungles. I expatiated upon the delights of an Ethiopian existence; I grew rapturous over the remembered ecstasy of mud-baths and lunches upon succulent lotus-stems by riversides where Nature kept free restaurant for pachydermatous gentlemen forever.

Ed was a man of strong social impulses, most kindly heart, and high appreciation of the beautiful. Yet at that moment, being ensconced in a tremendous munition of tomes, and supplied with stores of reading which might sustain the most protracted siege, pleaded preoccupation, and begged me to defer my lecture on the African far niente. I consented, with some indignation, however, at his lack of taste. I opened the door to leave his room for the sake of finding a more respectful auditor, when lo! to my shame, I had altogether mistaken my species, for I was the tallest giraffe that ever dallied amorously with a palm-bud. Abasing my exalted head to suit the dimensions of the door, I passed out, and was again restored to the human semblance.

VIII. Vos non vobis -- wherein the Pythagorean is a By-stander

The judgment that must be passed upon the hasheesh life in retrospect is widely different from the one which I formed during its progress. Now the drug, with all its revelation of interior mysteries, its glimpses of supernatural beauty and sublimity, appears as the very witch-plant of hell, the weed of madness. At the time of its daily use, I forgave it for all its pangs, for its cruel exercise of authority, its resistless fascination, and its usurpation of the place of all other excitement, at the intercession of the divine forms which it created for my soul, and which, though growing rarer and rarer, when they were present retained their glory until the last. Moreover, through many ecstasies and many pains, I still supposed that I was only making experiments, and that, too, in the most wonderful field of mind which could be opened for investigation, and with an agent so deluding in its influence that the soul only became aware that the strength of a giant was needed to escape when its locks were shorn.

In accordance with these facts, I did not suppose that I was imperiling any friend of mine by giving him an opportunity to make the same experiment which he beheld producing in me phenomena so astonishing to a mind in love with research. Several of my intimate associates applied to me for the means of experimentally gratifying their curiosity upon the subject, and to some of them, as favorable opportunities presented themselves, I administered hasheesh, remaining by their side during the progress of the effects. In no other experience can difference of temperament, physical and mental, produce such varieties of phenomena; nowhere can we attain so well defined an idea of this difference. I shall, therefore, devote this chapter to the relation of some of the more remarkable of these cases.

Upon William N----- hasheesh produced none of the effects characteristic of fantasia. There was no hallucination, no volitancy of unusual images before the eye when closed. Circulation, however, grew to a surprising fullness and rapidity, accompanied by the same introversion of faculties and clear perception of all physical processes which startled me in my first experiment upon myself. There was stertorous breathing, dilation of the pupil, and a drooping appearance of the eyelid, followed at last by a comatose state, lasting for hours, out of which it was almost impossible fully to arouse the energies. These symptoms, together with a peculiar rigidity of the muscular system, and inability to measure the precise compass and volume of the voice when speaking, brought the case nearer in resemblance to those recorded by Dr. O'Shaughnessy, of Calcutta, as occurring under his immediate inspection among the natives of India than any I have ever witnessed.

In William N----- I observed, however, one phenomenon which characterizes hasheesh existence in persons of far different constitutions -- the expansion of time and space. Walking with him a distance not exceeding a furlong, I have seen him grow weary and assume a look of hopelessness, which he explained by telling me that he never could traverse the immensity before him. Frequently, also, do I remember his asking to know the time thrice in as many minutes, and when answered, he exclaimed, "Is it possible? I supposed it an hour since I last inquired." His temperament was a mixture of the phlegmatic and nervous, and he was generally rather unsusceptible to stimulus. I was anxious at the time that he should be favorably affected, since he had been, and afterward was still more so, in an eminent degree, the kind-hearted assuager of my sufferings and increaser of my joys in many an experience of hasheesh. To him I ran, many a time, for companionship in my hasheesh journeyings, and always found in him full appreciation and sympathy.

I am now glad that he learned none of the fascination of the drug, for Heaven only, and not the hasheesh-eater in any wise, knows where it will lead him.

One of my friends in college was a man to whom it would have been physically, spiritually, and morally impossible ever to have borne any other name than Bob, the name by which he was called among all his intimates, and which has an air eminently expressive of his nature. Impulsive, enthusiastic in his affections, generous to a fault; excitable, fond of queer researches and romantic ventures, there is no other cognomen which would so typify him as to give more than a shadow image of his constitution -- none which would so incarnate him as not to leave some elbow of his inner being sticking out in the improper place. It is not surprising that a person of his temperament found much in the hasheesh condition that was strikingly attractive.

At half past seven in the evening, and consequently after supping instead of before, as I should have preferred, he took twenty-five grains of the drug. This may seem a large bolus to those who are aware that from fifteen grains I frequently got the strongest cannabine effect; but it must be kept in mind that, to secure the full phenomena, a much greater dose is necessary in the first experiment than ever after. Unlike all other stimuli with which I am acquainted, hasheesh, instead of requiring to be increased in quantity as existence in its use proceeds, demands rather a diminution, seeming to leave, at the return of the natural state (if I may express myself by a rather material analogy), an unconsumed capital of exaltation for the next indulgence to set up business upon.

From the untoward lateness of the hour at which the dose was administered, it was half past ten o'clock before any effects began to show themselves in this case. At that time Bob, and Edward, the reading man, to whose favorable notice I had presented myself under the guise of a hippopotamus, were both seated, together with myself, in a well-lighted room, conversing. Suddenly Bob leaped up from the lounge on which he had been lying, and, with loud peals of laughter, danced wildly over the room. A strange light was in his eyes, and he gesticulated furiously, like a player in pantomine. I was not in the least surprised by these symptoms, for I realized precisely the state of mind through which he was passing; yet my other companion was astonished even to terror with the idea that the experimenter would permanently lose his sanity. Suddenly he stopped dancing, and trembling, as with an undefinable fear, he whispered, "What will become of me?" This question distinctly recalled all the horrible apprehensions of my first experiment; and, though satisfied of the perfect harmlessness of the result, I saw the necessity of steadying the sufferer's mind upon my own firm assurance of his safety, for the sake of giving him quiet and endurance. I replied, "Trust me, however singularly you may feel, you have not the slightest cause for fear. I have been where you are now, and, upon my honor, guarantee you an unharmed return. No evil will result to you; abandon yourself to the full force of your feelings with perfect confidence that you are in no danger." Entirely new and unconceived as is the hasheesh-world, viewed for the first time, the man of greatest natural courage is no more capable of bearing its tremendous realities, unbraced by some such exterior support, than the most feeble woman.

The delirius, now rapidly mounting to its height, made it better that Bob should exert the supernatural activity with which he was endued out of doors, where the air was freer and less constraint was necessary. Clothing my words in as imaginative garb as I was master of, I therefore proposed to him that we should set out on a journey through the wonderful lands of vision. We were soon upon the pavement, he leaping in unbounded delight at the prospect of the grand scenery to come, I ready to humor to the utmost any pleasing fantasy which might possess him; and in the absence of such, or the presence of the contrary, to suggest fine avenues for his thought to follow-up.

It will of course be perceived that I labor under a great disadvantage from being compelled to relate the progress of subjective states from an objective point of view. My authority for all that I shall give in this case will be my own observation of outward phenomena and my friend's statement of interior ones, which he gave to me upon returning to consciousness. These latter were expressed with a height of ideality which I feel myself incompetent to give, and gave evidence of as remarkable an inner condition as I have ever known hasheesh to produce.

On our first leaving the steps of the building, a grand mosque rose upon his vision in the distance, its minarets flaunting with innumerable crescent- emblazoned flags. A mighty plain, covered with no other than a stinted grass, stretched between him and the mosque. Mounted upon Arab horses, with incredible swiftness we sped side by side toward the structure; and I knew when this imagination took place by the answers which he returned me upon my inquiry into the reasons of his prancing as we went. Before we reached the walls, arch and minaret had vanished, and, metamorphosed into an ostrich, he scoured the desert reaches, now utterly void of any human sign. Of this fact also I became aware at the moment from his own lips; for, although in perfect hallucination, the dual existence, as in me, was still perfectly capable of expressing its own states.

It is not one of the least singular facts of hasheesh that its fantasia almost invariably takes an Oriental form. This can not be explained upon the hypothesis that the experimenter remembers it as an indulgence in use among the people of the East, for at the acme of the delirium there is no consciousness remaining in the mind of its being an unnatural state. The very idea of the drug is utterly forgotten, and present reality shuts out all inquiry into grounds for belief. The only supposition which at all accounts for the fact to my own mind is that the hasheesh is the antecedent instead of the result of the peculiar characteristics of Oriental mind and manners. The Turk and the Syrian are indeed situated amid surroundings well calculated to stimulate the imaginative nature. A delicious sky, a luxuriant vegetation, and scenery like that of the Bosporous and Damascus are eminently calculated for fascination to dreams and poesy, but then hasheesh comes bearing an unutterably grander and richer gratification to the same music and odor haunted sense, and makes the highest tone in a harmony already beautiful almost beyond all that earth poseses.

To us, of a mistier atmosphere, yet far more lively perceptions of the very principle of beauty, the drug brings a similar wealth of visions, and, conjoining its influence with a greater scope of sight and strength of thought than the Oriental ever possesses, fills up all deficiencies of exterior sun and landscape by borrowing from the activities of the experimenter.

Eastern architecture, and, in fine, the sum total of Eastern manners, are all the embodiment and symbol of Eastern mind. That mind, or at least its specialty of condition, is very much the product of those stimulants which are in use throughout that portion of the world, and among these hasheesh holds the regency, as swaying the broadest domain of mind, and most authoritatively ruling all faculties within it. It is therefore the case that, wherever this drug comes into contact with a sensitive organization, the same fruit of supernatural beauty or horror will characterize the visions produced. It is hasheesh which makes both the Syrian and the Saxon Oriental.

That this hypothesis is more than mere vagary, it appears to me, may be proved by numerous parallels running through other nations than the Eastern. It is not mere murky weather, chill winds, and sudden changes of temperature which have built up the walls of reserve in manner and masonry in architecture around the Englishman. His national stimulus is beer, mildly toned by the moderate use of tobacco; his mental result is reticence, solidity, reflectiveness.

Nor does the newness of his country, the peculiarities of his climate, and the demand of his age for rapidity of action alone erect for the American his airy structures, rising with a fungus-vitality from basement to cope in a fortnight, and the pale fence of frankness, which permits insight into all his thoughts. His infants stretch supplicating hands from the cradle toward their father's tobacco-box; the olive-plants around his table are as regularly fumigated as if they were in a green-house; his gray-beard uncle (whenever an American takes time lo live so long) through all the house continually pipes a fragrant music, to which the remainder of the household do not refuse to dance, and from this most catholic transfusion of nicotine he results in that very anomalous, yet, on the whole, laudable product, our National Man. This man is a singular compound of the visionary and the actual: visionary, because (with other causes, to be sure) his stimulant makes him so; actual, because the necessity of hard work in the New World of intense activity demands it of him. His mind incarnates itself in structures whose decoration and rapidity of finish are accomplished at the risk of safety, permanence, and health, and in manners which caution and reserve only characterize when hard knocks against projecting angles of humanity have taught him the lesson of their needfulness.

His town house is the embodiment of the cigar, as the Briton's is that of the tankard, and the modes of living of both of them symbolize to a great degree the essence of their several stimulants.

In all civilized nations, the public works of architecture are an exception to this rule, for the design of the pile being more cosmopolitan, national idiosyncrasies are merged in the more comprehensive plan which contains within itself the garnered excellences of all worldly art. With the Turk it is not so; uncatholicized as is his nature, his mosque and his sultan's seraglio are as definite incarnations of generic peculiarity as his kiosk.

Excusing myself for this digression, I return to the details of the visions which I had commenced.

The night was much darker than it should have been for a hasheesh-eater's walk, who, it will be remembered, calls imperatively for light to tinge his visions. The hallucination of the ostrich still remaining, we passed out into the street through the stone gateway at the end of the college terrace. The sky above us was obscured by clouds, but the moon, now at her full, was about three breadths of her disk above the western horizon. I pointed through the trees to her radiant shield, and called Bob's attention to the peculiar beauty of the view. He clapped his hands in ecstasy, exclaiming, "Behold the eternal kingdom of the moonlight!" From that moment until the planet set, in this kingdom he walked. A silvery deliciousness transfused all things to his sight; his emotions rose and fell like tides with the thrill of the lunar influence. All that in past imaginings he had ever enjoyed of moonlit river views, terraces, castles, and slumberous gardens, was melted into this one vision of rapture.

At length the moon sank out of sight, and a thick darkness enveloped us in the lonely street, only relieved by the corner lamps, which dotted the long and drear prospective. For a while we walked silently. Presently I felt my companion shudder as he leaned upon my arm. "What is the matter, Bob?" I asked. "Oh! I am in unbearable horror," he replied. "If you can, save me!" "How do you suffer?" "This shower of soot which falls on me from heaven is dreadful!"

I sought to turn the current of his thoughts into another channel, but he had arrived at that place in his experience where suggestion is powerless. His world of the Real could not be changed by any inflow from ours of the Shadowy. I reached the same place in after days, and it was then as impossible for any human being to alter the condition which enwrapped me as it would have been for a brother on earth to stretch out his hands and rescue a brother writhing in the pains of immortality. There are men in Oriental countries who make it their business to attend hasheesh-eaters during the fantasia, and profess to be able to lead them constantly in pleasant paths of hallucination. If indeed they possess this power, the delirium which they control must be a far more ductile state than any I have witnessed occurring under the influence of hasheesh at its height. In the present instance I found all suggestion powerless. The inner actuality of the visions and the terror of external darkness both defeated me.

Again, for a short distance, we went without speaking. And now my friend broke forth into a faint, yet bitter cry of "Pray for me! I shall be lost!" Though still knowing that he was in no ultimate danger, I felt that it was vain to tell him so, and, granting his request, ejaculated, "Oh best and wisest God, give peace unto this man!" "Stop! stop!" spoke my friend; "that name is terrible to me; I can not hear it. I am dying; take me instantly to a physician."

Aware that, though no such physical need existed, there was still a great spiritual one if I would make him calm, I immediately promised him that I would do as he asked, and directed our course to the nearest doctor. Now, demoniac shapes clutched at him from the darkness, cloaked from head to foot in inky palls, yet glaring with fiery eyes from the depths of their cowls. I felt him struggling, and by main force dragged him from their visionary hands. The place wherein he seemed to himself to be walking wa a vast arena, encircled by tremendous walls. As from the bottom of a black barathrum, he looked up and saw the stars infinitely removed; they gazed mournfully at him with a human aspect of despairing pity, and he heard them faintly bewailing his perdition. Sulphureous fires rolled in the distance, upbearing on their waves agonized forms and faces of mockery, and demon watch-fires flared up fitfully on the impenetrable battlements around him. He did not speak a word, but I heard him groan with a tone that was full of fearful meaning.

And now, in the midst of the darkness, there suddenly stood a wheel like that of a lottery, surrounded by one luminous spot, which illustrated all its movements. It began slowly to revolve; its rapidity grew frightful, and out of its opening flew symbols which indicated to him, in refular succession, every minutest act of his past life: from his first unfilial disobedience in childhood -- the refusal upon a certain day, as far back as infancy, to go to school when it was enjoined upon him, up to the latest deed of impropriety he had committed -- all his existence flew before him like lightning in those burning emblems. Things utterly forgotten -- things at the time of their first presence considered trivial -- acts as small as the cutting of a willow wand, all fled by his sense in arrow-flight; yet he remembered them as real incidents, and recognized their order in his existence.

This phenomenon is one of the most striking exhibitions of the state in which the higher hasheesh exaltation really exists. It is a partial sundering, for the time, of those ties which unite soul and body. That spirit should ever lose the traces of a single impression is impossible. De Quincey's comparison of it to the palimpsest manuscripts, while it is one of the most powerful that even that great genius could have conceived, is not at all too much so to express the truth. We pass, in dreamy musing, through a grassy field; a blade of the tender herbage brushes against the foot; its impression hardly comes into consciousness; on earth it is never remembered again. But not even that slight sensation is utterly lost. The pressure of the body dulls the soul to its perception, other external experiences supplant it; but when the time of the final awakening comes, the ressurection of the soul from its charnel in the body, the analytic finger of inevitable light shall search out that old inscription, and to the spiritual eye no deep-graven record of its earthly triumphs shall be clearer.

The benumbing influences of the body protect us here from much of remorse and retrospective pining. Its weight lies heavily upon the inner sense, and deadens it to perception of multitudes of characters which, to be read, require acutest powers of discernment. When the body is removed, the barrier to the Past goes also.

This fact may perhaps be one of the final causes why the body exists at all. Why are we not born directly into the spiritual world, without having to pass through a weary preliminary experience hemmed in by the gross corporeal nature? May not the answer be something like this? Were the soul, at its first creation, introduced directly into the world where truth is an intuition, and stands in the dazzling light of its own essence, the dreadful sublimity of the view might prove its annihilation. We accordingly pass first through an apprenticeship, in which we have nothing colossal either to learn or to do; and eternal verities drawn on us slowly, instead of breaking in like lightning. The Phenomenal is at first all that we know; we have qualities and quantities, and through the period of infancy are content with novel acquisitions in this field. Next, we become aware of certain faculties of induction, investing us with the power of apprehending the Notional, which never comes within the grasp of Sense: we learn relations which exist only to the thought, yet are deemed still as valid experiences as if they were tasted or handled. Last of all, we mount into the Intuitional domain, and, without any of the props of Sense in any way to steady us, either by sensations perceived or suggesting relations, we know universal principles of Being face to face. Up this gradual stairway of Sense, Understanding, Intuition, we mount to that height from which we are able to behold, with some degree of calmness, the infinite fields of intuitive Beauty and Truth, when the screen of the bodily is removed, and the scope of vision belonging to our highest faulty is realized to be immeasurably beyond all that our most rapturous visions ever conceived it. Without this slow indoctrination, the soul might have flamed out in dazzling momentary irradiance, and then been extinguished in eternal nothingness.

If it be true that the bodily is thus our shield from the lethal glories of the purely spiritual world, and also from the full force of painful memories in the past, we can easily see how a most terrible retribution might be wreaked upon the soul by permitting it to stand through eternity without any covering to dim the events of its earthly time. Doubtless the spirit, interiorly in a state harmonious to the celestial concourse, will be invested with a spiritual body -- a body which, while it does not press heavily, like ours of the earthy, will still so condition states of mind as to permit no inflow but that of delightful impressions. But let the soul to which such societies and such garments are uncongenial, from the evils which he loves, stand bare in the presence of the Nemesis of his past life, with the wondrous light of the New World irradiating the terrors of her countenance, and all the symbols of fire and scorpion-stings will but faintly image the agonies of the view. Well, then, does Paul pray, "Not that I may be unclothed, but clothed upon."

I left the narration of my story while we were still walking toward the doctor's. At length, reaching there, we found him still sitting in his office, although it was now eleven o'clock.

I tried in vain to obtain the first word with him; for Bob, who seemed, according to the frequent nature of the hasheesh hallucination, suspicious of some wrong about to be done him, would not allow me to say any thing which might tinge the opinion of the physician. He persisted in affirming that he was at the point of death, although denying that he felt pain in any place which he could touch. He was totally unable to inform the doctor of the cause of his condition; but I at last managed to tell him myself. Like the great majority of practitioners, he knew nothing of the nature of the drug, and could only shake his head and presage evil from observing the singular phenomena which characterized his patient's outward conduct. He told Bob that he was very foolish to have made the experiment; was in imminent danger -- might die; would give him a powder -- ahem!

Whith such pre-eminent consolation he was poulticing the poor fellow's excited mind, when I took advantage of his going out for a dose of ipecac to follow him unostentatiously, feigning the intention of helping him to prepare the dose. The moment that we were in another room, I said, with as much vehemence as was possible without Bob's overhearing it, "For Heaven's sake, if you have any mercy, tell that man that he is in no danger! He is in none whatever. I have made the same experiment repeatedly, and I assure you that all he wants is the calm assurance of his safety."

My earnest manner satisfied him of my truth, and he accordingly went into the room where Bob was still sitting, and comforted him very much in the same manner that my doctor used with me when I was terrified in my first experiment. He told him, laughingly, to be in no apprehension whatever for results, as he would certainly recover from his present feelings intact.

In an instant Bob became perfectly calm, and the former state of happiness succeeded his agonies. We passed out of the doctor's office and began returning home. On the way he supposed himself a Mandarin freshly come from some triumph over invading tribes. Like myself, in the vision of my victorious march, he heard anthems of laud and glory pealing in his ears; but he did still more -- he played one of the instruments himself. Always a man of fine musical imagination, and quite a brilliant pianist, he now possessed a power of melodious creation unknown in his highest natural states. Setting his lips so as to send forth sounds in imiation of a bugle, he played in my hearing a strain of his own impromptu composition so beautiful that it would have done credit to any player upon wind instruments that ever obtained celebrity. For a quarter of a mile I enjoyed this unexpected rapture of music, in the utmost astonishment at a phenomenon I had never conceived of before.

We reached home. The experimenter lay down, and through all the night he was wrapped in visions of the utmost ecstasy. I sat beside his bed for hours, and always became aware of the moment of his highest exaltation by some strain after the manner of that which had cheered our way up the dark and lonely hill, bursting from his lips, even in sleep, with delicious melody. In the morning he awoke at the usual time; but, his temperament being perhaps more sensitive than mine, the hasheesh delight, without its hallucination, continued for several days. Bob never took it again.

The next case which I shall mention is that of my friend Fred W---
-, who, although now having abandoned hasheesh forever, still, from
the first experiment he made with it, was so delighted with the spell
that for several months he made trial of its powers, as successfully, if
never to the same extent, as myself. His temperament was the sanguine
and nervous commingled; his taste for the arts amounted to a passion.
The initiatory test of hasheesh which he made gave him only its space
and time expanding effects, but he had obtained a sufficient glimpse of
its weirdness to make him try again.

Upon many a bright moonlight night have I walked with him
through streets made balmy by the breath of the summer night, or
rowed our boat along the silvery river while he lay in ecstatic musing
upon the stern seat. In the dreams of such a man as he or the last one
whom I mentioned, by sympathy I lived almost as delicious a hasheesh
life as in my own. Once do I remember well, while we were floating
noiselessly between those twin welkins, the glorious sky above us, and
its image mirrored in the stream below, his beholding in the clouds that
lifted their beamy masses on the western horizon a resplendent city,
built amphitheatrically like Algiers, yet in every dome and architrave
beautiful with the taintless lustre of marble. And now he cried, "Sing!
my mood is congenial to the ethereal spirit of music." I softly hummed
"Spargi d'amaro pianto." "That is ecstasy!" he broke forth once more.
"Do you remember those words, 'Architecture is frozen music?' With
your ascending notes I saw grand battlements rise immensely into the
sky; with the descending tones they sank again, and through all your
song I have sat enamored of one delicious dance of Parian marble."

But his most wonderful experience -- wonderful for its exceeding
beauty, but still more so for the glimpse which it gave him of the
mind's power of sympathetic perception, was a vision which he had
after that which I have just related. Having taken hasheesh and felt its
influence already for several hours, he still retained enough of
conscious self-control to visit the room of a certain excellent pianist
without exciting the suspicion of the latter. Fred threw himself upon a
sofa immediately on entering, and asked the artist to play him some
piece of music, without naming any one in particular.

The prelude began. With its first harmonious rise and fall the
dreamer was lifted into the choir of a grand cathedral. Thenceforward it
was heard no longer as exterior, but I shall proceed to tell how it was
internally embodied in one of the most wonderful imaginative
representations that it has ever been my lot to know.

The windows of nave and transept were emblazoned, in the most gorgeous coloring, with incidents culled from saintly lives. Far off in the chancel, monks were loading the air with essences that streamed from their golden censers; on the pavement, of inimitable mosaic, kneeled a host of reverent worshippers in silent prayer.

Suddenly, behind him, the great organ began a plaintive minor like the murmur of some bard relieving his heart in threnody. This minor was joined by a gentle treble voice among the choir in which he stood. The low wail rose and fell as with the expression of wholly human emotion. One by one the remaining singers joined in it, and now he heard, thrilling to the very roof of the cathedral, a wondrous miserere. But the pathetic delight of hearing was soon supplanted by, or rather mingled with, a new sight in the body of the pile below him. At the farther end of the nave a great door slowly swung open and a bier entered, supported by solemn bearers. Upon it lay a coffin covered by a heavy pall, which, being removed as the bier was set down in the chancel, discovered the face of the sleeper. It was the dead Mendelssohn!

The last cadence of the death-chant died away; the bearers, with heavy tread, carried the coffin through an iron door to its place in the vault; one by one the crowd passed out of the cathedral, and at last, in the choir, the dreamer stood alone. He turned himself also to depart, and, awakened to complete consciousness, beheld the pianist just resting from the keys. "What piece have you been playing?" asked Fred. The musician replied it was "Mendelssohn's Funeral March!"

This piece, Fred solemnly assured me, he had never heard before. The phenomenon thus appears inexplicable by any hypothesis which would regard it as mere coincidence. Whether this vision was suggested by an unconscious recognition of Mendelssohn's style in the piece performed, or, by the awakening of some unknown intuitional faculty, it was produced as an original creation, I know not, but certainly it is as remarkable an instance of sympathetic clairvoyance as I ever knew.

Dan, the partner of my hasheesh-walk mentioned as occurring in the town of P-----, was, at the same time as myself, a member of the college. The Coryphæus of witty circles, and the light of all our festivals, he was still imaginative in higher spheres, and as worthily held the rostrum and the bard's chair as his place by the genial fireside or generous table. A poet, and an enthusiastic lover as well as performer of music, I supposed that the effect of hasheesh upon his susceptible temperament would be delightful in the extreme. But to such a result, the time at which he took the drug was one of the most unfavorable in the world -- when his nervous system was in a state of even morbid excitability. We had started together on a walk when the thrill came on. And such a thrill -- or, rather, such a succession of thrills -- it is wonderful how a human organism could sustain. At first a cloud of impenetrable mystery inwrapt him; then upon the crown of his head a weight began to press. It increased in gravity without gaining bulk, and at last, breaking through the barrier of the skull, it slid down the spinal column like lightning, convulsing every nerve with one simultaneous shudder of agony.

This sensation was repeated again and again, until, with horror, he called on me to return, as assured as I had ever been in my first experiments that death was soon to be the result of the shock. I instantly obeyed his wish, and on reaching his room he lay down. Of a sudden all space expanded marvelously, and into the broad area where he reclined marched a multitude of bands from all directions, discoursing music upon all sorts of instruments, and each band playing a different march on a different key, yet all, by some scientific arrangement, preserving perfect harmony with each other, and most exquisitely keeping time. As the symphony increased in volume, so also did it heighten in pitch, until at last the needle-points of sound seemed to concentre in a demon music-box of incredible upper register, which whirled the apex of its scream through the dome of his head, inside of which it was playing.

Now, on the wall of the room, removed to a great distance by the hasheesh expansion, a monstrous head was spiked up, which commenced a succession of grimaces of the most startling yet ludicrous character. First its ferociously bearded under jaw extended forward indefinitely, and then, the jaw shooting back, the mouth opened from ear to ear. Now the nose spun out into absurd enormity, and now the eyes winked with the rapidity of lightning.

Yet suffering in Dan bore an excessive over-ratio to mirth. In his greatest pain he had framed a withering curse against some one who had entered the room, but when he tried to give it utterance his lips failed in their office as if paralyzed. I gave him water when his thirst had become extreme, and the same sensations of a cataract plunging down his throat which I have before described occurred so powerfully that he set the glass down, unwilling to risk the consequences of his draught.

Returning to consciousness, he did not, however, recover from the more moderate hasheesh effects for months. The nervous thrills which I have related reappeared to him at intervals, and his dreams constantly wore a hasheesh tint. Indeed, in all cases which I have known, this drug has retained a more enduring influence than any stimulent in the whole catalogue.

A number of experiments made upon other persons with more or less success, yet none of them characterized by any phenomenon differing from those already detailed, prove conclusively that upon persons of the highest nervous and sanguine temperaments hasheesh has the strongest effect; on those of the bilious occasionally almost as powerful a one; while lymphatic constitutions are scarcely influenced at all except in some physical manner, such as vertigo, nausea, coma, or muscular rigidity. Yet to this statement there are striking exceptions, arising out of the operation of some latent forces of vitality which we have not yet included in our physical or psychical science. Until the laws which govern these are fully apprehended, hasheesh must ever remain a mystery, and its operation in any specific case an uncertainty.

IX. The Shadow of Bacchus, the Shadow of Thanatos, and the Shadow of Shame

Once more at the table I was seized by the hand of the hasheesh genie. Dinner was nearly over, and I escaped into the street without being suspected.

Street did I say? Ah no! That conventional synonym of all dust, heat, and garbage is unheard upon the sunny slopes of Mount Bermius, where I wandered Bacchus-smitten among the Maenades. Through the viny shades that embowered our dance of rapture, Haliaemon threw the gleam of his sky-bright waters, and the noon rays, sifted through leaves and clusters, fell on us softened like gold into the lap of Danae. Grapes above us, grapes around us, grapes every where, made the air fragrant as a censer. They dropped with the burden of their own sweetness; they shed volatile dews of ecstasy on every sense. Constellations of empurpled orbs, they dissolved the outer light of heaven by their own translucency; and from their hemispheres of silver down, which looked toward the sun, to those hemispheres which turned in upon our dance a gaze half of jet, half of sapphire, they transmitted the gentle radiance, until it bathed our cheeks and foreheads in the hue of autumn sunsets. Together with troops of Bacchantes I leaped madly among the clusters; I twirled my thyrsus, and cried Evoĕ Bacche with the loudest. On a delicious wind of fragrance the fawn-skin floated backward from my shoulders, and they viny leaves and tendrils of my garland caressed my temples lovingly. I drank the blood of grapes like nectar; I sang hymns to the son of Semele; I reeled under the possession of the divine afflatus. Around me in endless mazes circled beauteous shapes of men and women; with hands enclasped we danced and sang, and the Maenad houris overshadowed me with their luxuriant and disheveled hair.

Now, wandering from their throng in a rapture which, too high to be imparted, sought some solitude where it could shed itself forth unheard, I passed through the college gateway, and began traveling up the long walk which finally led into the woods toward the east -- finally, I say, for I remember even now the measureless stretch of the journey.

At length, reaching the borders of the stream which had before come to me the Nile, and which, through my whole hasheesh life, witnessed many a delirium of joy and torture, I sat down upon a high, precipitous bank which overhung the water, and gave myself up to my fantasia. The stream broadened and grew glorified: it was the Amazon, and on a towering bluff I was gazing down the liquid sweep toward the sea. Now a great ship came gliding past, lifting its top-gallant far above my post of observation, and men ran up the shrouds to peer curiously at me. With her long pennant flying and every inch of her courses shaken out, she passed me majestically, and I climbed down to the brink of the river to catch the last look at her, and see it returned from another inquisitive gazer at the taffrail.

I wandered completely through the woods, and came out into a broad field upon the farther side. Before me rose the buildings of a grand square, in some city whose name, whose nation I could not even imagine, so utterly foreign did it appear to any thing in the world of modern days. In the centre of the square a mighty host had assembled to inaugurate the equestrian statue of a hero, which, exquisitely carved in a rose-tinted marble, rose on its colossal pedestal far above their heads. I was drawn toward them by an irresistible impulse, for sculpture and architecture had reached, in that city, the highest ideal of art. I thought of the hero, and seemed to share the glory of his triumph.

Then out of the borders of the dense wood from which I had just emerged came a hot and hissing whisper, "Kill thyself! kill thyself!" Shuddering, I turned to see who spoke. No one was visible. Again, with still intenser earnestness, the whisper was repeated; and now unseen tongues syllabled it on all sides and in the air above me. To these words soon arguments were added, until the atmosphere seemed all aglow with fierce breathings of "Thou shalt be immortal; thou shalt behold the hidden things of God. The Most High commands thee to kill thyself." "My God!" I cried, "can this be true? I will obey thee, and drink in the eternities."

Feeling myself as mightily pressed on to do the deed as by a direct behest of Deity; daring not, for my soul's sake, to resist the utterances; and immeasurably exalted with the prelibation of the glories that, in moment, were to flow in upon me, in frantic fury I drew forth my knife, opened it, and placed it at my throat. Another heart-throb, and all would have been over.

It was just then that I felt the blow of some invisible hand strike my arm; my hand flew back, and, with the force of the shock, the knife went spinning away into the bushes. The whispers ceased. I looked up into heaven, and lo! from zenith to horizon, an awful angel of midnight blackness floated, with poised wings, on the sky. His face looked unutterable terrors into me, and his dreadful hand, half clenched, was hollowed above my head, as if waiting to take me by the hair. Across the firmament a chariot came like lightning; its wheels were rainbow-suns that rolled in tremendous music; no charioteer was there, but in his place flashed the glory of an intense brightness. At its approach the sable angel turned and rushed downward into the horizon, that seemed to smoke as he slid through it; and, thank God! from Azrael I was saved.

How many a temptation, which the ordinary grossness of the ear prevents us from ascribing to its true external source, and which we would fain persuade ourselves is nothing but our own thought, would come to us thus in a real demon-voice were the bands of the body but a little loosened! In how many attractions toward good and repulsions from evil would we then feel the touch of angel hands! The world at present is, to a great degree, Sadducee; it scoffs at the Spiritual, which for blindness it can not discern, and lives in meat and bone. The best men conservatively go half way to shake hands with the most unspiritual skeptic, and acknowledge with him that the most reasonable way to account for our wooings and our warnings is the reaction of soul upon itself. What these poor lovers of the earthy will do when they arrive among the realities of another world, it is hard to say. When this poor, mouldy, moth-eaten, time-tattered cloak of the corporeal, which for years has flapped about their heads in the gusts of worldly fortune, or tangled in its wet rags the feet of the soul that were trying to climb higher -- when this poor cloak falls off, and they stand transformed into that most dreader bugbear of their previous lives, spirit -- we may, perhaps, hear them cry out in agony, "Oh, my beloved garment! my best suit! what will become of thee?" and see them diving headlong off the battlements of light to recover the only part of their human wardrobe in which they can feel comfortable.

After my escape from death I returned to the border of the brook, and began pacing back and forth upon a long flat stone around which the shelve of the bank curved. My surroundings instantly became theatrical; the woods behind me changed into a back scene, and on a grand stage I was holding entranced a great audience, whom I beheld before me rising in colossal tiers from earth to sky. The part I was acting was that of a victorious soldier in some tragedy whose words I improvised, and, growing rapidly into the interest of my speech, I poured forth words -- now in prose and now in verse -- which swayed the hearers like a whirlwind. As my manner increased in earnestness, I saw a strange and dreadful look of suspicion overshadowing every face of the thousands in my audience. From the searching stare of the pit I sought relief in turning my face toward the boxes. The same stony glance from under eyebrows met me still, and when I raised my despairing countenance to the galleries, the same quenchless scrutiny poured down upon me. "Can it be?" I asked myself. "Oh! they know my secret!" and at that instant one maddening chorus broke from the whole theatre: "Hasheesh! hasheesh! he has eaten hasheesh!" Then, with one tumultuous uprising, the concourse fled. From the stage I crept away, consumed by an unutterable shame. I sought a place upon the bank of the stream still lower down, where a large hazel-bush leaned over the water, and beneath its branches I crouched. The helmet and corslet were gone. I looked at my garments, and beheld them foul and ragged as a beggar's. From head to foot I was an incarnation of the genius of squalidity.

Alas! even here I could not hide. I had chosen my asylum on the very pavement of a great city's principal thoroughfare. Children went by to school, and pointed at me in derision; loungers stood still, and searched me with inquisitive scorn. The multitude of man and beast all eyed me; the very stones of the street mocked me with a human raillery as cowered against a side wall in my bemired rags.

Now, mixing with the throng of passers-by, and no more real than they, two of my college friends came strolling along the brook. They saw and knew me, and my shame reached its unbearable height when I saw them approach me with looks which I thought also of sarcasm. But, as they drew nearer, they spoke to me kindly, and asked what was the matter with me, and why I sat hiding behind the hazel-branches. I hesitated for a moment, but, on their promise of secrecy, told them my latest experience. They sat down beside me, and in the diversion of talking the hallucination passed by.

Suddenly an unconquerable apprehension possessed me. There were certain secrets which for my right arm I would not have betrayed, and yet I felt imperatively called upon to speak them. I struggled against the impulse with the thews of a spiritual Titan. I was determined to conquer it, yet, that I might provide against a failure, I conceived this expedient. Picking up a withered leaf from the bank of the stream, I called the two to hold it, each by a portion of the rim, while I graped it by the stem. In this way we raised the leaf toward heaven, and with our other hands clasped in each other, I solemnly repeated this adjuration: "As this leaf shall be withered in the fiery breath of the final day, so may we be withered in the in the vengeance of the Eternal if aught that may be said here pass our lips without the consent of us all three." Here we all said "Amen," and once more I was at ease. I did not betray my own secrecy.

When I became calm the two left me and returned to their rooms. I wandered back to my old station on the high ledge, where I had seen the ship sweep by me, and sat down. When I looked into the sky between the tree-tops, the sun seemed reeling from his place, and the clouds danced around him like a chorus. I turned my eyes downward, and found that I was surrounded by warriors, who had come to bear me an invitation to the coronation of Charlemagne. "In a moment I will go with you," was my reply, "but first I must drink; I am dreadfully athirst." The stream was rattling away directly below me; my distance from it by the most easy roundabout descent was not more than fifty feet, yet I must relate, even at the risk of saying too much of the hasheesh expansion of distance, that in going to it I seemed passing down the league-long ridge of a mountain. I walked, I roamed, I traveled before reaching it, and at last, lying down upon the water's brim. I drank such streams of refreshment as appeared to lower the flood. On my return, after toiling up the weary steep, my escort had gone, and I certainly could not blame them, if the length of my unceremonious absence seemed to them half as great as it did to me.

Wandering through jungle, heather, brake, and fern -- through savanna, oak- opening, and prairie -- through all imagined and unimaginable countries -- now despairing of my ability ever to find my way, and now plucking heart to press on -- through many a day, or rather through one boundless perpetual day of journeying, I went until I reached home.

Throwing myself down upon a bed, I was immediately compensated for all past sufferings. In the middle of a vast unpeopled plain I stood alone. With one quick ravishment I was borne upward, as on superhuman wings, until, standing on the very cope of heaven, I looked down and saw beneath me all the worlds that God has made, not wheeling upon their beamy paths through ether, nor yet standing without significance like orbed clods.

By an instantaneous revealing I became aware of a mighty harp which lay athwart the celestial hemisphere, and filled the while sweep of vision before me. The lambent flame of myriad stars was burning in the azure spaces between its strings, and glorious suns gemmed with unimaginable lustre all its colossal framework. While I stood overwhelmed by the vision, a voice spoke clearly from the depth of the surrounding ether: "Behold the harp of the universe."

In an instant I realized the typification of the grand harmony of God's infinite creation, for every influence, from that which nerves the wing of Ithuriel down to the humblest force of growth, had there its beautiful and peculiar representative string.

As yet the music slept, when the voice spake to me again, "Stretch forth thine hand and wake the harmonies." Trembling, yet daring, I swept the harp, and straightway all heaven thrilled with an unutterable music. My arm strangely lengthened, I grew bolder, and my hand took a wider range. The symphony grew more intense; overpowered, I ceased, and heard tremendous echoes coming back from the infinitudes. Again I smote the chords, but, unable to endure the sublimity of the sound, I sank into an ecstatic trance, and was thus borne off unconsciously to the portals of some new vision.

X. Nimium
The Amreeta Cup of Unveiling

It was shortly after the last vision which has been related that I first experienced those sufferings which are generated by a dose of hasheesh taken to prolong the effects of a preceding one.

Through half a day I had lain quietly under the influence of the weed, possessed by no hallucination, yet delighted with a flow of pleasant images, which passed by under my closed eyelids. Unimaginable houris intoxicated the sense with airy ballet-dances of a divine gracefulness, rose-wreathed upon a state of roses, and flooded with the blush of a rosy atmosphere. Through grand avenues of overarching elms I floated down toward the glimpse of an impurpled sky, caught through the vista, or came glancing through the air over gateways of syenite, rose-tinted by the atmosphere, and in Egypt walked among the Caryatides. Up mystic pathways, on a mountain of evergreens, the priests of some nameless religion flocked, mitre-crowned, and passed into the temple of the sun over the threshold of the horizon. Now, "ringed with the azure world," I stood, a lonely hemisphere above me, a calm and voiceless sea beneath me; suddenly an island of feathery palms floated into the centre of the watery expanse, and gauze-winged sprites dropped down upon its shore. Now landscapes of strange loveliness slowly slid before me, but stopped at my will, that I might wander far up their music-haunted bays, and sit, bathed in sunlight, on the giant rock-fragments which lay around their unpeopled shores.

But once did I open my eyes and leap up in fear; for into the gardens of the Grecian villa where I walked among statues and fountains, an incongruous horde of Indian braves burst whooping, in their war-dance; and writhing in savage postures, with brandished club and tomahawk, they called upon my name, and looked for me through the olive-trees. Lying down again, I soared into the dome of St. Peter's, and, lighting on the pen of the apostle, laid my hand upon the angel's shoulder. A mighty stretch of arm indeed; yet, to the hasheesh-eater, all things are possible.

About the hour of noon I found the effects of my first dose rapidly passing off. It had been a small one, possibly fifteen grains, and, as I have said, produced no hallucination; yet so enamored had I become of the procession of pleasing images which it set in motion, that, for the sake of prolonging it, I took five grains more.

Hour after hour went by; I returned to the natural state, and gave up all idea of any result from the last dose. At nine o'clock in the evening I was sitting among my friends writing, while they talked around me. I became aware that it was gradually growing easier for me to express myself; my pen glanced presently like lightning in the effort to keep neck and neck with my ideas. At first I simply wondered at the phenomenon, without in the least suspecting the hasheesh which I had eaten nine hours before. At last, thought ran with such terrific speed that I could no longer write at all. Throwing down my pen, I paced the room, chafed my forehead, and strove to recover quiet by joining in the conversation of those about me.

In vain! intense fever boiled in my blood, and every heart-beat was the stroke of a colossal engine. Within me I felt that prophecy of dire suffering which the hasheesh-eater recognizes as unmistakably as were it graven by the finger of light, but whose signs, to all but him, are incommunicable. In agony of spirit I groaned inwardly, "My God, help me!"

The room grew unbearable with a penetrating glory of light. I mounted into it, I expanded through it, with a blind and speechless pain, which, in my very heart's core, was slowly developing itself into something afterward to burst forth into demoniac torture. I felt myself weeping, and ran to a looking-glass to observe the appearance of my eyes. They were pouring forth streams of blood! And now a sudden hemorrhage took place within me; my heart had dissolved, and from my lips the blood was breaking also.

Still, with that self-retent which a hasheesh eater acquires by many a bitter discipline, I withheld from my friends the knowledge of my torture, averting my face until the hallucination passed by. Indeed, as often occurs at such times, a paralysis of speech had taken place, which prevented me from communicating with others: not physical, but spiritual; for the recital of such pain seems to increase it tenfold by drawing its outlines more distinctly to the perception, and therefore did not dare to give it utterance.

And now a new fact flashed before me. This agony was not new; I had felt it ages ago, in the same room, among the same people, and hearing the same conversation. To most men, such a sensation has happened at some time, but it is seldom more than vague and momentary. With me it was sufficiently definite and lasting to be examined and located as an actual memory. I saw it in an instant, preceded and followed by the successions of a distinctly- recalled past life.

What is the philosophy of this fact? If we find no grounds for believing that we have ever lived self-consciously in any other state, and can not thus explain it, may not this be the solution of the enigma? At the moment of the soul's reception of a new impression, she first accepts it as a thing entirely of the sense; she tells us how large it is, and of what quality. To this definition of its boundaries and likenesses succeeds, at times of high activity, an intuition of the fact that the sensation shall be perceived again in the future unveiling that is to throw open all the past. Prophetically she notes it down upon the indestructible leaves of her diary, assured that it is to come out in the future revelation. Yet we who, from the tendency of our thought, reject all claims to any knowledge of the future, can only acknowledge perceptions as of the present or the past, and accordingly refer the dual realization to some period gone by. We perceive the correspondence of two sensations, but, by an instantaneous process, give the second one a wrong position in the succession of experiences. The soul is regarded as the historian when she is in reality the sibyl; but the misconception takes place in such a microscopic portion of time that detection is impossible. In the hasheesh expansion of seconds into minutes, or even according to a much mightier ratio, there is an opportunity thoroughly to scrutinize the hitherto evanescent phenomena, and the truth comes out. How any more such prophecies as these may have been rejected through the gross habit of the body we may never know until spirit vindicates her claim in a court where she must have audience.

At length the torture of my delirium became so great that I could no longer exist unsustained by sympathy. To Bob, as possessing, from his own experience, a better appreciation of that which I suffered, I repaired in preference to all others. "Let us walk," said I; "it is impossible for me to remain here."

Arm-in-arm we passed down the front steps. And now all traces of the surrounding world passed away from before me like marks wiped from a slate. When we first emerged from the building, I noticed that the night was dark, but this was the last I knew of any thing external. I was beyond all troubles from earth or sky; my agonies were in the spiritual, and there all was terrific light. By the flame of my previous vision the corporeal had been entirely burned off from about the soul, and I trod its charred ruins under foot without a remembrance that they had ever been sensitive or part of me. A voice spoke to me, "By the dissolution of fire hast thou been freed, to behold all things as they are, to gaze on realities, to know principles, to understand tendencies of being."

I now perceived that I was to pass through some awful revelation. It proved to be both Heaven and Hell, the only two states in the universe which together comprehend all free-agent creatures, whether in the Here or the hereafter. Of both I drank tremendous draughts, holding the cup to my lips as may never be done again until the draught of one of them is final.

Over many a mountain range, over plains and rivers, I heard wafted the cry of my household, who wept for me with as distinct a lamentation as if they were close at hand. Above all the rest, a sister mourned bitterly for a brother who was about to descend into hell!

Far in the distance rolled the serpentine fires of an infinite furnace; yet did this not seem to be the place to which I was tending, but only the symbol of a certain spiritual state which in this life has no representative. And now the principles of being, which the prophetic voice had foretold that I should see, suddenly disclosed themselves. Oh, awful sight! Iron, for they were unrelenting; straight as the ideal of a right line, for they were unalterable; like colossal railways they stretched from the centre whereon I stood. yet more were they to me than their mere material names, for they embodied an infinity of sublime truth. What that truth was I strove to express to my companion, yet in vain, for human language was yet void of signs which might characterize it. "Oh God!" I cried, "grant me the gift of a supernatural speech, that I may, if ever I return, come to humanity like a new apostle, and tell them of realities which are the essence of their being!" I perceived that this, also, was impossible. But vaguely, then, like some far-sighted one who points his brethren through the rack and tempest to a distant shore, should I ever be able to disclose what I had seen of the Real to men who dwelt amid the Shadowy.

For days afterward I remembered the unveiling. I myself knew that which it disclosed, yet could not tell it; and now all the significance of it has faded from my mind, leaving behind but the bare shard and husk of the symbols.

The railway which I saw appeared twofold: one arm led toward the far fires of my torture, the other into a cloudy distance which veiled its end completely from my sight. Upon the first I traveled, yet not on wheels, for I felt my feet still upbearing me through all the stages of an infinitely rapid progress.

Symbols -- symbols every where. All along my journey they flashed forth the apocalypse of utterly unimagined truths. All strange things in mind, which had before been my perplexity, were explained -- all vexed questions solved. The springs of suffering and of joy, the action of the human will, memory, every complex fact f being, stood forth before me in a clarity of revealing which would have been the sublimity of happiness but for their relation to man's tendencies toward evil. I was aware at the time (and I am no less so now) that, to a mind it its natural state, the symbols by which I was taught would be marrowless and unmeaning; yet so powerfully were they correspondences to unpreconceived spiritual verities, that I can not refrain from giving one or two of them in this recital.

Hanging in a sky of spotless azure, within the walls of my own heart, appeared my soul as a coin flaming with glories, which radiated from the impress of God's face stamped upon it. This told me an unutterable truth of my being. Again the soul appeared as a vast store of the same coin shed prodigally upon the earth. Through clefts in the rocky wall which rose beside my way were thrust, in a manner expressive of wondrous craft, barbed talons, which, grasping the coin one by one, as a fish-hook holds the prey, drew them slowly i, while I stood helpless, shrieking in the desert loneliness. As each piece of my treasure slid through the crevices, I heard it fall, with a cruel metallic ring, upon the bottom of some invisible strong-box, and this ring was echoed by a peal of hollow laughter from within. Another truth, though not the most evident one which now suggests itself, but far more dreadful, was taught me by this symbol.

Again, my heart was a deep well of volatile blood, and into it buckets perpetually descended to be drawn up filed, and carried away by viewless hands to nurture the flames which writhed in the distant furnace. Through all this time I was witnessing one more tremendous truth. But one of the representatives still retains its full significancy to my mind, and is communicable also to others.

Standing upon a mountain peak appeared a serene old prophet, whose face was radiant with a divine majesty. In his look, his form, his manner, was embodied all that glorifies the sage; wonderfully did he typify the ideal of the bard --

"His open eyes desire the truth;
The wisdom of a thousand years
Is in them."

All that science, art, and spotless purity of life can do to ennoble humanity, had ennobled him, and I well-nigh knelt down before him in an ecstasy of worship. A voice spoke to me from the infinitides, "Behold man's soul in primeval grandeur; as it was while yet he talked with God."

Hurried away through immensity, I came, somewhere in the universe, upon a low knoll, flaunting in a growth of coarse and gaudy flowers. Half way down its slope sat a hideous dwarf, deformed in body, but still much more terrible in the soul, which ogled me through his leaden eyes, or broke in ripples of idiotic laughter over his lax and expressionless lip. One by one he aimlessly plucked the flowers among which he was sitting; he pressed them to his bosom, and leered upon them, as a maniac miser looks upon his treasures, and then, tearing to pieces their garish petals, tossed them into the air, and laughed wildly to see them whirling downward to strew his lap. In horror I averted my face, but a strange fascination drew it back to him again, when once more the terrible voice sounded over my shoulder, "Behold thine own soul!" In an agony I cried, "Why, oh why?" Sternly, yet without a thrill of passion, the voice replied, "Thou hast perverted thy gifts, thou hast squandered thine opportunities, thou hast spurned thy warnings, and, blind to great things, thou playest with bawbles. Therefore, behold thyself thus!"

In speechless shame I hid my face and turned away. Now, as with the descent of a torrent, all my violations of the principles which I saw revealed fell down upon my head from the heights of the Past. It was no bewailing over the inexpediency of any deed or thought which I then uttered; from the abysses of my soul a cry of torture went up for discords which I had caused in the grand harmony of universal law. The importance to mere temporal well-being of this act or that, made no difference in the inconceivable pain which I felt at its clear remembrance. Whether, in the Past, I was confronted with a deliberate falsehood or a fictitious addition, for the sake of symmetry, to an otherwise true recital, the horror was the same. It was not consequences to happiness that troubled me, but something of far mightier scope, for I looked upon some little pulse of evil which, at its time, had seemed to die away in the thought, and lo, in all the years since then it had been ceaselessly waving onward in consecutive circles, whose outer rim touched and invaded the majestic symphony of unalterable principles of Beauty and Truth. Before the presence of that beholding there was no such thing as a little wrong in all the universe.

And now, in review, there passed before my mind all those paradoxes of being which, to our natural sense, forever perplex the relations between God and Man -- God, the omnipotent; Man, the free agent, the two concentric wheels of self-determining will which turn the universe. How can these things be?

In an instant I saw that hitherto unattainable How. Out of the depths of mystery it broke forth and stood in grand relief upon its midnight veil. Between truths there was no longer any jar; as on a map, illustrated by eternal light, I beheld all their relative bearings, and in the conviction of an intuition cried out, "True, true, divinely true!"

Do you ask me to give the process? As well might I attempt to define sight to a being born without eyes as to image, even to myself, at this moment, the mode of that apocalypse. Had memory of it as aught else than a fact remained to me, I had long since been consumed, as a red-hot needle dissolves away in oxygen. As it is, I remember not the manner, except that it was Sight; at the moment it was incommunicable by any human language. Yet the stamp of the intuition remains so indelibly upon my soul, that there is no self- evident truth which I could not more easily abjure than the undimmed and perfect harmony which, in that dreadful night, I beheld as an intuition.

After this I suffered hellish agonies, prolonged through an infinity of duration. As they were all embodied in symbols, I recall them but dimly, and the endeavor to relate them would be painful and profitless.

At the end of my representative road, arriving through growing distances, times, and tortures, God-drawn, I was hurried back to be launched forward in the direction of the other, the celestial tendency. The music of unimaginable harps grew clearer with every league of speed; symbols were turned to their most ravishing uses; the gleam of crystal gates and empyrean battlements flashed on me with increasing radiance; the sky breathed down a balm which signified love, love -- quenchless love. At the end of this journey I arrived also; and, between towers of light, was about to pass through into a land resounding with infinite choruses of joy. I was detained. Again the voice spake to me, "The thing is too great for thee; seek not to enter. As thou wast preserved at the end of thy former way from going into the fires to which it led, so also now do I guard thee from beholding the fatal glories of the Divine face to face." With inconceivable grief I hid my face in my hands and returned, weeping bitterly.

At this moment, for the first time since coming from my room, I became aware of the external world. My friend still walked by my side, supporting me through the darkness. We had not come half a mile while I passed through all that awful vision!

Presently we came to a short bridge. Little conceiving the state of mind from which I had just emerged, Bob said to me, with the impression that the novelty of the idea would give me an attractive suggestion of adventure, "See the Styx." Groaning in spirit, I looked down upon that dark and sullen watter which rolled below me, and saw it mightily expanded beneath horrible shadows toward a shore which glowed with the fires of my earlier vision. "My God!" I cried, "am I again journeying toward the Infernal? Yes, it must be so; for even this man, who has learned nothing of my past tortures, knows and tells me this is one of the rivers of Hell!"

Bob caught a glimpse of the pain he had innocently caused me, and assured me, for the sake of my peace, that he had only been jesting. "This is not the Styx at all," said he, "but only a small stream which runs through Schenectady." By pointing out to me familiar surroundings, by persuasion, by entreaty, he at length prevailed upon me to cross the bridge; yet I only did so by concealing my eyes in his bosom and clasping his hands with the clutch of a vice.

Supposing that light and the restorative influence of wine would relieve me, he led me to a restaurant, and there, sitting down with me to a table, called for a glass of Port. In the unnatural shadow which inwrapped all things and persons, a man was standing near the door, and in the conversation which h was carrying on with another I heard him use the word "damn."

In an instant my mind, now exquisitely susceptible, took fire from that oath as tinder from steel. "There is, indeed," I soliloquized, "such a thing as damnation, for I have seen it. Shall I be saved?" This dreadful question forced me to determine it with an imperative fascination. I continued. "Oh thou Angel of Destiny, in whose book all the names of the saved are written, I call on thee to open unto me the leaves!"

Hardly had I spoken when upon a sable pedestal of clouds the dread registrar sat before me, looking immeasurable pity from his superhuman eyes. Silently he stretched out to me the great volume of record, and with devouring eyes I scanned its pages, turning them over in a wild haste that did not preclude the most rigid scrutiny. Leaf after leaf flew back; from top to bottom I consumed them in my gaze of agony. Here and there I recognized a familiar name, but even my joy at such revelations took nothing from the cruelty of the suspense in which I looked to find my own. With a face cold as marble I came to the last page, and had not found it yet. Drops of torture beaded my brow as with eye and finger I ran down the final column. One, two, three -- I came to the bottom -- the last. It was not there!

My God! nothing but thine upbearing arms at that moment kept me from eternal annihilation. In stony horror I sat dumb.

After the Angel of Destiny took back his book and shut it with the echo of doom, I know not what time elapsed while I dwelt in that unfathomable abyss of despair. I saw Eternity, like a chariot out of which I had fallen, roll out of sight upon the bowed and smoking clouds to leave me, a creature of perdition, in an inanity of space and out of the successions of duration. Familiar faces were around me, yet the thought of obtaining relief from them never crossed my mind. They were powerless to help a sufferer of the immortal pangs.

If, as I sat at the table, a caldron of boiling lead had been brought in and set beside me, I would have leaped into it with exultant haste, to divert my mind from spiritual to physical sufferings. Through a period which the hasheesh-eater alone can know, I sat speechlessly beside my friend.

Suddenly upon the opposite wall appeared a cross, and Christ the Merciful was nailed thereon. I sprang from my seat; I rushed toward him; I embraced his knees; I looked intensely into his face in voiceless entreaty. That sad face sweetly smiled upon me, and I saw that my unspoken prayer was granted. through my soul, as through a porous film, swept a wind of balm, and left it clean. The voice that had attended me through all past journeyings, now changed from stern upbraiding to unimaginable love, spoke gently, "By the breath of the Spirit thine iniquities are borne utterly away." To colossal agonies peace as great succeeded, and, thus sustained, I returned to my room.

Yet all my sufferings had not yet been fulfilled. The moment that I reached home I threw myself down upon my bed. Hardly had I touched it when, from all sides, devouring flame rolled upward and girt me in with a hemisphere of fire. Shrieking, I leaped up and ran to my friends, who cared for me till the wrathful hallucination was overpast.

At this day it seems to me almost incredible that I ever survived that experience at all. Yet, inexplicable as it may be, when I awoke the next morning, I was as free from all traces of suffering as if I had been, all the evening previous, cradled in a mother's arms.

XI. The Book of Symbols

Of all experiences in the hasheesh state, my indoctrination into spiritual facts through means of symbols was the most wonderful to myself. In other visions I have reveled in more delicious beauty, and suffered horrors even more terrible; but in this I was lifted entirely out of the world of hitherto conceivable being, and invested with the power of beholding forms and modes of existence which, on earth, are impossible to be expressed, for the reason that no material emblems exist which even faintly foreshadow them.

Among men we communicate entirely by symbols. Upon any thought which has not its symbol in the Outer, "untransferable" is stamped indelibly. A certain relation between two thoughts is beheld by one human mind. How shall the man inform his neighbor of this relation? There is no meatus for it through any of the labyrinths of material sense; it can not be seen, heard, felt, smelt, or tasted. What is to be done?

A flock of cranes are assembling from the four quarters of heaven to hold their aerial council on some tall crag above him. Into our thinker's mind flashes a bright idea. Those birds shall mediate for his relation a passage into his brother's understanding. The cranes (grues) are coming together (con), and in this visible symbol he embodies his invisible relation, and the name henceforth that passes for it among men is "congruous."

Yet there is one condition beyond the mere discovery of an apt symbol which is necessary before that symbol can be circulated as the bank-note which bases its security on the intangible coin within the spiritual treasury. That coin must be universally felt to exist, or the bill will be good for nothing. In the present instance, the idea of the relation expressed by "congruous" must already have been perceived by the communicatee, or the communicator will be unable to express himself intelligibly. Rather should we say, the idea of the possibility of this relation must exist before the former can perceive it; for, if he recognizes such a possibility, then, by virtue of this very capacity, he will immediately actualize the possible, and on the communication of the symbol perceive the idea of "congruity," though it be for the first time.

The question now arises, What state of mind lies back of, and conditions the capacity to recognize, through symbols, the mental phenomena of another? Plainly this: the two who are in communication must be situated so nearly upon the same plane of thought that they behold the same truths and are affected by the same emotions. In proportion as this condition is violated will two men be unappreciating of each other's inner states.

Now in hasheesh it is utterly violated. In the hasheesh-eater a virtual change of worlds has taken place, through the preternatural scope and activity of all his faculties. Truth has not become expanded, but his vision has grown telescopic; that which others see only as the dim nebula, or do not see at all, he looks into with a penetrating scrutiny which distance, to a great extent, can not evade. Where the luminous mist or the perfect void had been, he finds wondrous constellations of spiritual being, determines their bearings, and reads the law of their sublime harmony. To his neighbor in the natural state he turns to give expression to his visions, but finds that to him the symbols which convey the apocalypse to his own mind are meaningless, because, in our ordinary life, the thoughts which they convey have no existence; their two planes are utterly different.

This has not only occurred in my own case, but in several others - - in persons upon whom I have experimented with hasheesh. At their highest exaltation, so earnest has been the desire to communicate the burden which overpowered them, that they have spoken forth the symbols presented to their minds; yet from these symbols men around them, in the unexalted state, drew an entirely different significance from the true one, or, perceiving none at all, laughed at what was said as an absurdity, seeing nothing in the name of some ordinary thing or mode of being to excite such emotions of terror or ecstasy as were produced in the hasheesh-eater. Yet many a time, as I stood near, by these symbols thus expressed, have I been able to follow the ecstatic wanderer, and recognize the exact place in his journey at which he had arrived as something which I had once seen myself.

It is this process of symbolization which, in certain hasheesh states, gives every tree and house, every pebble and leaf, every footprint, feature, and gesture, a significance beyond mere matter or form, which possesses an inconceivable force of tortures or of happiness.

Perhaps one of the most difficult things to convey to a mind not in the hasheesh delirium, by the symbols which there teach the manner of its process, or by any others, is the interchange of senses. The soul is sometimes plainly perceived to be but one in its own sensorium, while the body is understood to be all that so variously modifies impressions as to make them in the one instance smell, in another taste, another sight, and thus on, ad finem. Thus the hasheesh-eater knows what it is to be burned by salt fire, to smell colors, to see sounds, and, much more frequently, to see feelings. How often do I remember vibrating in the air over a floor bristling with red-hot needles, and, although I never supposed I came in contact with them, feeling the sensation of their frightful pungency through sight as distinctly as if they were entering my heart.

In the midst of sufferings unfathomable or raptures measureless, I often thought of St. Paul's God-given trance, and the Never was I more convinced of any thing in my life than that our translation, "which it is not lawful for a man to utter," is wholly inadequate. It should be, "which it is impossible to utter to man;" for this alone harmonizes with that state of intuition in which the words are "speechless words," and the truths beheld have no symbol on earth which will embody them. Though far from believing that my own ecstasy, or that of any hasheesh-eater, has claim to such inspiration as an apostle's, the states are still analogous in this respect, that they both share the nature of disembodyment, and the soul, in both, beholds realities of greater or less significance, such as may never be apprehended again out of the light of eternity.

There is one thought suggested by the symbolization of hasheesh which I can not refrain from introducing here. In some apocalyptic states of delirium like that which I have mentioned, and others succeeding it, there were symbols of an earthly nature used, which not only had never before conveyed to me such truth as I then saw, but never had expressed any truth at all. Things the least suspected of having any significance beyond their material agency were perceived to be the most startling illustrations and incarnations of spiritual facts.

Now where, among created things, shall we set the boundaries to this capacity for symbolizing. In view of that which I saw, especially upon the last detailed memorable night, I felt, and still feel, forced to the conclusion that there is no boundary. If, as the true philosopher must believe, the material was created for the spiritual, as the lower for the higher, the means for the end, it is impossible that any minutest lichen should exist as mere inert matter, lessonless to the soul of all creation's viceroy -- man.

What a world of symbols, then, lie sleeping in expectancy of the approaching times which shall bring some translator to their now unnoticed sermons, and bid them speak of unconceived beauties and truths!

Following out the perverted tendencies of a pseudo-science, we are now forever seeking some reason for the existence of the outer world as it is, which will utterly insphere it within the ends of material well-being. Plainly perceiving that respect for the Creative Wisdom will not permit us to suppose that any thing, however microscopic, has been made aimlessly, we belabor our brains with attempts to find out some physical good arising out of the being of every object in all the terrene kingdoms. Such a thing was created that man might be cured of the headache; such another, that his food might be varied; still another, that a convenient circulating medium might be in his power. Doubtless such corporeal goods were among the final causes of some portions of the creation. Our trouble is not our activity in the discovery of these, but that beyond their petty circle discovery does not dare to set her foot, for fear of being called visionary.

Doubtless, when God has lent us a tenement to lodge in, albeit for a few days and nights, it is our duty to find out and apply all those materials of repair which will keep it in good order till we pass finally from its low door-step into our palace; as honorable tenants, and for the sake of our own better preservation, this is both duty and right, so far as it may be done without bespangling and frescoing our wayfaring house as if it were to be our perpetual home. Yet what effort can be meaner, what more unworthy of Spirit, than studiously to degrade the whole sublime Kosmos into one colossal eating- house, wardrobe, or doctor's shop for the body? Good men, perhaps wise men, are forever looking for something medicinal in the scorpion, or edible in the fungus, to vindicate God's claim to an intention. Most ingeniously do they fabricate supposititious purposes for outer things; hopelessly writhe in the folds of perplexity when, with all their far-fetched hypotheses, they can not see what material good is to come out of some obstinate resistant to their analysis.

Blind philosophers! Nature refuses to cramp herself within your impossible law; she rejects your generalization; she throws off the shackles of your theory! For the sake of mere physical well-being, it had doubtless been far better that never a centipede had been created; that the most formidable snake had been the harmless garter; that the euphorbus had never put forth a leaf, nor the seleniuret a vapor. Yet this is not the grand aim of the system of things, but that man might, for the present, have symbols for the communication of manly thought; that God himself, for the future, might have symbols for the revelation of Divine Truth, when, in the grand unveiling, rocks, trees, and rivers -- yea, the smallest atom also -- shall come thronging up along all the was of the Universe to unseal their long- embosomed messages, and join in the choral dance of the Spiritual -- the only science -- to the Orpheus-music of the awakened soul.

XII. To-day, Zeus;
to-morrow, Prometheus.

At what precise time in my experience I began to doubt the drug being, with me, so much a mere experiment as a fascinating indulgence, I do not now recollect. It may be that the fact of its ascendency gradually dawned upon me; but, at any rate, whenever the suspicion became definite, I dismissed it by so varying the manner of the enjoyment as to persuade myself that it was experimental still.

I had walked, talked, and dreamed under the hasheesh influence; I would now listen to music and see acting, that, under such circumstances, I might note the varying phenomena, if any occurred.

To reach New York for the purpose I would go by water, sailing down the glorious Hudson under the full moon; and this would still be another opportunity for experimenting.

Upon one of the largest and most beautiful of the steamers which ever glided down the shining pathway of the river upon a moonlight night of summer, I stepped, at eight o'clock in the evening, accompanied by several of my friends, and carrying in my pocket a box of boluses. The gang-plank was drawn in, and we were on our way.

In the few moments which elapsed before the steward appeared, brandishing his noisy harbinger of things edible, I managed to swallow, unseen, a number of the spheroids contained in my box.

On regaining the deck from that savory, subaqueous cavern where, amid sepulchral lights, five hundred Americans of us had, for the incredible space of fifteen minutes, been fiercely elbowing each other in insane haste to secure that grand national end, indigestion, we found the broad disk of the moon just above the horizon, and, on arm-chairs taken forward, sat down, with our toes thrust into the bulwark-netting, for our post-coenatial smoke. Cigars and studently habits of thinking impelled us toward song, and for two hours, at least, the low rocks which skirt the upper channel echoed with "There is music in the air," "Co-ca-che-lunk," and other collegiate harmonies.

The Opera, with its glory of lights, passionate song, orchestral crashes, and scenery, whirls the soul on with it, indeed, in a bewildering dance of delight; the ballad we love, sung feelingly by the woman we love, at that hour when to lift the curtains would only let in more twilight, is a calm rapture which is good for the heart; if it be not too near, the bugle discourses rich melody and spirit-stirring among the mountains of its birth; yet, beyond all other music, grant me a song trolled from manly throats, which keep good chord and time, and first learned within those homely walls which, to the true American collegian, are dearer than all the towers of Oxford.

Reverend Union! it is not thine to deck thyself in the outworn trappings of feudal pomp; not even is it thine to bear upon thy brow the wrinkles of unnumbered years, though long before thou lackest such prestige its sign shall come upon thee. Thou hast no high places for lineage nor fat tables for gold; thou art beautiful neither in marble nor carved workmanship. Yet art thou the mother of thinkers and workers - - high souls and brave hearts, which make their throb felt in the giant pulses of a great nation. To these Gracchi of thine dost thou point and say, "Behold my jewels." With the love of thy sons thou art crowned more royally than turrets might crown thee; and better than all the remembrance of coronets upon thy calendar and ermine in thy halls is the thought that, grasping thy protectress hand, merit hath so often struggled up to fame out of the oblivion of namelessness and the clutch of poverty.

It is in the American college, with its freedom from fictitious distinctions, its rejection of all odious badges, which set genealogy and money over mind and heart; its inculcation of manly self-government rather than the fear of tyrannic espionage; its unrestrained intercourse between congenial souls, and its grouping of congenialities by society bonds, that the most perfect development of the social and individual man takes place. here it is that, by attrition of minds, unworthy eccentricities are rubbed off, while the personal and characteristic nature of the man is solidified and polished into higher symmetry. And here, last, though far from least, among all the true purposes of education, the heart gets its due in the attainment of those unworldly associations which, many a year after the actual presences which they symbolize have dropped down into the "long ago," send up the hallowed savor of friendship and disinterestedness through the dust and cobwebs which choke will-nigh every other memory.

It is not wonderful that, out of such free and intimate converse among young men as we find in our colleges, song should spring up as a most legitimate and accredited progeny. He who should collect the college carols of our country, or, at least, those of them whose spice would not be wholly lost in the transplantation from their original time and place, would be adding no mean department to the national literature. Piquant, fresh-imaged, outwelling, and sitting snug to their airs, they are frequently both excellent poetry and music. Whether they ring through the free air of a balmy summer evening from a row of sitters on a terrace or a green, who snatch fragrant puffs of old Virginia between staves, or gladden a college room through the long evenings of winter, they are always inspiriting, always heart-blending, and always, I may add, well sung.

I have rambled round the complete circle of my digression to the place where I left my friends seated upon the forward deck and singing in the incipient moonlight. By the time that we had grown tired of singing, the river was very beautiful with the clear reflection of the sky, turning the spray of our prow to silver beads, and giving still snowier lustre to our wake. The excitement of music had put off that of hasheesh, but I was not surprised to feel the well-known thrill as our voices died away.

In a moment I became the fairy monarch. Etherealized and beautified, I was gliding upon my will-borne pleasure-vessel through the moonlit kingdom over which I was supreme. Now whippoorwills chanted me a plaintive welcome from the dreamy, wooded shores; fire-flies illuminated, with triumphal lights, their palace fronts among the shadowy elms; and the little moon-glorified islands, that caught our waves upon their foreheads, sent back a delicious voice of laud and joy.

In this ecstasy I sat reviewing my domain until the moon stood at the zenith, and then pacing through the long saloons, I reveled in the ownership of gorgeous tapestry and panelings, and from the galleries looked proudly upon my retinue of beautiful women and brave men who sat or walked below.

When I shut my eyes I dwelt in a delicious land of dreams. Charging at the head of ever-victorious legions, I drove millions of laughing foes in playful rout through an illimitable field of roses. Down the mountains of Congo a whole universe of lithe and shapely negro children ran leaping, with their arms full of elephants' tusks, boxes of gold-dust, and fresh cocoanuts, to be the purveyors of my palace. On the wings of a speechless music I floated through the air, and in the cloud-valleys played hide-and-seek with meteors.

A little after midnight I felt the hasheesh effects decreasing, and not having yet recognized that law of the drug which forbids prolonging its dreams by a second dose (nor, indeed, did I recognize it until several bitter experiences had taught me), I took five grains more.

Gradually more and more the hasheesh influence wore off. I went to my state- room, and now, perfectly restored to the natural state, lay down, and all night slept quietly.

Upon awaking with the early sunlight I found that we were midway past the Palisades. Upon the eastern bank of the river the signs of suburban life had become visible in terraces, lawns, and verandas, and bells were audible down the bay.

It was not until we reached the pier that I felt the effect of my last bolus. I stepped ashore, and, for the first time, separated for a season from my fellow-voyagers. The morning already gave most earnest promise of a day which was to be one of the hottest of summer, and as I walked up that unsheltered quay alone, and with the sun streaming full upon me, I suddenly felt my heart catch fire. There was no premonitory, no mystery, no thrill; and this gave a more terrible tone to my suffering, for I burned among acknowledged and familiar realities without the possibility of remembering any former state of a calmer nature upon which to steady myself.

Most fully did I then realize the hell of Eblis and its inextinguishable pangs, as, walking through the thronged streets of the great city, I laid my hand upon my heart to hide its writhings, and saw in every face of the vast multitude who hurried past tokens of something despairing and diabolic. The well-known long rows of palatial shops and gaudy windows swept by me as I paced along. The hurrying crowds of men upon the pavement who went to their businesses, and the fluctuating stream of carriages and omnibuses which rolled down the street, seemed, in their mere matter, nothing unusual to me. Yet the spirit which pervaded all things was that of the infernal. I wandered through a colossal city of hell, where all men were pursuing their earthly tendencies amid pomp and affluence as great as ever, yet stamped upon their foreheads with the dreadful sign of all hope of better things forever lost.

At all times the thoroughfare of a large town is a wilderness to me. In desert loneliness, on mountain tops, or by the side of an unfrequented stream, there is no such hermit conceivable as the hermit of a crowd. The study of character in faces, of universal human nature in its elbowings and windings toward its aim, may be pursued upon a city's pave to the greatest advantage; yet overtopping all the external aspects of society found there is the solitude which inspheres the wanderer within himself, as he perceives not one being within the distance of miles to whom he is bound by any dearer interest than our common humanity.

But at this time how singularly, how especially was I a hermit! Still conscious of retaining some of the attributes of a man, I was surrounded by infernal forms and features, shaped, indeed, like my own, but with the good- will, the hope, the confidence of our common life forever evaporated from them. Every one of the beings that hastened by me in hum and tumult looked under his eyebrows, with dreadful superstition, at his neighbor and at me. The ideal of hell, where all faith hath perished, and in endless mutation of couples the wretched sneer and glare at each other continually, was realized in that scene.

I could not bear the pavement, and so stepped into an omnibus, that I might behold less of that terrible ebb and flow of Life in Death. As we rolled heavily over the stones of the street, I felt my heart transferred to some flinty road-bed, a fathom below the surface, where it writhed beneath the jar of wheels, and the puncture of the cruel rock-fragments yet communicated all its sufferings to me by slender cords of conduction, whose elastic fibre stretched more and more as we rode on, and grew tenser with an unutterable pain. At the same time, all my fellow-passengers in the omnibus seemed staring at me with hot and searching eyes; in one corner I cowered from their glance, and sat with my hand upon my face. They whispered; it was myself of whom they talked, and I distinctly heard them use the word "hasheesh."

I got out of the omnibus and again took the pavement, realizing that there was nowhere any relief for my pangs. It would be vain to detail all the horrors through which I passed before I took shelter in the house of a friend. Among them not the least were a heart on fire, a brain pierced by a multitude of revolving augers, and the return, amid dim inner flames, of the fearful symbolization and the demon-songs of former visions.

Arriving at my friend's, I pleaded fatigue, and lay down. Hours were wretchedly passed in falling asleep, and then darting up in terror at some ideal danger. Sometimes a gnashing maniac looked at me, face to face, out of the darkness; sometimes into rayless caverns I fell from the very heavens; sometimes the lofty houses of an unknown city were toppling over my head in the agonies of an earthquake. Agonies, I say, for their throes seemed like human sufferings.

Out of this woe I emerged entirely by noon, but began to be aware that I should never again, in the hasheesh state, be secure in the certainty of unclouded visions. The cup had been so often mingled, that its savor of bitterness would never wholly pass away. Yet ascribing all the pain which, in this instance, I had endured, to some unfavorable state of the body (I had not yet realized the law of a second dose), I supposed that, by preserving a general healthy tone of the system, hasheesh might be used harmlessly.

XIII. Eidola Theatri and
the Prince of Whales.

Waiting until the next day at evening I took a moderate bolus, say twenty-five grains, and repaired to the theatre.

In the action of the pieces which were performed I lived as really as I had ever lived in the world. With the fortunes of a certain adventurer in one of the plays my mind so thoroughly associated me that, when he was led to the block and the headsman stood over him, I nerved myself for the final stroke, and waited to feel the steel crash through my own neck. He was reprieved, and, in his redemption, it was I who exulted.

The effect of some rich-toned frescoing above the stage was to make me imagine myself in heaven. Yet "imagine" is not the proper word, for it does not express the cloudless conviction of reality which characterized this vision. There were no longer any forms or faces visible below me, but out of the wondrous rosy perspective of the upper paneling angels came gliding, as through corridors hewn of ruby, and showered down rays of music, which were also beheld as rays of color.

A most singular phenomenon occurred while I was intently listening to the orchestra. Singular, because it seems one of the most striking illustrations I have ever known of the preternatural activity of sense in the hasheesh state, and in an analytic direction.

Seated side by side in the middle of the orchestra played two violinists. That they were playing the same part was evident from their perfect uniformity in bowing; their bows, through the whole piece, rose and fell simultaneously, keeping exactly parallel. A chorus of wind and stringed instruments pealed on both sides of them, and the symphony was as perfect as possible; yet, amid all that harmonious blending, I was able to detect which note came from one violin and which from the other as distinctly as if the violinists had been playing at the distance of a hundred feet apart, and with no other instruments discoursing near them.

According to a law of hasheesh already mentioned, a very ludicrous hallucination came in to relieve the mind from its tense state. Just as the rapture of music, lights, and acting began to grow painful from excess, I felt myself losing all human proportions, and, spinning up to a tremendous height, became Cleopatra's Needle.

A man once remarked to young Dumas, "My poor friend, M. Thibadeau, returned home, took off his spectacles, and died." "Did he take off his spectacles first?" asked Dumas. "Yes, truly," replied the other; "but why?" "Merely how delightful it must have been to be spared the grief of seeing himself die!"

About as absurd a duality as that inferred for Monsieur Thibadeau, if he had kept on his spectacles, was the duality with which I looked up and saw my own head some hundred feet in the air. Suddenly a hasheesh-voice rang clearly in my ear, "Sit still upon thy base, Eternal Obelisk!" Ah me! I had not realized till then how necessary it was that I should preserve the centre of gravity. What if I should go over? One motion on this side or that, and dire destruction would overwhelm the whole parquette. From my lofty top I looked down upon responsible fathers of families; innocent children; young maidens, with the first peach-bloom of womanhood upon their cheeks; young men, with the firelight of ambitious enterprise new-kindled in their eyes. There was absolutely no effort which I was unwilling to make to save them from destruction. So I said to myself, "Be a good obelisk and behave yourself, old fellow; keep your equilibrium, I entreat you. You don't want to clothe all the families of New York in mourning, I know you don't; control yourself, I beg." Bold upright and motionless I sat, until it pleased the gods to alter my shape, most opportunely, when I was just giving out, to the far more secure pyramid, after which all hallucinations gently passed away.

The hasheesh state, in its intensest forms, is generally one of the wildest insanity. By this I do not mean to say that the hasheesh-eater at such a season necessarily loses his self-control, or wanders among the incoherent dreams of a lawless fancy, for neither of these propositions is true. As I have heretofore remarked, self-government during the delirium, from being at first apprehended as a necessity, grows up at length into a habit, and the visions that appear before the shut or open eyes of the ecstatic have an orderly progress and a consistent law according to which they are informed, which elevate them above the prodigal though meaningless displays of fancy into the highest sphere of imagination.

Yet, after all, there are reasons for calling the state an insanity, and a wild insanity, which will defend the name to all who can realize them from a description, and far more completely to those who have known them by experiment.

In the first place, when self-control has reached its utmost development, and the tortured or exultant spirit restrains itself from all eruptive paroxysms of communication among those people to whom its secret would be unwisely imparted, there is still a sense of perfect passivity to some Titanic force of life, which, for good or evil, must work on through its seeming eternity. Hurried through sublimest ascending paths, or whirled downward through ever- blackening infinitudes, longing for a Lemnos where the limbs may rebound from solid ground, even though shattered by the shock, there is no relief for the soul but to endure, to wait, and through a time of patience but faintly imaged by the nine days of the headlong Hephaestus. When the Afreet who was of old your servant becomes your lord, he is as deaf to petitions as you were avaricious in your demand for splendors.

Again: at the moment of the most rapturous exultation, the soul hears the outcry of the physical nature pouring up to its height of vision out of the walls of flesh, and the burden of that cry is, "I am in pain; I am finite, though thou art infinite!" The cords which bind the two mysterious portions of our duality together have been stretched to their ultimate tensity, and the body, for the sake of its own existence, calls the soul back into the husk which it can not carry with it. Oftentimes, in the presence of the most ravishing views, have I felt these cords pulling me downward with as distinct a sensation as if they were real sinews, and, compelled to ask the question "Is this happiness or torture?" soul and body have returned opposite verdicts.

These two facts constitute hasheesh a most tremendous form of insanity

At intervals, however, in the enchanted life which I led under the influence of the drug, there occurred seasons of a quieter nature than the ravishment of delirium, when my mind, with a calm power of insight, penetrated into some of its own kingdoms, whose external boundaries only it had known before, reflected, marveled, and took notes as serenely as a philosophic voyager.

In the department of philological discovery I sometimes reveled for hours, coming upon clews to the geneaology of words and unexpected affinities between languages, which, upon afterward recalling them (though only in a few cases was I able to do this), I generally found substantiated by the authorities of science, or, if they had not before been perceived by any writers who I had at hand, at least bearing the stamp of a strong probability of correctness.

I mention but one of them as with me merely conjectural, for it bases its plausibility upon a root in the Sanscrit, with which language I do not pretend to be acquainted.

I remembered during one of these calm, suggestive states that the Latin cano (to sing) and candeo (to shine) were supposed to derive their origin from a common Sanscrit root, whose signification was "to dart forth, as the sun his rays of light." The thought struck me, Might not other vocal utterance than singing be found cognate with the out-darting of light also? I would see. The Latin "fari," "to speak," referred me back to its Greek equivalent, . The verb "to shine" was "." So far, in sound at least, the two were affiliated. It now occurred to me that "" was both "a light" and "man," in his prerogative of speech, with a slight variation of accent in the different cases. I had here four words (dividing the last by its two meanings), all of whose original roots must have been something very nearly like . On referring to authorities, I found that the fountain-head of the Greek "" is supposed to be the Sanscrit "bhâ," "to shine forth." Following out the result of my previous argument, I connected all the words with this root, and in this conjecture saw both light and speech as effluences from Brahm, the great giver of all radiance, and man not merely an effluence from him, but, in virtue of speech, a "shiner" also, a reflector of Him from whose radiance he came, and into whose glory he should be absorbed. Now all this process (be its result true or false) was accomplished internally in a hundredth part of the time which it will take to read it -- nay, almost instantaneously, and with a sense of delight in the mental activity which carried it on such as the creation of his highest ideal by an artist gives him when he stands mute before his marble.

Another field through which I sometimes wandered was sown with those sound- relations between words which constitute the pun. For hours I walked aching with laughter in this land of Paronomasia, where the whole Dictionary had arrayed itself in strophe and antistrophe, and was dancing a ludicrous chorus of quirk and quibble. If Hood had been there, the notes which he would have taken had supplied him with materials for the Comic Annuals of a cycle. Rarely did the music of a deeper wit intermingle with the rattling fantasies of the pun-country; never was any thing but the broad laugh heard there, and the very atmosphere was crazy with oxygen. Were it possible to transport to a country such as this those grave professors of the moralities who have been convicted of contempt of the court of Mirth, and high treason to the King of Misrule, how delightful would it be to behold their iron diaphragms vibrating perforce, and the stereotyped downward curves at the corners of their mouths reversed until they encroached upon the boundaries of their juiceless cheeks! But, in hasheesh states, temperament and previous habit so much decide tendencies, that the transport-ship which bore these convicts would float inevitably to the mouth of Acheron, or strand midway upon some reef upraised by a million of zoophytic Duns Scotuses. Out of the number of double-entendres which appeared to me (and they probably amounted to thousands), I recollect but very few. To recall them all would e nearly, if not quite as difficult as to remember the characteristics of each separate wheat-head in a large harvest-field after having but once passed through it. I give two of them.

A youth, not at all of that description which "maketh a glad father," was seen standing at the counter of a gaudy restaurant. Glass after glass of various exhilarating compounds was handed to him by the man in waiting, and as quickly drained. I did not observe that the genius of decanters received any compensation for the liquors consumed from the young man who demanded them, and modestly asked him how he had been induced to purvey to the drinker's thirst on so liberal a scale. With arms akimbo, and casting upon me a most impressive look, the official replied, "Like the man in Thanatopsis, I am

"'Sustained by an unfaltering trust.'"

Upon the steps of the post-office stood another young man, who had been disappointed in a remittance from the parental treasury. "What are you doing there?" I asked. "I am waiting patiently until my change come."

Occasionally there intervened between the vagaries of pun and double-entendre some display of comic points in human nature, which were as amusing as the puns themselves. For instance, I remember the representation to me of a man of remarkable self-esteem, who happened, as he sat in my presence, to appease the irritation of his scalp with his digit. Just then a peal of thunder shook the sky above us. "Heavens!" cried our friend, "to think that it should thunder because a man scratched his head!"

I feel that these things lose very much of their original effervescence in the relation, for at the time they none of them seemed so much told to me as acted before me; nor was it the action of a stage, but of a vivified picture, where fun, in all its myriad mutations, was embodied to sight, and the joke was as much apprehended by the eye as by the feeling. Every gesture of the figures that passed before me told more of raillery than tongue could utter, and it was this fact that sometimes made pantomime upon the stage a perfect feast of mirth to me as I sat seeing it in the appreciative state induced by hasheesh. At such seasons, not the faintest stroke of humor in look or manner escaped me, and I no doubt often committed that most gross error in any man, laughing when my neighbors saw fit not to be moved.

At one time, in my ramble through the realm of incongruities, I came to the strand of the Mediterranean, and beheld an acquaintance of mine standing close beside the water. With a tourist's knapsack upon his back, and a stout umbrella in his hand, to serve the double purpose of a walking-stick, he drew near and accosted me. "Will you go with me," said he, "to make a call upon a certain old and valued friend?"

"Most willingly, if you will let me know his name."

"It is the Prophet Jonah, who still occupies submarine lodgings in a situation, to be sure, rather cold and damp, yet commanding a fine water privilege." "There is nothing," I replied, "which would please me more; but how is it to be accomplished?" ,"Be patient, and you shall see." Just then a slight ripple ridged the surface of the sea, bubbles appeared, and then there followed them the black muzzle of Leviathan, who, with mighty strokes, pushed toward the shore. Arriving there, his under jaw slid half way up the beach, and his upper jaw slowly rose like a trap-door, disclosing a fearful chasm of darkness within. I looked down the throat of the beast, and beheld descending it a rickety wooden staircase, which was evidently the only feasible access to interior apartments. Hardly would I have dared to trust myself to the tumble-down passage but for the importunate hand of my companion, which pressed me along beside him through the doorway and down the steps. The monster let down his grisly portcullis behind us, and in total darkness we groped to the bottom of our way, where we emerged into the most shabby room that ever dawned upon the eyes of the visiting committee of a benevolent association.

The central figure was an unutterably lean and woe-begone looking man, who, on a rush-bottomed chair, the only one in the room, sat mending his sole pair of unmentionables by the aid of a small needle-book which I was informed his mother had given him on leaving home.

"Mr. Jonah, Mr. Fitz-Gerald," said my friend, sententiously. "Very happy to know Mr. Fitz-Gerald," returned the seer; though, as I took his lank and ghostly fingers in mine, he looked the very antipodes of happy. Decayed gentleman as he was, he shuffled around to do the honors of his mansion, and offered us the chair in which he had been sitting. We refused to dispossess him, and took our seats upon the shaky pine table, which, with one battered brazen candlestick, holing an inch of semi-luminous tallow, and a dog's- eared copy of Watt's Hymns, also a gift from his mother, completed his inventory of furniture.

"How do you like your situation?" asked my friend.

"Leaky," replied Jonah; "find the climate don't agree with me. I often wish I hadn't come."

"Can't you leave here when you want to? I should think you would clear out if you find it uncomfortable," said I to our entertainer.

"I have repeatedly asked my landlord to make out his bill and let me go," replied the gentleman; "but he isn't used to casting up his prophets, and I don't know when I shall get off."

Just then Leviathan, from the top of the stairs, by a strange introversion looked down into his own interiors, and in a hoarse voice called out to know whether we were going to stay all night, as he wanted to put down the shutters.

"Be happy to give you a bed, gentlemen, but I sleep on the floor myself," woefully murmured the poor seer. "You mustn't neglect to call on me if you ever pass through Joppa, and -- and -- I ever get back myself." We wrung Jonah's hand convulsively, rattled up the crazy stairs, and ran out upon the sand just as Leviathan was about shoving off into deep water.

It may, perhaps, be hard to conceive how this incongruous element of the hasheesh visions should comport with all I have said upon the subject of those delicious raptures of beauty and sublime revelations of truth which break upon the mind under the influence of the drug.

How, it will be asked, as oftentimes it has been asked me already, can you put any confidence in discoveries of unsupposed significancy in outer things, and wonderful laws of mental being, attained during the hasheesh state, when you have also beheld vagaries of fancy which Reason instantly pronounced absurd? You do not believe that you really saw Jonah; how, then, can you believe that you saw truth?

I would answer thus: The domains of intuition and those of a wild fancy were always, in my visions, separated from each other by a clearly-defined and recognized boundary. The congruous and the incongruous might alternate, but they never blended. The light which illustrated the one was as different from that shed upon the other as a zenith sun is from lamplight. Moreover, at the time of each specific envisionment, I beheld which faculty of mind was working as distinctly as in the simplest tests of his laboratory the chemist knows whether cobalt or litmus is producing a certain change of color. The conviction of truth in the one case was like that of an axiom; in the other, such only as is drawn inferentially from mere sense.

We very little realize in our daily life that there are two species of conviction felt at various times by every man, yet a moment's reflection will show that it is so. I look, for example, at a piece of silk, and pronounce it black; if I were now to turn away without any further inspection, I should not be at all astonished to hear afterward, from some one who had examined the fabric more closely and in a better light, that it was not black, as I had pronounced it, but a dark shade of blue. I would be very willing to abjure my previous conviction, and, in this willingness, would show that I ascribed no absolute infallibility to the proofs of sense. Yet if the same man should assure me that the silk was both wholly black and wholly blue at the same time, I should instantly reject his assertion as absurd, for the reason that it was a violation of the very law of possibility. There would be no need of going back to test his truth, for it is denied by an entirely different conviction from that of sense -- the conviction arising from an insight into necessary and universal law.

Between the convictions of reality in the different hasheesh states, the boundary-lines are drawn even more distinctly than in the natural; and not only so, but the hasheesh-eater beholds those lines and acknowledges them, as the ordinary observer never does, from the fact that the practical wants of life make it convenient, nay, even imperative, that the data of sense should be treated as valid for the basis of action. We have neither time nor power in our present day-labor to secure the same unerring verdict upon objects of sense which the axiom gives us upon objects of intuition.

Nor is it necessary that in this life such a power should be possible. In a former part of these pages we have suggested a reason why it would not be best for the soul, thus early in its career, to have its intuitional domain enlarged. We may here, by another process, get at some of the final causes why this domain is just so large as it is. We have a sufficient scope of intuition for all our earthly purposes. Those truths are imparted to us as axioms which are necessary for the shaping of our habitual conduct. In the thousands of constantly-recurring cases where, to direct our course wisely, it is necessary to know that a straight line is the shortest distance between two given points, that the whole is equal to its parts, and numerous similar facts, it would greatly hinder action were it necessary to take the rule and the balance into each specific consideration, and make a measurement according to sense. These truths, therefore, stand before every man in a light which shows them to be universal and necessary; they are every where assented to upon their mere statement. The animal is not God's grand laborer, but man's; he, therefore, needs no such faculty as intuition, the work of his little day requiring neither dispatch nor accuracy; and when he is impressed for human uses into the harness or the mill, the intuitions of his master guide him through the rein and the halter.

Doubtless, as our field of action widens, our intuitional eyesight shall be increased also; not only because otherwise we should be mortified and saddened by our purblindness and the sense of making no progress proportional to the pace of our circumstances, but because God will never leave the workmen of his purposes hampered in their action among the colossal plans of the eternal building.

There is one more fact to which I would advert in this rather rambling portion of my narrative, which characterizes the hasheesh state at times when it does not reach the height of delirium. I refer to a lively appreciation of the feelings and manners of all people, in whatever lands and ages -- a catholic sympathy, a spiritual cosmopolitanism. Not only does this exhibit itself in affectionate yearnings toward friends that are about one, and an extraordinary insight into the excellencies of their characters, but, taking a wider sweep, it can understand and feel with the heroism of philanthropists and the enthusiasm of Crusaders. The lamentation of the most ancient Thracian captive is a sincere grief to the dreamer, and the returning Camillus brought no greater joy to Rome, as he threw his defiant sword into the scale, than over the chasm of ages he sends thrilling into the hasheesh- eater's heart. Whether it is the Past or the Present that is read or heard, he sorrows in all its woes and rejoices in all its rejoicings. He understands all feelings; his mind is malleable to all thoughts; his susceptibilities run into the mould of all emotions.

Sitting in this fused state of mind, I have heard the old ladies of the Latin time, as they sat gossiping over spindle and distaff, keep up their perpetual round of "inquit" and "papæ" with as distinct and s kind appreciation as were they our own beloved American aunts and grandmothers, knitting after tea amid the interchange of "says he" and "do tell." For Epaminondas, coming glorious from Leuctra, I could have hurrahed as enthusiastically as any Thebian of them all, or hobnobbed with Horace over his

"Pocula veteris Massici"

with a true Roman zest and full-heartedness. At such times no anachronism seems surprising; time is treated as an insignificant barrier to those souls who, in the element of their generous humanity, possess the only true bond of conjunction, and a bond which, though now so elastic that it permits years and leagues to keep souls apart, shall one day pull with a force strong enough to bring all congenialities together, in place as well as in state, and every man shall be with those whom, for their inner qualities, he has most deeply lived through all his life.

XIV. Hail! Pythagoras

The hemisphere of sky which walls us in is something more than a mere product of the laws of sight. It is our shield from unbearable visions. Within our little domain of view, girt by the horizon and arched by the dome of heaven, there is enough of sorrow, enough of danger, yes, enough of beauty and of mirth visible to occupy the soul abundantly in any one single beholding. That lesser and unseen hemisphere which bounds our hearing is also amply large, for within it echo enough of music and lamentation to fill all susceptibility to the utmost. In this world we are but half spirit; we are thus able to hold only the perceptions and emotions of half an orb. Once fully rounded into symmetry ourselves, we shall have strength to bear the pressure of influences from a whole sphere of truth and loveliness.

It is this present half-developed state of ours which makes the infinitude of the hasheesh awakening so unendurable, even when its sublimity is the sublimity of delight. We have no longer any thing to do with horizons, and the boundary which was at once our barrier and our fortress is removed, until we almost perish from the inflow of perceptions.

One most powerful realization of this fact occurred to me when hasheesh had already become a fascination and a habit. In the broad daylight of a summer afternoon I was walking in the full possession of delirium. For an hour the expansion of all visible things had been growing toward its height; it now reached it, and to the fullest extent I apprehended what is meant by the infinity of space. Vistas no longer converged; sight met no barrier; the world was horizonless, for earth and sky stretched endlessly onward in parallel planes. Above me the heavens were terrible with the glory of a fathomless depth. I looked up, but my eyes, unopposed, every moment penetrated farther and farther into the immensity, and I turned them downward, lest they should presently intrude into the fatal splendors of the Great Presence. Unable to bear visible objects, I shut my eyes. In one moment a colossal music filled the whole hemisphere above me, and I thrilled upward through its environment on visionless wings. It was not song, it was not instruments, but the inexpressible spirit of sublime sound -- like nothing I had ever heard -- impossible to be symbolized; intense, yet not loud; the ideal of harmony, yet distinguishable into a multiplicity of exquisite parts.

136

I opened my eyes, but it still continued. I sought around me to detect some natural sound which might be exaggerated into such a semblance; but no, it was of unearthly generation, and it thrilled through the universe an inexplicable, a beautiful, yet an awful symphony.

Suddenly my mind grew solemn with the consciousness of a quickened perception. And what a solemnity is that which the hasheesh-eater feels at such a moment! The very beating of his heart is silenced; he stands with his finger on his lip; his eye is fixed, and he becomes a very statue of awful veneration. The face of such a man, however little glorified in feature or expression during his ordinary states of mind, I have stood and looked upon with the consciousness that I was beholding more of the embodiment of the truly sublime than any created thing could ever offer me.

I looked abroad on fields, and waters, and sky, and read in them a most startling meaning. I wondered how I had ever regarded them in the light of dead matter, at the farthest only suggesting lessons. They were now, as in my former vision, grand symbols of the sublimest spiritual truths -- truths never before even feebly grasped, and utterly unsuspected.

Like a map, the arcana of the universe lay bare before me. I saw how every created thing not only typifies, but springs forth from some mighty spiritual law as its offspring, its necessary external development -- not the mere clothing of the essence, but the essence incarnate.

I am aware that, in this recital, I may seem to be repeating what I have said before of my dreadful night of insight; but between the two visions there was this difference, the view did not stop here. While that music was pouring through the great heavens above me, I became conscious of a numerical order which ran through it, and in marking this order, I beheld it transferred to every movement of the universe. Every sphere wheeled on in its orbit, every emotion of the soul arose and fell, every smallest moss and fungus germinated and grew according to some peculiarity of numbers which severally governed them, and was most admirably typified them in return. An exquisite harmony of proportion reigned through space, and I seemed to realize that the music which I heard was but this numerical harmony making itself objective through the development of a grand harmony of tones.

The vividness with which this conception revealed itself to me made it a thing terrible to bear alone. An unutterable ecstasy was carrying me away, but I dared not abandon myself to it. I was no seer who could look on the unveiling of such glories face to face.

An irrepressible yearning came over me to impart what I beheld, to share with another soul the weight of this colossal revelation. With this purpose I scrutinized this vision; I sought in it for some characteristic which might make it translatable to another mind. There was none. In absolute incommunicableness it stood apart. For it, in spoken language, there was no symbol.

For a long time -- how long a hasheesh-eater alone can know -- I was in an agony. I searched every pocket for my pencil and note-book, that I might at least set down some representative mark which would afterward recall to me the lineaments of my apocalypse. They were not with me. Jutting into the water of the brook along which I then wandered, and which, before and afterward, was my sole companion through so many ecstasies, lay a broad, flat stone. "Glory in the highest!" I shouted, exultingly; "I will at least grave on this tablet some hieroglyph of what I feel. Tremblingly I sought for my knife; that, too, was gone! It was then that, in a phrensy, I threw myself prostrate on the stone, and with my nails sought to make some memorial scratch upon it. Hard, hard as flint! In despair I stood up.

Suddenly there came a sense as if some invisible presence walking the dread paths of the vision with me, yet at a distance, as if separated from my side by a long flow of time. Taking courage, I cried, "Who has ever been here before me? who, in years past, has shared with me this unutterable view?" In tones which linger with me to this day, a grand, audible voice responded "Pythagoras!" In an instant I was calm. I heard the footsteps of that sublime sage echoing upward through the ages, and in celestial light I read my vision unterrified, since it had burst upon his sight before me.

For years previous I had been perplexed with his mysterious philosophy. I saw in him an isolation from universal contemporary mind for which I could not account. When the Ionic school was at the height of its dominance, he stood forth alone the originator of a system as distinct from it as the antipodes of mind.

The doctrine of Thales was built up by the uncertain processes of an obscure logic; that of Pythagoras seemed informed by intuition. In his assertions there ad always appeared to me a grave conviction of truth, a consciousness of sincerity which gave them a great weight, though I saw them through the dim refracting medium of tradition, and grasped their meaning imperfectly. It was now given to see, in their own light, the truths which he set forth. I also saw, as to this day I firmly believe, the source whence their revelation flowed.

Tell me not that from Phoenicia he received the wand at whose signal the cohorts of the spheres came trooping up before him in review, unveiling the eternal law and itinerary of their revolutions, and pouring on his spiritual ear that tremendous music to which they marched through space. No. During half a lifetime spent in Egypt and India, both mother-lands of this nepenthe, doubt not that he quaffed its apocalyptic draught, and awoke, through its terrific quickening, into the consciousness of that ever-present and all- pervading harmony "which we hear not, because the coarseness of the daily life hath dulled our ear." The dim penetralia of the Theban Memnonium, or the silent spice-groves of the upper Indus, may have been the gymnasium of his wrestling with the mighty revealer; a priest or a gymnosophist may have been the first to anoint him with the palæstric oil, but he conquered alone. On the strange intuitive characteristics of his system; on the spherical music; on the government of all created things, and their development according to the laws of numbers; yes, on the very use of symbols, which could alone have force to the esoteric disciple (and a terrible significancy, indeed, has the simplest form to a mind hasheesh-quickened to read its meaning) -- on all of these is the legible stamp of the hasheesh inspiration.

It would be no hard task to prove, to a strong probability, at least, that the initiation to the Pythagorean mysteries, and the progressive instruction that succeeded it, to a considerable extent consisted in the employment, judiciously, if we may use the word, of hasheesh, as giving a critical and analytic power to the mind, which enabled the neophyte to roll up the murk and mist from beclouded truths till they stood distinctly seen in the splendor of their own harmonious beauty as an intuition.

One thing related of Pythagoras and his friends has seemed very striking to me. There is a legend that, as he was passing over a river, its waters called up to him, in the presence of his followers, "Hail! Pythagoras." Frequently, while in the power of the hasheesh delirium, have I heard inanimate things sonorous with such voices. On every side they have saluted me, from rocks, and trees, and waters, and sky; in my happiness filling me with intense exultation as I heard them welcoming their master; in my agony heaping nameless curses on my head as I went away into an eternal exile from all sympathy. Of this tradition of Iamblichus I feel an appreciation which almost convinces me that the voice of the river was indeed heard, though only by the quickened mind of some hasheesh-glorified esoterie. Again, it may be that the doctrine of the metempsychosis was first communicated to Pythagoras by Theban priests; but the astonishing illustration which hasheesh would contribute to this tenet should not be overlooked in our attempt to assign its first suggestion and succeeding spread to their proper causes.

A modern critic, in defending the hypothesis that Pythagoras was an imposter, has triumphantly asked, "Why did he assume the character of Apollo at the Olympic games? Why did he boast that his soul had lived in former bodies, and that he had first been Æthalides, the son of Mercury, then Euphorbus, then Pyrrhus of Delos, and at last Pythagoras, but that he might more easily impose upon the credulity of an ignorant and superstitious people?" To us these facts seem rather an evidence of his sincerity. Had he made these assertions without proof, it is difficult to see how they would not have had a precisely contrary effect from that of paving the way to a more complete imposition upon popular credulity. Upon our hypothesis it may be easily shown, not only how he could fully have believed these assertions himself, but also have given them a deep significance to the minds of his disciples.

Let us see. We will consider, for example, his assumption of the character of Phoebus at the Olympic games. Let us suppose that Pythagoras, animated with a desire of alluring to the study of his philosophy a choice and enthusiastic number out of that host who, along all the radii of the civilized world, had come up to the solemn festival at Elis, had, by the talisman of hasheesh, called to his aid the magic of a preternatural eloquence; that while he addressed the throng, whom he had chained into breathless attention by the weird brilliancy of his eye, the unearthly imagery of his style, and the oracular insight of his thought, the grand impression flashed upon him from the very honor he was receiving, that he was the incarnation of some sublime deity. What wonder that he burst into the acknowledgment of his godship as a secret too majestic to be hoarded up; what wonder that this sudden revelation of himself, darting forth in burning words and amid such colossal surroundings, went down with the accessories of time and place along the stream of perpetual tradition?

If I may illustrate great things by small, I well remember many hallucinations of my own which would be exactly parallel to such a fancy in the mind of Pythagoras. There is no impression more deeply stamped upon my past life than one of a walk along the brook which had so often witnessed my wrestlings with the hasheesh-afreet, and which now beheld me, the immortal Zeus, descended among men to grant them the sublime benediction of renovated life. For this cause I had abandoned the serene seats of Olympus, the convocation of the gods, and the glory of an immortal kingship, while by my side Hermes trod the earth with radiant feed, the companion and dispenser of the beneficence of Deity. Across lakes and seas, from continent to continent we strode; the snows of Hæmus and the Himmalehs crunched beneath our sandals; our foreheads were bathed with the upper light, our breasts glowed with the exultant inspiration of the golden ether. Now resting on Chimborzao, I poured forth a majestic blessing upon all my creatures, and in an instant, with one omniscient glance, I beheld every human dwelling-place on the whole sphere irradiated with an unspeakable joy.

I saw the king rule more wisely; the laborer return from his toil to a happier home; the park grow green with an intenser culture; the harvest-field groan under the sheaves of a more prudent and prosperous husbandry. Adown blue slopes came new and more populous flocks, led by unvexed and gladsome shepherds; a thousand healthy vineyards sprang up above their new-raised sunny terraces; every smallest heart glowed with an added thrill of exultation, and the universal rebound of joy came pouring up into my own spirit with an intensity which lit my deity with rapture.

And this was but a lay hasheesh-eater, mysteriously clothed in no Pallas-woven, philosophic stole, who, with his friend, walked out into the fields to enjoy his delirium among the beauties of a clear summer afternoon. What, the, of Pythagoras?

It was during this walk that one of the strangest phenomena of sight which I have ever noticed appeared to me. Every sunbeam was refracted into its primitive rays; wherever upon the landscape a pencil of light fell, between rocks or trees, it seemed a prismatic pathway between earth and heaven. The atmosphere was one network of variegated solar threads, tremulous with radiance, and distilling rapture from its fibres into all my veins.

It is singular in how many ways, during the hasheesh life, the harmony of creation was typified to me. The harp of the universe, which I have already mentioned, was itself once repeated invision; other representations, on a scale perhaps even as grand, have left but a dim outline upon my memory; yet there is one which, though at least thrice repeated, lost no glory by growing familiar, but more and more deepened its first impress of awe and rapture. The first time that it occurred to me was when, at the close of my walk amid the majesty of apotheosis, I sat quietly at the window of my room looking out upon the sunset which bathed the gigantic landscape before me. As yet the magnifying effect of the drug had not begun to decrease, and I gazed with fascinated eyes upon mountains which scaled heaven, and a river which was oceanic, in a breathless exultancy which vibrated on the diamond edge of pain.

Suddenly the landscape floated out of sight, and in its place there sat on the trembling ether a tremendous ship, which within itself included every portion of created being. Not a God-born essence, not a microscopic atom, but was builded up into some bulwark, beam, or spar of the colossal vessel. its marked outline was traced with the more glorious things of creation, the baser formed its inner and hidden parts. Its sides, its stern, its bow were wrought of mighty stars whose rays interlaced; its masts were similar constellations, that at their heads, a million leagues above me, yet still distinctly radiant, bore systems of suns for lanterns. Like lanterns flashed far off upon the prow, and dazzling clouds and nebulae, filled out with the breath of an omnipotent will, strained the crystal yards upon which they hung.

Now I was transferred to the deck of this infinite ship; her name was whispered in my ear, "The Ship of the Universe," and the helm was put into my hand. With unutterable symphonies we floated out upon the boundless space, and on the distant bows there broke in music the waves of resplendent ether. It was at this post of pilotage, steering out into the unknown void, that I felt human nature within me grow godlike to an insane excess. The helmsman, the master of all being but the Divine, I burst into a chant of triumph, which shook the starry lights above me till their clusters rained glory like wine.

I bethought me, forgetful of the infinity of the ocean we were traveling, that I might mark the rate of our progress, and so drew out my watch. Its second- hand had stopped. I held it to my ear and heard it tick. Again I looked at it; the hand was motionless. Continuing my gaze, I saw it at length move slowly through one of the second-spaces, when it stopped once more. Still I looked, and at last became aware that, by the hasheesh expansion of time, I was enabled to realize as a quite prolonged and definite period -- a period as great as in our ordinary state a whole minute, at least, would appear -- that almost infinitesimal instant during which a second-hand actually is motionless at the end of its vibration between two consecutive ticks.

XV. "Then Seeva opened on the Accursed One his Eye of Anger"

In the agonies of hasheesh, which now became more and more frequent, a new element began to develop itself toward a terrible symmetry, which afterward made it effective for the direst spiritual evil. This was the appearance of Deity upon the stage of my visionary life, now sublimely grand in very person, and now through the intermediation of some messenger or sign, yet always menacing, wrathful, or avenging, in whatever form or manner the visitation might be made. The myriad voices which, earlier in my enchanted life, I had heard from Nature through all her mysterious passages of communication, now died down forever, or, rather, became absorbed into one colossal and central voice, which spoke with the force of a fiat, and silenced my own faint replies like the sentence of inevitable doom.

At first I was calmly warned. Repeatedly, as I sat in an elysium of rosy languor, banqueting upon all that could exalt the inner sense into the serenest ecstasy, the hand that wrote upon the wall has invaded the sanctity of my feast, and its dread tracery has made me suddenly afraid. In characters of light I have seen it written, "Beware how thou triflest with a mysterious power of the Most High!" and an audible voice, whose divinity at the moment I no more doubted than my own humanity, has added its injunction, "Beware! beware!" Anticipating nothing but an uninterrupted procession of sublime images and the choral music which had so often ravished me out of the walls of sense, I have in an instant shuddered with unutterable terror as I felt the unlooked-for finger of some awful presence marking out downward channels for my upwelling thought, and solemnly forcing its streams into them with a power which bore no doubtful tokens of irresistibleness, but commanded even my own assent to the impossibility of escape.

At length the reasons of my punishment were shown me. Here again, as audibly as man talks with man, I was told, "Thou hast lifted thyself above humanity to peer into he speechless secrets before thy time; and thou shalt be smitten -- smitten -- smitten." As the last echo of the sentence died away, it always began its execution in Promethean pangs. At last even the faintest suggestion of the presence of Deity possessed a power to work me ill which hardly the haunting of demons had been able to produce before. At one time I well remember beholding a colossal veiled figure part the drapery of sombre clouds which hung over the horizon, and appear upon a platform which I supposed to be the stage of the universe. No sound, no radiance issued from behind the veil, yet when the mysterious figure lifted his hands, I cried, "It is the Day of Judgment, and my doom is being pronounced!" Then I fled for my soul, and cowered in the darkest spot that I could find.

One tremendous vision occurred to me during the progress of one of these peculiar states, which, while it filled me with the agony of despair for my own fate, still gave me an inconceivable pain for another being. In the heavens I heard a voice of weeping; no plaintive wail like that of woman in affliction, no passionate cry like that of a strong man riven by distress, but some nameless agony, foreshadowed by a solemn voice of woe, which spoke of universal creation suffering fearfully at its centre, life drying up at its fountain-head of being. "Who weeps?" I cried in terror. And the answer was returned to me out of the viewless air, "The Mighty One, who was of old held supreme, hath discovered that his supremacy is void. Fate, blind Fate, that hath no ear for thy yearnings, sits mover of the spring of all things, and He to whom thou prayest is a discrowned King." Ah! well might there be such weeping in the heavens! After all, we had no Lord, no God but Destiny. And I saw dynasties rush down in aimless ruin; good and evil met in eternal shock; there should be no prevalence to Right; the souls of all humanity were but atoms hurled onward through an infinite, lawless Chaos. In my own spirit there sounded an echo to the celestial groaning, and with tearless horror I went straying through the rayless abyss of accident, a tortured creature without a goal. "My God," I whispered, "annihilate me!" Words of accursed folly! God no longer lived.

I threw myself upon the earth, and clutched its dead, ungoverned dust in my writhing fingers. I called no longer upon God, and was dumb because Fate was deaf. I cursed the day that I was born -- meaningless, still meaningless, since there was no power who could authenticate the curse. I lay balancing the chances of being blotted out. Somewhere in the eternities a crash might end me. Forever? What if my disrupted being should float together in cycles measurelessly on? Reunited, I should wander once more a godless wretch!

From horizon to horizon there flashed a quick glory; heaven rang through all its dome with a multitude of tremendous bands, and a sound of chanting joined in the symphony. "Ah! what is this?" I said, and started up. "I hear a harmony, and Fate knows only discords." Again the aerial voice responded, but now in a triumphant song, "After all, there is a Supreme; he rules whose right it is; there is no destiny but God, and he is over all forever." I leaped into the air -- I shouted for joy. The hope of the ages was sure -- there was a God!

Yet few of my visions of the Divine, as bitterly I tested in many a trial of fire, were to have an issue so blessed as this.

Through the watches of a long and lonely night I had been sitting, with no other companion than my crusted lamp, and the shapes of strange men and things passed by me ceaselessly in tides of pain and pleasure. At length I found myself in the highest story of an unknown and desolate house, surrounded by blank walls, and lighted by a single narrow window. "This room," spoke the hasheesh voice, "is that which thou callest Time. Outside the whirl the resistless, the unbounded winds of Eternity."

I went to the window, and, looking out, saw nothing; but the heavy roar of a storm-lashed atmosphere shook the panes. A strange fascination tempted me to draw nearer to the tempest. I threw up the sash; in one moment the wind of eternity came rushing in; the foundations of my building shook, and straightway, by those stormy wings, every atom of it was winnowed out of sight, and, houseless, I found myself alone among the infinitudes. For a while I was blown hither and thither unconsciously. Then, coming to myself, I found that I had been wafted to the door of a certain friend of mine, who doubtless would care for me in my bewilderment of suffering.

It was now four o'clock of a midsummer morning, and the western hills, that I could see through a hall window, began to be impurpled by reflection from the opposite horizon of the dawn. My friend was an early riser, and he would, perhaps, be willing to walk with me, for I could not endure to sit still for a moment. "Baldwin!" I cried; "Baldwin, it is necessary that I should speak with you," at the same time knocking stoutly until I aroused him from sleep.

It was at first very difficult for me to persuade him how intensely I was suffering, for my habit of self-control subdued even my face. At last we were in the open air, and I walked clinging to Baldwin's arm. I said little, for I had no power to speak above a whisper, and in disjointed sentences. Coming to the steps which led from my own entry, we sat down for a few moments' rest. All familiarity of appearance was utterly dissipated from the place, and the buildings in view had become to me the temples and pylons of disentombed Memphis. Awful Egyptian gateways frowned down upon me with a wrathful meaning, which they had not lost in all their centuries of sepulchral dust since the Pharaohs, and the grisly stare of Sphinx and Caryatid appalled me, on all sides shutting out relief through change of view. But, worse horror yet, beneath pedestal and foundation, under the lowest stone of the deepest-based temple of all the adamantine group, supporting its weight, bursting with a torture in which it could not writhe, lay my own, my living heart, unreached and never to be reached by the instrument of the resurrectionist of ages!

It was the wrath of God which had whelmed that city; my heart, therefore, lay under that wrath. Yet I would appeal submissively to the Supreme, that he might perchance have mercy on me. I looked heavenward, but what a vision there unveiled itself! In the most intimate recess of a sable, cloudy cavern flamed vengefully two burning, soul-penetrating eyes. Their gaze dissolved me, and, turning away, I hid my face in my friend's lap.

When he sought the cause of my pain, I could not tell him. At that moment I would not have embodied in words the infinity of wrathful menace which I had seen on high for the endowment of coined words.

When at length I dared to look out from my lurking-place, my sight chanced to fall upon the vapory banks which skirted the gleaming western horizon. In mercy my vision was here changed to one of peace. As if to heal the pangs of my spirit, I saw, flowing down to me through a rift in the clouds, a silvery river of unutterable balm. Unknown trees drooped, prodigal of wondrous fruit and odors, over its enameled margin; and rare beings floated, with their beaming girdles streaming on the breeze, above the crystal waters, or stooped to drink of them along the edge; and the hasheesh voice whispered me, "The River of the Water of Life." If heaven be like that, the stake and the rack are worth while to bear on the way to it!

Slowly the celestial aspect of the vision passed away. The river still remained, but on its banks a great city lifted her walls, and I knew that the river was Simois, and the city Troy. As yet the inner citadel rose fair and vase, and the broad gates stood firm.

Upon the bank of the stream I saw a dead face turned up toward the morning sky. The agony of the death-struggle had plowed no furrows upon brow or cheek, and a mysterious, matchless loveliness slept in the features chiseled without fault. More than I had ever been with life I was ravished with death -- nay, I had given my own life to print a kiss upon the serene lips of the sleeper, or to pluck a lock from the wavy wealth which flowed out of his helmet, whose clasps, now unbound, hung idly to the earth beside him.

A warrior still living came into my view. With shield thrown on the ground and spear trailing through his arm in all the negligence of grief, with owed crest and hands intensely clasped, he stood silently gazing upon the dead, and his look was so instinct with a superhuman grief that I wept in sympathy with him.

Again the hasheesh voice spoke to me, "This is Achilles standing over the slain Patroclus," and my grief was changed into a sublime awe of mystery as I beheld that some unknown power had borne me over the bridgeless abyss of three thousand years to sorrow in the sorrowing of one of the grandest children of the epic Past.

I have sometimes lamented that in my hasheesh experience visions of ecstasy almost always followed those of pain, and, indeed, generally concluded the trance, whether I walked or slept. With opium-eaters or drinkers of liquor the case is ordinarily different. Their happiness comes first, and the depression that follows brings with it shame, repentance, and at least a feeble aim at some new life. When they have become satiated with their pleasure, they have to pay for it, and of all things which it is odious to pay for, a luxury enjoyed in the past is the most so. If, in my own experience, such a disgust and loathing, such reaction of body and spirit, had succeeded the hasheesh indulgence, I had possessed much stronger motives for renouncing it. But with me ecstasy had always the last word, and, on returning to the natural state, I remembered great tortures to be sure, but only as the unnecessary adjuncts to a happiness which I fondly persuaded myself was the legitimate effect of the drug. I said, I have suffered, but only because certain unfortunate circumstances came in to pervert my condition, and I will, in the future, avoid them. In the instance just related this fact fully obtained. For days afterward I never looked toward a certain quarter of the heavens without shuddering, as I remembered that it was there I met the gaze of the burning eyes, and my hand involuntarily went to my heart as I saw the site of the disentombed city, in imagination, once more occupied by its ponderous and cruel piles of granite. But from such memories as these my mind glanced with an elasticity as yet undiminished by its many shocks to the healing waters of the celestial river, or the face of mortal loveliness which has never, even now, passed thoroughly from my dreams.

After this, therefore, I took hasheesh many times; nay, more, life became with me one prolonged state of hasheesh exaltation -- a very network, singularly varied, of golden and iron strands, and throughout this life I ever and anon bore hours of wretchedness from superhuman threatenings such as I would not, if I could, transcribe entire, unless called by most imperative duty to hand down a legacy of admonition to all who may seek by other than the appointed means to mount into a life above the utterly material. I shall not, therefore, detail in their order of time all the visitations of horror which afflicted me, but will endeavor here and there to cull those which may most graphically foreshadow that "last state of a man which is worse than the first."

Repeatedly, as I have said, was I menaced by voices. Yet the threatening sometimes took other forms, and none of them were more terrific than the exhibition to me, as frequently occurred, of all nature abominating me, sometimes for the reason clearly set forth that I had tampered with a mystery which encroached on the prerogative of God, and sometimes for the sake of a nameless crime -- nameless because too horrible to be named -- whose nature or aggravation I did not know, but which lurked for me in some covert by the wayside, ready to spring upon me with the sword of Nemesis as I came by.

Through the whole of one breezy summer afternoon I had been wandering through the woods which I have so often mentioned, happy to delirious excess, and sustained by the arm and the conversation of a congenial friend, whom I now found it wisest to take with me as a precaution against wild vagaries, whenever I walked in the hasheesh state. Our pathway led over a thick carpet of fallen pine leaves, and my delight was heightened by the aromatic odors which exhaled from them in the warm winds which fanned us as we went. In this perfume was luxuriant suggestion of Indian spice-groves, and nothing more marked than such a mere suggestion does the hasheesh-eater need to build up for him the fabric of a most amazing and odorous dream. Straightway a grand procession of Burmese priests wound down the slope of a distant hill; solemnly, yet joyously, they approached me with music, and the air was loaded with the breath of their swinging censers. At a vast distance above me I could catch glimpses through the tree-tops of a radiant sapphire sky, and rose-tinged clouds floated dreamily therein, yet the incense vapors reached and blended with them even at that grand height. I stopped the foremost of the sacerdotal train, and spoke with him in his own language. He answered me, and we understood each other through a prolonged conversation, while my friend stood waiting by my side, in speechless marvel at an exhibition of my delirium for which he could not see even as much cause as usually explains conduct in the hasheesh state.

Our conversation over, the procession passed on. I now felt, as suddenly as if it had fallen upon me from heaven, and as assuredly as if Heaven had spoken it, that that priestly multitude were the last of human kind that should ever endure my presence. My companion abhorred me, and nothing but his sense of duty forced him to accede to my request that he should lead me to my room. On the way back we passed a radiant and balmy knoll, whereon, amid a tropical excess of flowers and foliage, a group of Burmese children were dancing to stringed instrument. They saw me, and instantly rushed out of sight in precipitate agony of loathing.

Reaching home, I entered my room. Wherever, upon tables or chairs, on the bed or on the floor, there was any possible space, stood a coffin, with lid let down, disclosing the face of some one among the well-remembered dead. Though never feared death, I always knew well the feeling of our ancient sire, who prayed the sons of Heth, saying "Give me a burying-place with you, that I may bury the dead out of my sight." Yet at this moment I crouched between the coffins as in an asylum, a demon, indeed, in nature, yet exulting in the security of possessing a hiding-place among the ruins which had once held holy souls. My God! could the dead still know me and my dreadful state? Over every one of those cold faces passed a ripple of dire agony! They feared me, after having been lifeless for many years! Distinctly I saw them convulsed with a tremendous shudder. One by one they turned upon their faces, and eagerly snatched with their hands behind them to close the lids which let in my accursed sight.

And now the two most loving friends who remained to me alive came walking toward me with tears streaming from their eyes. They had come on foot from a far city to fall upon their knees and beseech me, by all that I held sacred in the dearness of our relation, by the most precious future of my soul, to abandon hasheesh. The moment that their faces met my own, with a piercing cry of pain they fled out of my sight.

I ran out of my room and came to the house of an old and intimate companion. In a work-shop which he had fitted up as the place for his recreation he was busily engaged, as I came in, upon some mechanical contrivance, commenced when I had last seen him. His back was turned, and, to attract his attention, I called him by name, "Edward!"

Suddenly he faced me, smiling to recognize my voice; but, as the change of horror came over his features, he flung the hammer which he held in his hand at my head. It just missed its aim, and I saw that he had delivered the weapon, not in anger, but as the last boon he could give me to deprive me of my infernal life. The next moment he leaped through the lofty window of the room, and fathoms below I heard him crushed upon the pavement.

In a former agony I had suddenly obtained relief from the view of a certain name written in soft tints upon the sky. It was the name of a beautiful, good, and beloved girl; and as I saw it, it represented to me such lovely qualities of innocence, that beneath it I took sweet refuge as under an aegis. In an instant I grew calm, and the devil-voices that boomed after me died away.

Remembering this, I now bethought me to image that protectress' name in the same way as before, and therefrom promised myself speedy comfort. I sought to picture it before me, a name as simple as it was beautiful both in itself and its associations. It was "Mary," and I fled to it as never hunted murderer fled to grasp the skirts of Our Lady, the holy namesake of this most pure child.

In the first place, I tried to set the whole word before my eyes. This I found impossible. Then my endeavor was, letter by letter, to behold it in succession. I tried to get the first letter. And now came the inexplicable affliction of a perfect capability to think of the one which I wanted without being able to represent its form even to my inner sight. Backward and forward I boxed the whole alphabet. With inconceivable rapidity, every character beginning with A flew past me, but when the flight came to L there was one inevitable void between it and N. At Z I took the trail of the alphabetic whirl; in the same way, from N the letters leaped to L. At length, after a countless multitude of trials, I madly dashed myself upon the ground before that rushing demon font of type, and cried to Heaven, "An M! an M! for the love of my soul, grant me an M!"

My prayer was not heard, but without warning I was lifted from the earth, and on a burning wind wafted like a dry leaf into the sky. Whither and wherefore I was going I knew not until a dreadful voice hissed close beside my ear, "On earth thou didst triumph in superhuman joys -- now shalt thou ring their knell. It is thine to toll the summons to the Judgment."

I looked, and lo! all the celestial hemisphere was one terrific brazen bell, which rocked upon some invisible adamantine pivot in the infinitudes above. When I came it was voiceless, but I soon knew how it was to sound. My feet were quickly chained fast to the top of heaven, and, swinging with my head downward, I became its tongue. Still more mightily swayed that frightful bell, and now, tremendously crashing, my head smote against its side. It was not the pain of the blow, though that was inconceivable, but the colossal roar that filled the universe, and rent my brain also, which blotted out in one instant all sense, thought, and being. In an instant I felt my life extinguished, but knew that it was by annihilation, not by death.

When I awoke out of the hasheesh state I was as overwhelmed to find myself still in existence as a dead man of the last century could be were he now suddenly restored to earth. For a while, even in perfect consciousness, I believed I was still dreaming, and to this day I have so little lost the memory of that one demoniac toll, that, while writing these lines, I have put my hand to my forehead, hearing and feeling something, through the mere imagination, which was an echo of the original pang. It is this persistency of impressions which explains the fact of the hasheesh state, after a certain time, growing more and more every day a thing of agony. It is not because the body becomes worn out by repeated nervous shocks; with some constitutions, indeed, this wearing may occur; it never did with me, as I have said, even to the extent of producing muscular weakness, yet the universal law of constantly accelerating diabolization of visions held good as much in my case as in any others. But a thing of horror once experienced became a "," an inalienable dower of hell; it was certain to reproduce itself in some -- to God be the thanks if not in all -- future visions. I had seen, for instance, in one of my states of ecstasy, a luminous spot on the firmament, a prismatic parhelion. In the midst of my delight in gazing on it, it had transferred itself mysteriously to my own heart, and there became a circle of fire, which gradually ate its way until the whole writhing organ was in a torturous blaze. That spot, seen again in an after vision, through the memory of its former pain instantly wrought out for me the same accursed result. The number of such remembered fagots of fuel for dire suggestion of course increased proportionally to the prolonging of the hasheesh life, until at length there was hardly a visible or tangible object, hardly a phrase which could be spoken, that had not some such infernal potency as connected with an earlier effect of suffering.

Slowly thus does midnight close over the hasheesh-eater's heaven. One by one, upon its pall thrice dyed in Acheron, do the baleful lustres appear, until he walks under a hemisphere flaming with demon lamps, and upon a ground paved with tiles of hell. Out of this awful domain there are but three ways. Thank God that over its alluring gate way is not written,

"Lasciate ogni speranza voi ch'entrate!"

The first of these exits is insanity, the second death, the third abandonment. The first is doubtless oftenest trodden, yet it may be long ere it reaches the final escape in oblivion, and it is as frightful as the domain it leaves behind. The second but rarely opens to the wretch unless he pries it open with his knife; ordinarily its hinges turn lingeringly. Toward the last let him struggle, though a nightmare torpor petrify his limbs -- though on either side of the road be a phalanx of monstrous Afreets with drawn swords of flame -- though demon cries peal before him, and unimaginable houris beckon him back -- over thorns, through furnaces, but into -- Life!

XVI. An Oath in the Forum of Madness

Having been threatened many times with an utter isolation from human kind, it now became my practice, the moment that I began to feel the hasheesh change come over me, to run for sympathy to some congenial friend, and thus assure myself that the sentence had not yet been carried out. I entered his room. I told him of my state; and, before increasing delirium had any power to pervert my thoughts, pledged him to care for me, never to leave me, always to interest himself in my welfare to the end. Frequently this step prevented any under-current of horror from breaking up through my delightful tides of vision. Frequently, when I beheld the fearful Afreet invade the sanctity of my rejoicing with drawn cimeter, was that remembered pledge to me as the ring of Abdaldar, and straightway

"There ceased his power; his lifted arm,
Suspended by the spell,
Hung impotent to strike."

The penal renunciation of me by God and man was the grand prevailing shadow which now lowered about the horizon of my visions, and thrice happy was I when, in this way, I could keep it from blackening the whole sky. I mean more by this word "blackening" than mere metaphor, for, fully awake and at unclouded noonday, I have seen both heavens and air grow sable suddenly with a supernatural eclipse, and I walked by no beacon save that of fiery eyes which "glared upon me through the darkness."

Yet the spell was not always powerful. There occurred seasons when I was beyond the power of man, and, as I thought, also an outcast from man's league with God. Man could not, God would not, keep faith with me.

In the ecstasy of a serene uplifting I came one afternoon to the room of an acquaintance who had often expressed a wish to witness the hasheesh state in some walk with me while I was under the influence of the drug. By the pledge of sympathy I bound him, and felt assured -- doubly assured; for, as he prepared to accompany me out, without premonition there flashed into my mind that grand line of Festus,

"Tis not my will that evil be immortal."

Not only did this line suggest to me a great future of good and happiness throughout my hasheesh eternity, but I saw the triumphant reign of right established forever among men. A sublime emancipation from the thraldom of the ages had been declared to earth, and in visible and audible joy Creation leaped and sang. Should I not, then, be happy, since God had pronounced it? I had no fears. Taking the arm of my friend, I passed into the open air.

We had hardly gone fifty feet when I heard the dreadful voice distinctly speak to me: "This is an imaginative man; if you are happy, he will powerfully sympathize with you; he will be fascinated, he will become like yourself a hasheesh-eater. To save him from this, it is necessary that you should become an exemplar of agony. Are you content?" Knowing well what should ensue, aware of the tortures that lay prepared in the intimate abyss of the hasheesh hell, could I, as aught less than a God, say "Yes?" Unable to bring myself to this height of superhuman heroism, I only forced my lips to murmur, "The will of God be done."

Then the voice answered, "Horribly shalt thou suffer, suffer, suffer, more than tongue can tell, more than thou hast dreamed."

I clenched my fists, I shut my teeth, I nerved my whole being for the flood of agony which was about to pour upward on me from the depths. I felt within me the prophecy of such pangs as would bring me to the very portals of nothingness.

The sentence began to be fulfilled. From the fence beside which we walked came hot blasts, as from a furnace, and, looking at its base, I saw fiery rifts in the ground whence the tornado issued. I withered to a parchment sack, which bound in my heart as the sensitive fuel for more torments.

And now through that heart glided a delicate saw, of innumerable blades, each sharpened to the ultimate thinness of steel, and each glowing with a red heat. Slowly as a marble-saw the dreadful engine passed back and forth, hissing through the writhing muscle, and, as I pressed my hand upon my breast, it was scorched by the intense heat of the laminae. From the walls of houses, black talons darted forth to clutch my skirts; they left a scar like the touch of moxa. And still I burned unquenchably.

For a while I kept silence, shutting my mouth with Promethean self- control. Not only did my acquired habit of suffering speechlessly restrain me, but my pride could not endure the thought of acknowledging to him who walked by my side the vengeful infliction which had fallen upon me, in place of the mantle of rapture which my promise had prepared him to see.

The voice then said, "Confess! confess!" In desperation, I set my lips like a vice, and in my soul replied, "No! I will not!"

"Wilt thou not confess?" wrathfully the voice returned.

"Thou shalt then know bitterer agonies."

Now in my brain, moved by the same hellish machinery which was driving the saws through my heart, a murderous red-hot auger began turning round. Its speed increased, and with it a tremendous roar that shook my being. In every nerve I was agonized with an agony such as no martyr can ever have known. Head and heart both flaming, both riven by steel, the heavens looking wrathfully down, the earth opening up dreadful views of her demon-peopled deeps. Oh, here was a hell in which how could I live!

To the man at my side I whispered my confession. I told him all. I revealed to him the reasons of my punishment. I adjured him by all my own immortal tortures never to tamper with the insane spell.

And then, in piteous accents, I besought him to put out my fire.

To the first restaurant at hand we hastened. Passing in, I called for that only material relief which I have ever found for these spiritual sufferings -- something strongly acid. In the East the form in use is sherbet; mine was very sour lemonade. A glass of it was made ready, and with a small glass tube I drew it up, not being able to bear the shock of a large swallow. Relief came but very slightly -- very slowly. Before the first glass was exhausted I called most imperatively for another one to be prepared as quickly as possible, lest the flames should spread by waiting. In this way I kept a man busy with the composition of lemonade after lemonade, plunging my tube over the edge of the drained tumbler into the full one with a precipitate haste for which there were mortal reasons, until six had been consumed.

And now, almost entirely restored, I assured myself that I had expiated my full penal term, and passed out rejoicing. Baseless hope! In a moment my heart caught fire again, and now it was a huge cathedral organ wrapped in a garment of flame, and played upon mysteriously by the fingers of the element which was burning it up. Every stop that could sound like the despairing shrieks and groans of a human soul was open; nay, it was human; it lived in this slow and cruel death, and I felt its torture. A devil-choir sang anthems of mockery to its accompaniment, and I grew phrensied as I recognized the voices which ages back in the measureless past had blasphemed over my white-hot cradle and rocked me with the lullaby of hell. As we came along the broad terrace which extends before the colleges, I looked into heaven, and lo! upon rosy coursers serene angels were riding like an army, with incredible swiftness, upon some expedition of succor. Behind them trailed on winds that blew from the gates of Paradise resplendent garments of cloud ermine dotted with stars. In an ecstasy which upbore me above my demoniac pangs, I clasped my hands and shouted, "It is I whom they are coming to save!"

Just then a black hand parted the top of heaven and shook at me menacingly. Talk not to me of faces instinct with spiritual expression; that hand, slowly brandished and then withdrawn, held more expression than the most facile face. It told me all things of terror and of doom.

Until we arrived at the door of my entry I was speechless. Here my companion left me, and once more I gathered strength to burst into a bitter cry, "O God, if it be possible, let this cup pass from me." I used the prayer of the Divine One with a most reverent soul, and hoping that the remembered words of his Son might move the heart of the Father.

I added also a promise, "Save me, and I will never take hasheesh again." Once more the voice spoke and answered me, "Many a time hast thou promised this before. Speak! how hast thou kept thy vow?"

This was true. Repeatedly during the seasons of my suffering I had resolved, yes, sworn, that if I ever escaped with life and reason from the then present delirium, I would abjure the weed of madness forever. On returning to the natural state I always recollected having made a promise, but regarded it as the act of an unphilosophic fear in irresponsible circumstances, and moved by a suffering which it was perfectly possible to prevent by sufficient attention to general health and spirits as elements materially modifying the effect of the drug. Holding it, therefore, not at all binding, I had broken it as I would if it had been made in some terrific dream. Yet always when the hasheesh suffering brought me into the same court before whose awful bar I had bound myself at my last similar trial, I was charged by the prosecuting voice with my breach of faith, convicted, sentenced by my own soul, and after that the pangs were sharp with the blade of Nemesis. I writhed not under affliction, but under penalty.

At this moment I answered the voice, "I have not kept my vow, but for this once be merciful, and I will sin no more."

Again my accuser spoke: "Once more shalt thou go free -- remember -- once!"

I accepted this promise as the safe-conduct of Deity; my pain ceased, and I walked fearlessly.

But, oh unbearable! In an instant it seized me again, and I groaned out, "Hath even faith perished in the Divine? O God, hast thou broken faith with me?" I received no reply. For a few moments I paced up and down an empty room into which I had entered, with my hand upon my struggling heart, and feeling its mighty beats blend with the throbs of the devilish enginery.

Then I came out into the entry. From the opposite door a man was approaching me. I stood still, and he also stopped. I walked forward, and he came to meet me. I turned away, and he followed behind me. I faced him -- we were foot to foot -- it was myself! Yes, there stood my double, resembling me as face answereth to face in water. Another being for whose crimes I had to answer, whose wrathful portion I should suffer! It was too much to endure. I fell upon my knees, and called out to Heaven, "Oh! do I not dream? Tell me, tell me, am I indeed more than one?" I was answered, "Thou are Legion!" I looked away toward the stairs. Crouching upon a step, glaring upon me between the posts of the balustrade, clutching at me like a tiger-cat, sat -- myself again! I rushed toward the door of another room; I would lock myself in from my multitude of being. At that door, tearing his hair, gnashing his teeth, smiling with a maniac smile of pain, stood once more myself!

The remainder of my personalities I was spared from seeing. One more would have driven me forever mad.

For the last time I cried to Heaven, "How shall I be saved?" I was now finally answered, "Thy goodness extendeth not to God. To man must thou repay thy fault in that thou hast sought to lift thyself above humanity. Go find a man who will believe thy promise and thou shalt be saved."

Hard condition. So many of my friends had known the former vows, and seen how I had kept them, that I bitterly feared I should never be able to fulfill it.

But as in this lay my last hope, I rushed up the staircase to find the man who would accept my security. The first I met was at the top of the farthest stairs. There he was sitting, as if in anticipation that I should come, on the throne of a solemn tribunal.

Yet not a tribunal of severe and unrelenting justice. The courtly appanage of the scene which surrounded him was necessary for my very sense of security, since, in bringing my case to any other than the most august judication, I should have felt that I was trifling with immeasurable destiny.

160

Moreover, the man was my bosom friend. In his truthful and serene eyes nothing but love for me had ever sat, nothing but most brother pity was in them now. I loved him for himself -- I reverenced him for what he was, the calm, the thoughtful, the wise, the sincere. Heaven had sent him now to hear me, and both in his affection and his character I put my trust.

"Robb, my dear, my priceless friend, have pity on me. Accept my pledge. I will take hasheesh no more."

I spoke to him as if he knew what he did not know, my previous suffering. So he replied sadly, "Ah! you have said that many times before." I began to fear he might refuse me. I looked around, and standing not three paces off stood a cold shadow, and with its lip and finger it mocked me, saying plainly without words, "You are mine; he will not believe you." It was Insanity.

Once more I turned, and looking at him as such a sight along could make one look, I simply said, "Believe me!" This was all, but the intensity of that one expression contained in it enough meaning to show what a dire spiritual necessity there was that he should grant my request. With emphasis he answered, "I do believe you." With a look of baffled hellish malice the shadow fled away.

After this I was but once more in pain. As a great chimney, I had grown hundreds of feet into the air; with pitch and fagots of wood, with all things inflammable, I was completely filled. Suddenly some one approached and held a lighted torch to the draught below. In an instant, from basement to spiral jets, my head was crowned with flame and plumed with smoke, and far down in the middle of the blazing mass my heart lay cracking and singing in agony.

"Water!" I shouted; "I am on fire! Help, for the love of heaven!" They tore my clothes from me in the most precipitous haste. From head to foot they deluged me with water. I heard within me the coals hiss and the cinders fall down dead into the grate below, as in an extinguished furnace.

And then I grew calm.

XVII. Down with the Tide.

For days after the last-mentioned suffering I adhered sacredly to my vow. Fortified by the sympathy of my friends, nerved by the images of a fearful memory, staying myself on the Divine, I battled against the fascinations of the drug successfully. At last there came a time when nothing but superhuman endurance could withstand and conquer.

As I have frequently said, I felt no depression of body. The flames of my vision had not withered a single corporeal tissue nor snapped a single corporeal cord. All the pains induced by the total abandonment of hasheesh were spiritual. From the ethereal heights of Olympus I had been dropped into the midst of an Acherontian fog. My soul breathed laboriously, and grew torpid with every hour. I dreaded an advancing night of oblivion. I sat awaiting extinction. The shapes which moved about me in the outer world seemed like galvanized corpses; the living soul of Nature, with which I had so long communed, had gone out like the flame of a candle, and her remaining exterior was as poor and meaningless as those wooden trees with which children play, and the cliffs and chalets carved out of box-wood by some Swiss in his winter leisure.

Moreover, actual pain had not ceased with abandonment of the indulgence. In some fiery dream of night, or some sudden thrill of daylight, the old pangs were reproduced with a vividness only less than amounting to hallucination. I opened my eyes, I rubbed my forehead, I arose and walked: they were then perceived to be merely ideal; but the very necessity of this effort to arouse myself, a necessity which might occur at any time and in any place, became gradually a grievous thraldom.

But harder to endure than all these was a sudden flash of that supernatural beauty which had so often tinged my past experience -- a quick disclosure of the rosy hasheesh sky let in upon me by some passing wind which fanned aside the dense vapors of my present life -- a peal of the remembered mighty music pouring through the gratings of my voiceless prison, and dying sadly away against its granite walls. Ah! well may the most rigid moral critic forgive me, if, looking upward to my former peak of vision, I spoke to my past self as if it were still sitting there.

"So mayst thou watch me where I weep,
As unto vaster motions bound,

162

The circuits of thine orbit round
A higher height, a deeper deep."
Like Eblis, I refused to worship earth when I had seen heaven, and once more dared to assume his pride even with his pangs.

I returned to hasheesh, but only when I had become hopeless of carrying out my first intention -- its utter and immediate abandonment. I now resolved to abandon it gradually -- to retreat slowly from my enemy, until I had passed the borders of his enchanted ground, whereon he warred with me at vantage. Once over the boundaries, and the nightmare spell unloosed, I might run for my life, and hope to distance him in my own recovered territory.

This end I sought to accomplish by diminishing the doses of the drug. The highest I had ever reached was a drachm, and this was seldom necessary except in the most unimpressible states of the brain, since, according to the law of the hasheesh operation which I have stated to hold good in my experience, a much less bolus was ordinarily sufficient to produce full effect at this time than when I commenced the indulgence. I now reduced my daily ration to ten or fifteen grains.

The immediate result of even this modified resumption of the habit was a reinstatement into the glories of the former life. I came out of my clouds; the outer world was reinvested with some claim to interest, and the lethal torpor of my mind was replaced by an airy activity. I flattered myself that there was now some hope of escape by grades of renunciation, and felt assured, moreover, that since I now seldom experienced any thing approaching hallucination, I might pass through this gradual course without suffering on the way.

I did not reveal to my friends the fact of my once more eating hasheesh. To no one who had not participated in my sufferings could I have shown adequate reasons for doing so. I should have pleaded an excuse which none but myself could feel; I should have been answered by the earnest entreaty to cleave to my first purpose -- perhaps by the expressed or tacit distrust of my intention to abjure the indulgence at all. But I felt no danger of betraying myself, since from the meditations and the ecstasies in which I now sat I could arouse myself at need, talk and act naturally, or perform any of the duties to which I might be called. I do not think there was a person beside myself who once suspected, at this time, my return to the indulgence. I was not even questioned upon the subject.

Once, and once only, was I in peril of making known my secret. With two or three of my friends I had made an agreement that on a certain afternoon, as was our wont, we should speak in turn, and subject to each other's criticism, for the sake of improvement in oratory. When the time arrived, I found myself not only adequate to any amount of speech-making, but liable to adorn my sentences with an Oriental luxuriance of imagery which would infallibly disclose the fact of my having taken hasheesh two hours before, for the dose, although not extending in size beyond the boundary I had set myself, had still operated with an unusual power.

When my friends called for me I knew not what to do. There was no sickness to plead -- the animation with which every word was uttered would have belied that; other engagement I had not, for the appointment had been made unconditionally and some time before. If I went with them, it amounted almost to a physical certainty that I would break forth into some rapture which would let me out. Yet there was no time to be lost. I resolved to go, and giving into he hand of Will the curb of Passion, started with them down the street.

The struggle which I made to keep silent, or, at furthest, to talk in a practical way, was among the hardest of my lifetime. There is a game of forfeits, to most of my readers no doubt well enough known, which consists in walking three times diagonally across a room, bearing a lighted candle, and repeating the most absurd formula to a person who meets you similarly furnished, without moving a muscle of the face. There is also a legend, woven into the Arabian Nights, of a young man who, in fulfillment of some enterprise, descended through a demon-haunted cavern where, though assailed on every side by sights of astoundment most provocative of speech, he was compelled to seal his lips under pain of a terrible retribution.

The nature only, and not the degree of self-control demanded by my circumstances, is foreshadowed by these illustrations. I was assailed with every possible temptation to laughter and to open amazement. At the very commencement of my walk, for the first time in several months I was in China. All the roofs turned up at the corners, and amorphous dragons flaunted in red, green, and gold from their peaks. The air smelt of orange-blossoms, and boys hawked fruit about the streets in the dialect of Whampoa.

But the Chinese hallucination did not long continue. I presently remembered the old familiar town in which I was walking, yet what a singular change in manners had passed over it! Every house had been to dancing-school, and returned educated into the most excruciating politeness. They were all paying me their salutations as I passed with a knowledge of good-breeding absolutely overwhelming.

A spruce brick tenement, evidently a new-comer, and, on account of the insecurity of his social position, particularly anxious to ingratiate himself with the habitues, made me a profound bow, even unto his doorstep.

A respectable old house, that had been there since the last war, looked stiffly over the walls which flanked his chimneys, and slightly inclined himself with a rigid courtliness -- a very Roger de Coverley in stone and mortar.

A fast-looking house of a particularly vivid color, conscious of containing all the modern improvements, and profusely ornamented in gingerbread-carved workmanship, took upon himself to be easy in his address as a soi-disant fashionable, and nodded to me familiarly, at the same time saying at his front door, "How are you, old fellow?" "Curse his impudence!" said I to myself, and walked on.

The next was a maidenly little cottage, who modestly dropped her second-story window-sashes, and blushed up to her eaves-trough as we came by, at the same time courtesying clear into her back yard.

A church smiled condescendingly on me from its belfry, bowed forward, and immediately took it back by making another bow backward, with a look which said, "I hope you take care of yourself, young man."

A shop bowed blandly and inquiringly, with a what-d'ye-buy air, and even a poor lawyer's office abased its cornice cautiously, as if it feared to commit itself. In all these salutations there was something which gave me a half-consciousness that after all it was only an emblematical show, yet it required all my self-constraint to refrain from returning the compliment in a succession of bows. I mentally represented to myself my circumstances as nearly as I could make them natural. I painted the necessity of keeping still with all the picturesqueness of which I was capable, and so succeeded in controlling all outbreaks of my feeling.

At length we arrived at the place of our appointment (a church to which we had the key), and one after another my friends spoke, and I listened quietly until my own turn came. With a terrible effort I held myself in, and walked to the platform still guiltless of my own betrayal. If I could resist a few moments more, I was safe.

Hardly had I uttered my first sentence before I awakened to the consciousness that I was Rienzi proclaiming freedom to enthralled Rome. I portrayed the abased glories of the older time; I raised both the Catos from their graves to groan over the present slavery; I hurled fiery invective against the usurpations of Colonna, and pointed the way through tyrant blood up to an immortal future. The broad space below the tribune grew populous with a multitude of intense faces, and within myself there was a sense of towering into sublimity, as I knew that it was my eloquence which swayed that great host with a storm of indignation, like the sirocco passing over reeds.

Strange to say, I did not even here reveal my state. That vigilant portion of my duality which had controlled me hitherto, guarded me from any unwarrantable excess even in the impassioned character of Rienzi.

For a number of weeks I continued this moderate employment of hasheesh, sometimes diminishing the doses, then returning to the boundary, but never beyond it. As the diminutions went on by a tolerably regular but slow ratio, I flattered myself that I was advancing toward a final and perfect emancipation. But the progress was not that painless one with which I had flattered myself. There was much less to endure than in the worst part of the former period of indulgence, yet it could have been many times diminished in intensity without descending to the plane of ordinary physical or spiritual suffering.

One of the most bitter experiences of hasheesh occurred to me about this time, and since it is the only one which in my memory stands in peculiar distinctness of outline from the vague background of alternating lights and shadows, I give it as powerful and recompensing contrast to the formerly-detailed vision in which I triumphed as the millennial king.

It was now with Christ the crucified that I identified myself. In dim horror I perceived the nails piercing my hands and my feet, but it was not this which seemed the burden of my suffering. Upon my head, in a tremendous and ever-thickening cloud, came slowly down the guilt of all the ages past and all the world to come. By a dreadful quickening, I beheld every atrocity and nameless crime coming up from all time on lines that centred in myself. The thorns clung to my brow, and bloody drops stood like dew upon my hair, yet these were not the instruments of my agony. I was withered like a leaf in the breath of a righteous vengeance. The curtain of a lurid blackness hung between me and heaven; mercy was dumb, and I bore the anger of Omnipotence alone. Out of a fiery distance demon chants of triumphant blasphemy came surging on my ear, and whispers of ferocious wickedness ruffled the leaden air about my cross. How long I bore this vicarious agony I have never known; from the peculiarity of the time in such states, it would be impossible to know.

But, in general, while feeling the full effect of the dose, I sat in solitude, with closed eyes, enjoying the tranquil procession of images, especially those of scenery, which I could dispel at will, since they did not reach the reality of hallucination. Or, if my quiet was broken by the entrance of others, by an effort conversation was possible with them, so long as care was taken to prevent the introduction of any powerfully-agitating subject. This care I found to be extremely necessary, as the peculiar sensitiveness to impression which is induced by hasheesh made sympathy so deep as to be painful. In one instance this fact discovered itself with sufficient clearness to warn me ever afterward. To comply with the request of a friend, I read him some verses upon doubts of human immortality. Upon arriving at a passage where one of our primeval fathers is introduced as speaking in agony of his dread of advancing death, I felt that agony becoming, by sympathy, so strongly my own emotion, that, lest I should completely identify myself with the sufferer, I was forced to lay down the manuscript, and plead some excuse for not continuing the reading.

XVIII. My Stony Guardian

It was during this period that I spent a short time at Niagara. In the hurry of setting out upon my journey thither, I left behind that traveling companion, which was more indispensable than any article or all possible articles of luggage, my box of boluses. Too late to repair the error, too late for my own serenity, I found out that my staff of life was out of reach at a place on Lake Ontario where the most concentrated cannabine preparation is the jib-stay of a fore-and-after.

At the Falls, however, and once grown enthusiastic, I fared much better than I had expected. The only trace of suffering at first perceptible was left in the shape of a somewhat nervously-written name on the entry-book of the hotel. The excitement of a sublimity which, to say the least, is extra-natural, for a while sustained me above pain for the loss of the super-natural.

Moreover, a material support came in to augment the spiritual. As lemon- juice had been sometimes an effectual cure for the sufferings of excess, I now discovered that a use of tobacco, to an extent which at other times would be immoderate, was a precentive of the horrors of abandonment. Making use of this knowledge, I smoked incessantly when out of the immediate presence of the waters -- never could I bring myself, however needy, to puff in the face of Niagara -- a blasphemy of deed only second to one of word which came to my notice during this visit.

For an hour of one glorious morning I had been looking down from the balcony of the Goat Island tower upon the emerald crown in all the luxury of solitude. A heavy footstep from within sounded upon the staircase, breaking up my dream, and the next moment flashed upon the platform a man who had come to "do" the falls, with the odors of metropolis still cleaving to his garments, and rotund in all the plenitude of corporeal well-being -- an Omphalopsychite by necessity, since he found it impossible to look down at all without resting his eyes upon that portion of his individuality tangent to the lower border of the waistcoat. The utmost that I could ask from this adipose formation was to keep silence: he did not even do that. Turning his face toward the wind to get its full tonic effect, for a while he drank it in copious draughts, and then enthusiastically broke forth to me, "What a splendid thing to give a man appetite for his dinner!" Sensitive as my state made me at that moment, I so far controlled myself as to answer nothing. It was well that I had not been hasheesh-glorified when he made his assault, or, notwithstanding he no way lacked in the bodily, he might not have been heard of again till he was fished out of Ontario.

It has always been surprising to me that the Falls are so much the theme of lovers of the sublime to the almost entire exclusion of the Rapids. The Rapids have a majesty of their own, which, to my mind, has never yielded at all to the very different one of the Falls. Trying to resolve this difference by analysis, it seems to be this: in the precipitous brink over which takes place the final leap of the waters, we find a reason for the grand power of the descent. Higher up the river the slope of the flood is comparatively imperceptible; the headlong crash of the waves becomes to us a result of some inner will rather than of soulless gravity; and by the putting forth of power from this mysterious will we are overwhelmed, seeming to find our cause in spirit and not in matter. Quite as holy a place does the upper point of the Island appear to me, looking forth, as it does, upon the oceanic wrath of that resistless billowy soul, from the silent eddy where it cleaves itself for the last maddening throes, far up to the line of its trembling in the first consciousness of ingathered strength against the farther sky, quite as holy as any station beside the shifting pavement of flecked and molten porphyry below the Fall, where the spray is forever floating back upon the headlong wall like marble-dust wind-driven from the floor of the Great Sculptor.

There is still another element in the sublimity of the place too little noticed, or noticed only as a curiosity. This is the Profile Rock, in the edge of the American Fall nearest to Goat Island. So little is it known, that many persons go there unaware of its existence, and come away without having had it pointed out to them. Indeed, by a mere superficial looker at, and not a student of Niagara, it would be, in all probability, passed over. Were I not near-sighted, I should be ashamed to confess that I did not see it myself until my eyes were called to it by a most sincere and ardent lover of all that is noble in nature, a very near and dear friend, whom I was so fortunate as to have beside me in most of my walks.

Sustaining the weight of those vast waters upon his half-bowed head, the stony figure stands, visible under the veil, or visible at least above the waist, yet no more is needed than the face, with its look of calm endurance, to suggest for him a whole history of Fate. At that time of which I have been speaking, I myself felt enough need of fortitude to give me an intense yearning toward this emblem of heroic patience, and as I looked upon him I more and more felt myself loving him even humanly. In many a vision afterward did he appear to me as a silent consoler, when Niagara itself had become an affliction to my memory; and as side by side we stood, he under his flood, I under mine, I gathered strength from his moveless eye to bear unto the end all which should finally be given to the triumph of resignation.

Alone and unable to sleep, though the late night heard nothing to break its stillness but the ceaseless rush of the river, I felt myself thus "flowing in words" to that mute face of forbearance:

> Niagara! I am not one who seeks
> To lift his voice above thine awful hymn;
> Mine be it to keep silence where God speaks,
> Nor with my praise to make his glory dim.
>
> Yet unto thee, shape of the stony brow,
> Standing forever in thine unshared place,
> The human soul within me yearneth now,
> And I would lay my head beside thy face
>
> King, from dim ages of God set apart
> To bear the weight of a tremendous crown,
> And feel the robes that wrap thy lonely heart
> Deaden its pulses as their folds flow down;

What sublime years are written on the scroll
  Of thine impereal, dread inheritance,
Man shall not read until its lines unroll
  In the great hand that set thy stony trance.

Perchance thy moveless adamantine look
  For its long watch o'er the abyss was bent
Ere the thick gates of primal darkness shook,
  And light broke in upon thy battlement.

And when that sudden glory lit thy crown,
  And God lent thee a rainbow from His throne,
E'en through thy stony breast flashed there not down
  Somewhat of His joy also made thine own?

Who knoweth but He gave thee to rejoice
  Till man's hymn sounded through the time to be,
And when our choral coming hushed thy voice,
  Still left thee something of humanity?

Still semest thou a priest -- still the veil streams
  Before thy reverent eyes, and hides His light,
And thine is as the face of one who dreams
  Of a great glory now no more his right.

Soon shall I pass away; the mighty psalm
  Of thine o'ershadowing waters shall be heard
In memory only; but thy speechless calm
  Hath lessons for me more than many a word,

Teaching the glory of the soul that bears
  Great floods, a veil between him and the sun,
And, standing in the might of Patience, dares
  To bide His finishing who hath begun.

I have said that Niagara itself became an affliction to me. More especially was this the case after my total abandonment of hasheesh; but I must not anticipate. Every one of sensitive mind has noticed the permanency of impressions left by grand scenery, of none more so than Niagara. Indeed, I have acquaintances who for months, in all their day-dreams as well as those of sleep, were haunted by the Falls in a manner almost like optical illusion. Their visions were always delightful. Fancy now a mind naturally very impressible by scenery, rendered numberless times more sensitive by a process which left it a permanent photographic plate, and then exposed to such lights as those reflected from that supernatural river: you will then have the condition in which I left Niagara -- a condition continuing for many a month afterward. So slowly did the traces of that imagery fade on my mind, that I have never, even now, wholly lost them. At times the terrors of the brink and the cataract still echo in dreams with a hasheesh mystery, and appall me as the presence of their real danger could hardly appall.

Upon returning to a place where hasheesh was within reach, I fled to it for relief as into an ark. By considerable self-government, I conquered the tendency to excess produced by long deprivation of the stimulus, and indulged in it within my stated boundaries only.

I now began to find that gradual was almost as difficult as instant abandonment. The utmost that could be done was to keep the bolus from exceeding fifteen grains. From ten and five, which at times I tried, there was an insensible sliding back to the larger allowance, and even there my mind rebelled at the restriction. While there was no suffering from absolute intellectual lassitude, there still, ever and anon, arose a longing more or less intense for the former music and ecstatic fantasia, which could not be satisfied by a mere panoramic display of internal images, however beautiful, dissolved in a moment by opening my eyes.

Yet I struggled strenuously against the fascination to a more generious ration, and hoped against hope for some indefinite time at which the dangerous spell might be entirely unbound.

XIX. Resurgam

One morning, having taken my ordinary dose without yet feeling its effect, I strolled into a bookseller's to get the latest number of Putnam's. Turning over its leaves as it lay upon the counter, the first article which detained my eyes was headed "The Hasheesh Eater." None but a man in my circumstances can realize the intense interest which possessed me at the sight of these words.

For a while I lingered upon them with an inexplicable dread of looking further into the paper. I shut the book, and toyed with my curiosity by examining its cover, as one who receives a letter directed in some unfamiliar hand carefully scrutinizes the postmark and the envelope, and dallies with the seal before he finally breaks it open. I had supposed myself the only hasheesh-eater upon this side of the ocean; this idea of utter isolation had been one element in many of my horrors. That some one among my acquaintance had been detailing a fragment of my own experience, as viewed by him from without, was my first hypothesis. Although, in itself considered, there was nothing very improbable in the acquirement of the habit by another person, the coincidence of my having fallen upon this article, with the hasheesh force still latent within me, seemed so remarkable that I could not believe it. Then I said to myself, I will not read this paper now. I will defer it to another time; for, if its recital be one of horrors, it may darken the complexion of my awaited vision. In pursuance of this purpose, I passed out of the shop and went down the street.

I was not satisfied. Whichever way I turned I was followed by a shadow of fascination. By an irresistible attraction I was drawn back to the counter. If the worst were there, I must know it. I returned, and there, as before, lay the unsealed mystery. With a trembling hand I turned to the place; again I scrutinized the caption, to see if some unconscious illusion of a hasheesh state, which had ensued before I was aware, had not made objective the words which so many a day had stamped upon my brain. No; plainly as eyes could read them, they stood upon the page. I would read the article from beginning to end. This resolution, once formed, was shaken, but not broken, by an unavoidable glance ahead, which told me that the recital was one of agonies.

It was only a moment before I found that I was not this hasheesh-eater. Yet as, with the devouring gaze of a miser, I read, dwelt upon, and re-read every line, I found such startling analogies to my own past experience that cold drops started upon my forehead, and I exclaimed, "This man has been in my own soul." We both had been abandoned of Heaven; had climbed up into the prerogatives of Deity, thence to be cast down; had drawn the accursed knife at the whispers of a frightful temptation; had been the disowned, the abominated, the execrated of men. Should I carry the parallel further? He had forever abandoned hasheesh. How terribly this question shook my soul! In an instant, like some grand pageant, the glories of the enchantment streamed before my eyes. Out of the past came Memory, swinging delicious censers; upon the fragrant vapor, as it floated upward, was traced a sublimer heaven, a more beauteous earth, from the days gone by, than ever Sorcery painted upon the Fate-compelling smoke for a rapt gazer into Futurity. There the pangs of the old time had no place; all was serenity, ecstasy, revelation. Should I forego all this forever?

So help me God, I would!

The author of that article I did not know. Of his name I had not even the faintest suspicion. Yet for him I felt a sympathy; yes, though it be unworldly, an affection such as would move me to the highest office of gratitude. Into my hitherto unbroken loneliness he had penetrated; unconscious of each other's presence, we had walked the valley of awful shadows side by side. As no other man upon the earth could feel for me, he could feel. As none other could counsel me, he might counsel. For the first time in all the tremendous stretch of my spell-bound eternity heard I the voice of sympathy or saw I an exemplar of escape. Though I might never look upon his face on earth, disenthralled from the bodily I should know him immediately, for I was bound to him by ties spun from the distaff of a supernatural hand.

I returned homeward, bearing in my mind almost the exact words of that vivid and most truthful recital. So powerfully did its emotion possess me as to supplant entirely that of the drug, which did not once render itself perceptible.

There is a rich lesson of deep springs of human action taught by the old history, wherein he who in after years was to make the name of Carthage glorious among the peoples uplifted his hand of adjuration in the presence of his father. From him out of whose original fount he came, and in whose depths his earliest waves of being found their noblest, their truest echo of response, most naturally did he draw that full tide of strength which through all barriers was to bear him on until he whelmed in the deluge of inherited vengeance the territory of his foe.

No Hannibal was I, but the struggling sufferer under long soldered thrall of sorcery, groaning for a deliverance which I just dared to tempt; no Hamilcar wert thou, my father, for the hands with which thou supportedst mine in their final vow of liberty were wet, not with the blood of war, but the tears of a most precious compassion; and as before thee, on that last night of my bondage, I took the oath which opened up my prison-doors, from thy presence I won a sustaining force of will which, through many a day of fray and weariness, was to press me on (in all reverence to the majestic memorials of past time) against a mightier, a subtler enemy than Rome!

After thus sealing my deliverance, my next step was to discover the author of the article in Putnam's, which had determined me to it at first. This, through the kind courtesy of some of its presiding minds, I was in a few days enabled to do. To the author I then wrote, trusting to no other introduction than that of our common ground and the sympathies of human nature. I asked counsel upon the best means of softening the pathway of my escape, for I had seen enough in my former effort to assure me that it would be a very hard one. Moreover, the simple possession of a letter from one who had been so instrumental in originally effecting my release would be a powerful aid toward rendering it permanent.

A very short time elapsed before I received an answer to my inquiries. My anxiety could not have made it more full than it was of information and assistance; my gratitude could not have exaggerated the value of its sympathy and encouragement. But for the sacredness which to a mind of any refinement invests a correspondence of such nature, I could not refrain from here giving it publicity. It strengthened my resolution, it opened for me a cheering sky of hope, it pointed me to expedients for insuring success, it mitigated the sufferings of the present. It is, and ever will be, treasured among the most precious archives of my life.

Thus supported humanly, and feeling the ever-near incitement and sustenance of a Presence still higher, I began to feel my way out of the barathrum of my long sojourn, and its jaws closed behind me, never since then, never hereafter till there be no more help in heaven, to open for my ingress. Out of its tremendous Elysium, its quenchless Tartarus, its speechless revelations, I came slowly into a land of subdued skies and heavier atmosphere. The jet of flame and fountain grew dimmer behind me in the mists of distance; broader, in the land from which I had long wandered, before me grew the shadows of the present life. Yet among all the lights which, unobscured by vapor, from afar led me on my way, was one which gleamed with a promise that in the days hereafter, the soul, purified from the earthy, should once more, painlessly, look on the now abandoned glories of its past apocalypse.

XX. Leaving the Schoolmaster, the Pythagorean sets up for himself.

During the progress of the events which have hitherto occupied my narrative, I had become a graduate of my college. Willing for a while to defer the prosecution of more immediately professional studies, I cast about for some employment which for a year might engage a portion of my efforts, and leave, at the same time, a reasonable amount of leisure for private reading. As is the case with so many of our newly-fledged American alumni, my choice fell upon the assumption of the pedagogic purple. There were doubtless, somewhere in the States, candidates for induction into the mysteries of the Greek and Latin tongues -- some youths of promise who burned for an acquaintance with the arts of address, and who would not scorn to receive, even from the hands of an own countryman, the crumbs of literature which fall from the Gallic table. If my horoscope had not failed me, I could find them out.

Accordingly, at the bar of my college, whither petitions for instruction very frequently came in from the benighted world, I lodged an application for the most eligible situation of the kind above stated which should present itself. Before long a letter reached me, offering a post of teachership, situated somewhere between the Hudson and Fort Laramie, in a village glorified with some name of Epic valor, mighty in the appanage of ten dwelling-houses and a post-office, and, like all places sanctified by the presence of the educational genius, "refined, salubrious, and highly religious." As to the first item in this latter statement, there was every reason to be satisfied of its truth, since the writer of the letter was evidently a gentleman, and, to judge from the size of the place, he was a very large integral portion of its population. Upon the second point it was rather more difficult to be assured, since any number of deaths possible to the dimensions of the village might have occurred there without their wave of agitation reaching the shore that acknowledges the jurisdiction of bills of mortality. Finally came the question of "highly-religiousness." On this head, nothing could have given my doubts a more decisive quietus than the fact that the community wanted a teacher, since, just then looking through the Lorraine-glass of enthusiasm for a chosen occupation, I saw a peculiar force and beauty in the words, "Science, the handmaid of Religion." Yet one thing there was which stood as a slight obstacle in the way of accepting the position. I had determined, for the year to come, to be independent for a support of all aid save my own exertions. Entire self-sustenance was a very dear project with me. Could I hope for it there?

177

My correspondent informed me that no very great pecuniary inducements could be offered, but seductively added that, to a young man of excellent principles, who desired to establish himself as a moral centre in the community, no opening could be more promising. As he did not go on to advise me whether, in his portion of the country, "moral centres" were gratuitously fed, lodged, and clothed, besides being generously presented, as a slight token of popular esteem, with their laundry-bills, fuel, lights, and stationery, I concluded not to close with his offer, thus forever losing, for the basest of earthly considerations, the priceless opportunity of radiating circular waves of an unctuous excellence through it is impossible to tell how large an area of uninhabited timber-region. Whether any sufficiently self-sacrificing incumbent has been found to fill the rejected vacancy, from want of data is uncertain; if not, the place with the Homeric name wanders in heathen ignorance to this day.

Another application which came to me, seeming in all points satisfactory, was accepted. In the town of W----, in the State of New York, a cry had gone up for a teacher, who might be absorbent as well as radiant, and one, moreover, who might indulge the hope of moderate leisure for his own self-disciplinary purposes.

There, as I began arranging matters for my departure from home, I flattered myself that a stated occupation should absorb me from regrets over the loss of my old indulgence; quiet, books, and a regular life should create in me a new stimulus and energy. The department of pedagoguery over which I was to be installed was congenial to long-consolidated tastes -- the ancient and the English classics. Thus I should gradually emerge out of shadows into a being with new motives, and by moderate cares blunt the pains of progress. How far I harvested my hope the sequel will show.

Having reached the scene of my labors, I found myself associated with a teacher who, like myself, was a new-comer, yet not, like myself, a neophyte in the profession, for he had grown venerable in the priesthood of Minerva, having, in all probability, during his previous life, offered up numerous hecatombs of youthful victims, both male and female, upon her altar. At the same time that I congratulated myself upon possessing the aid of his experience, I discovered that I must look elsewhere for congenial sympathies, since he was one of those persons whose metal is not annealed. In youth he had indulged a happy disposition, but now saw the folly of it. Through some fault of my own early training, I was unable to discover the necessary connection between sanctity and acridity, a heart like Enoch and a face like Sphinx.

Yet upon external sympathy I did not expect to be very dependent. The institution in which I was resident offered that invaluable advantage, a large and well-selected library, where I hoped to find all those choice attachments which from without my position might deny me.

In a good library how swiftly time melts away! Not merely in the sense of its rapid passage through our absorption in other interests, but as an element in any consideration, it becomes entirely neglected. In practical business the present is our only actuality; the past has been cast down like a ladder whose rounds have helped us up to a height whence we never again expect to descend. Among books, all temporal successions are obliterated; Plato and Coleridge walk arm-in-arm; genial Chaucer and loving Elia shake hands; with them, with all, we stand enraptured upon the same plane of time, in one age, the ceaseless age of the communion of souls. Well did Heinsius say, as he locked himself into the library of Leyden, Nunc sum in gremio sæculorum! -- "Now I am in the lap of eternity!"

But gradually the increasing pressure of duties connected with my new vocation more and more deprived me of leisure for enjoying any other literature than that of text-books. Long after the last noisy foot had pattered down the front steps of the school building did my table groan with incorrigible exercises which demanded correction, one leaf of which, laid upon the grave of any worthy -- Molière, for instance -- who spoke the language which it assassinated, would have brought up as deep a groan from the depths below as when the mandrake is uprooted.

I had promised myself regular habits; but the wanderer who was so unfortunate or so eccentric as to be shelterless at that hour, might have seen, at two or three o'clock of almost every morning, the light of my lamp shining through one of the tall windows that looked upon the street. Not that I rose early, but that I retired early -- in the morning. It was not the mere sense of duty and responsibility which impelled me to such labors for the school, although, indeed, these had their just, perhaps their exorbitant weight with me. An element more selfish entered into the consideration -- the dread of being haunted on the morrow by unappeased ghosts of business. The accumulative nature of work distressed me; the slightest thing left unfinished at the close of one day added itself to the labors of the next, and it had grown mightily during the night. There are some people so constituted that they can not slur matters if they would. No one else may notice the mint, anise, and cummin which they have forbone to tithe, but they can no more themselves overlook the deficiency than if they had neglected the weightier matters of the law.

It will be easily understood that late hours, hard work, and an almost total cessation from bodily exercise were not the best means that could have been taken to restore tone and elasticity to a mind struggling with the horrors of an abandoned stimulus. Without cares of some kind, I had doubtless been at this time a most unhappy being; yet, under such pressure as I then felt, an overtasked mind had no opportunity to recover itself, but rather grew sensitive daily to the loss of its former support. Perhaps, however, even such a state of things was better than an absence of all absorbing employment; for, although I dreaded a return to hasheesh as an upright man dreads the violation of his most sacred oath, I had not reached a point at which I could utterly execrate the drug. The only feat of righteous indignation which was then possible was to think ill of it, as the lover of a faithless mistress whom he must abandon, or as the patriot of his fatherland, swayed by vile rulers, when, "fallen upon evil times," he flies it in voluntary exile. Unemployed with daily and perplexing duties, I might have heard the former siren-voice floating into my careless quiet, and, step by step, have been almost unconsciously led back into the old snares.

As it was, the fascinations of the past were hard enough to resist. If ever for a moment I granted myself leisure to sit still and think -- if, especially, I resigned myself with closed eyes to the train of meditations set in motion by good music, I was infallibly borne back into the hasheesh world, and placed face to face with its now irretrievable glories. In quick flashes the old empurpled heights for a moment broke upon me, or amid cloud battalions in their rainbow armor I floated through a tremendous heaven. Or the far windings of some wondrous river allured me into the luxuriant shadows which trembled over its brink, and I sighed for an instant with an unutterable yearning as I thought that its waves were never more to upbear my shallop of gramarye. The embodied temptation of exquisite houris swam in ethereal dance down a garden of Gul: never more were their rosy arms to embrace me. Grand temples reared their spotless pediments into a sapphire sky; a lake that answered back in its own hue the look of heaven, kissed, dimpling with a fairy laughter, the steps that ascended to their portals -- portals eternally barred on me. And sometimes, more solemnly alluring than all these, for an instant I caught a view of that light wherein I had of old read the sublime secrets of things by unbearable apocalypse. At such a season, well -- oh! unspeakably well was it that hundreds of miles stretched between me and the nearest box of hasheesh, for, had I possessed the means, I should have rushed to the indulgence, though it were necessary to swim a whirlpool on the way.

I made acquaintances at W---- who could play cunningly upon an instrument, that universal one, the piano, especially. Knowing that there was no possibility of yielding to the allurement, I, often as possible, had them play for me, while I sat almost unconscious of any thing outward, abandoning myself to music-inspired visions. Yet even then, perfectly assured that I had no power to gratify the hasheesh appetite, I have started up from my seat to dispel by walking and the sight of familiar objects a rapture which was enchanting me irresistibly.

Constantly, notwithstanding all my occupation of mind, the cloud of dejection deepened in hue and in density. My troubles were not merely negative, simply regrets for something which was not, but a loathing, a fear, a hate of something which was. The very existence of the outer world seemed a base mockery, a cruel sham of some remembered possibility which had been glorious with a speechless beauty. I hated flowers, for I had seen the enameled meads of Paradise; I cursed the rocks because they were mute stone, the sky because it rang with no music; and the earth and sky seemed to throw back my curse.

An abhorrence of speech or action, except toward the fewest possible persons, possessed me. For the sake of not appearing singular or ascetic, and so crippling my power for whatever little good I might do, I at first mingled with society, forcing myself to laugh and to talk conventionalities. At last associations grew absolutely unbearable; the greatest effort was necessary to speak with any but one or two to whom I had fully confided my past experience. A footstep on the stairs was sufficient to make me tremble with anticipations of a conversation; every morning brought a resurrection into renewed horrors, as I thought of the advancing necessity of once more coming in contact with men and things. Any man who has felt the pangs of some bitter bereavement can understand this experience when he remembers how many a time he awoke after his affliction, and for a moment remained forgetful that it had fallen upon him. Then suddenly gathering a fearful strength, the knowledge of the reality flashed upon him, and he groaned aloud as if some fresh arrow had entered his soul. At times the awakening was so terrible an experience to me that from any other than my own hand I would have courted death as a mercy. The death which was but another birth and possible, the death which was utter extinction and an impossibility, seemed either of them preferable to that illusion into which the light aroused me, which men called life, but which was, after all, but death in its most horrible form, death vivified, stalking about in hollow pageantry, breathing meaningless utterances, interchanging salutations, mocking spirit by gestures without spirit, and unable to return to its legitimate corruption.

Aware as I was that this terrible state was the revenge of the rejected sorceress, and feeling it grow bitterer every day to bear, I began to struggle against two temptations, yielding to either of which seemed to offer some change of suffering, if not a permanent relief. One of these was self-destruction, the other return to hasheesh, and I can hardly pronounce which of the two was the most abhorrent idea. Either of them ultimately led in the same direction. My argument with myself was, that there must be some turning point, some lowest depth to the abyss which I was descending; the hope I could not see, but faith clung to it desperately, and ever kept repeating,

"Behold! we know not any thing;
I can but trust that good shall fall
At last -- far off --"

But, though day was terrible, night was often as much so. While indulging in hasheesh, none of its images had ever been reproduced in dreams, provided that I retired to sleep thoroughly restored from the last dose. Indeed, it is a singular fact, that although, previously to acquiring the habit, I never slept without some dream more or less vivid, during the whole progress of the hasheesh life my rest was absolutely dreamless. The visions of the drug entirely supplanted those of nature.

Now the position of things was transposed. Day was a rayless blank, night became frightful with fire. The first phenomenon which I began to notice, as I entered this condition, was the peculiar susceptibility of the brain to its last impression before my chamber was darkened. Did I look at the flame of the lamp before putting it out? -- for an hour afterward I lay tossing and sleepless, because one fiery spot burned unquenchably upon the surrounding blackness. Did I shut the pages of a book immediately before lying down? -- the last sentence I had read was as distinctly printed on the dark as it could have been upon a scroll, and there for half the night I read it till it grew maddening. Well was it for me if the words were not of gloomy import, for I could endure with measurable patience even the wearily monotonous assurance of good cheer; but one night I was forced to rise and relight my lamp to blot out the sight of such an awful sentence as this:

"Depart, ye cursed!"

At length I used the habitual precaution, borrowed from my former usage in the hasheesh state, of keeping one wick of my lamp burning while I slept. At first this was very painful to my eyes; but so much better was any pain than the horror of that last permanency of the final impression, that I bore it willingly.

Gradually my rest began to be broken by tremendous dreams, that mirrored the sights and echoed the voices of the former hasheesh life. In them I faithfully lived over my past experience, with many additions, and but this one difference. Out of the reality of the hasheesh state there had been no awakening possible; from this hallucination of dreams I awoke when the terrors became too superhuman.

What has been said in an earlier part of this narrative upon the indelible characteristic of all the impressions of our life seemed to find illustration here. Doomed to re-read the old, yet, though sometimes forgotten, never obliterated inscriptions, I wandered up and down the halls of sleep with my gaze fixed upon the mind's judicial tablets. Not always were the memories in themselves painful; where of old I had felt ecstasy, in the same place I rejoiced wildly now; yet the close of that season of rejoicing was often tinged with most melancholy dye, for, from my recollection of the former order of succession, I could infallibly tell what was coming next, and many a time was it a vision of pain.

All the facts of a recalled experience took their regular relative position save one -- I never dreamed of taking hasheesh. I was always seized suddenly by the thrill; it came upon me unexpectedly, while walking with friends or sitting alone. This ignorance of any time when I took the dose did not, however, absolve me from self-convicting pangs. Invariably my first cry was, "I have broken my vow! Alas! alas!" Then followed furious exultancy. I rushed like a Maenad through colossal scenery; I leaped unhurt down measureless cataracts; I whirled between skies and oceans, both shining in fiery sapphire; I stood alone amid ruined piles as vast as the demon-built palaces of Baly. Then an undefined horror seized me. I fled from it to find my friends, but there were none to comfort me. Finally, reaching the climax of pain, I caught fire, or saw the approach of awful presences.

Then I awoke. But not always into the delicious comfort of a calm reality -- I may almost say, never; ordinarily to cry out to Heaven for the boon of an unpeopled darkness; always to find the beating of my heart either totally stopped, or so swift and loud that I could hear it with the utmost distinctness, like a rapid, muffled hammer; frequently to discover that the idea of fire had some ground in a raging fever, which parched my lips, and swelled the veins upon my forehead till they projected in relief. At such times my course was to rise and walk the floor for an hour, if need were, at the same time bathing my head until the heat was assuaged.

If memory, still blunted by the body, could thus clearly and faithfully read her old records, in what astonishing apocalypse shall they stand forth at the unerring wand of the disembodying change!

I have spoken of additions to the original scroll of visions. It remains to mention some of them.

The region around W---- is a limestone formation, tunneled in one place by a rather extensive and remarkable cave. I have never found there any of those lofty halls and vast stalactites which render certain other caverns famous; the calcareous depositions are very much in miniature, but some of them of a most delicate beauty. One, in particular, is a most perfect statuette (if the term may be allowed in such a connection) of Niagara Falls; the Rapids, Goat Island, with its precipitous battlement toward the lower river, the American Fall, the Horse-shoe, all are there, exquisitely carved, on a scale of not quite an inch to the foot. Another is a Gothic monastery, with its shrine and Madonna just outside the grille, and a cresset hanging from the point of the portal's arch. The chambers are often narrow and sinuous; there is nothing there to astound any one who has visited Weyer's Cave or the Mammoth; but as this was the only one that I had ever seen, it was there that I found my cavernous ideal.

My guide through it was a young man of the neighborhood, whose gratification in obliging a stranger was the only recompense which he would not refuse; yet dear enough was the price which I paid for my visit.

185

It was no less than the punishment of being cavern-haunted for weeks. Nightly I was compelled to explore the most fearful of subterraneous labyrinths alone. Now climbing crags which gave way behind me, hanging to round projections of slippery limestone, while I heard the dislodged débris go bounding down from ledge to ledge of a yawning pit of darkness and reaching no bottom. Now crawling painfully like a worm, pushed on through winding passages no wider than a chimney, by a Fate whose will I doubted ever to bring me back. Now beholding far above my head the rifted ceiling tremble with the echo of my least footstep, in momentary agony to see it fall. Now joyfully hastening toward a glimpse of daylight, coming up to it, and falling backward just in time to save myself from plunging down some sheer wall of measureless height, upon which the labyrinth opened.

From that visit to the W---- cave I suffered that which only the hasheesh-eater and a soul in the other hell can suffer. In time, however, I slowly outgrew its memory, but only to replace it by others almost as fearful. I cite but one more in this place.

I had been sitting upon the window-sill one day, with my body partly outside, for the purpose of performing some repair upon the sash. My sleep thereafter was scared by a vision of a house supernaturally high, upon whose topmost window-sill I stood, holding on by a projecting cornice with one hand, while with the other I sought to perform some impossible purpose, which prevented it from assisting its mate. Still the cornice kept crumbling. I grasped it by a fresh projection. That also gave way; another, and that was broken by my grasp. This position was brought to a crisis in several ways. Sometimes by a powerful impulse I swayed myself inside, and the current of the dream changed. Sometimes, without my knowing how, the vision passed utterly away. Once the whole building on whose side I stood from basement to cap-stone took fire in an instant; I leaped to the more merciful, to avoid the more cruel death, and, awaking, found myself upon the floor in one of those feverish states of which I have spoken.

That night I slept no more. At dawn I laid myself down for an hour of disturbed slumber, to awake again to a day which was as much to be dreaded as the night.

XXI. Concerning the Doctor; not Southey's, but mine.

At the time of my greatest need, I was so fortunate as to make the acquaintance of one man whose sympathy was, for months of trial, one of my strongest supports. Half discouraged in my attempts at self-rescue, I passed an hour in conversation with him, and fortitude came to me anew; for soul and its connection with the body had so long been his study that he knew how, with the utmost delicacy, to turn thought out of unwholesome channels; moreover, he had the heart as well as the brain for doing good. I need not say that he was a doctor.

I can not resist the temptation to a digression in this place for the purpose of giving my testimony, for the highest that it is worth, to one fact of past experience. It is this: if I have ever met a man before unknown to me, whose sympathies flowed instinctively toward distress, whose self-sacrifice had become an inseparable part of nature, whose comprehensive interest in all that might ennoble our kind was equaled only by his loving patience with its present infirmities, I have called him "doctor," and, nine times in ten, have not been mistaken.

Society has now grown old enough, for the sake of self-respect at least, to despise and abandon those stale jokes upon doctors which tickled her childish ear. With her superstition of the value of a horse-shoe as prophylactic against witches, let her also put aside the inanities which she talks, in her less sombre mood, of the physician in league with the sexton, and the solemnity of mock-learning which reigns over a circle of gold-headed canes. When frightened, she is ever ready to send for the doctor; she stops joking as soon as she is parturient, apoplectic from last night's surfeit, or appalled at the consequences of having swallowed a button.

True, there are empirics in medicine. There are men who tamper with the delicate springs of life upon no other authority than that of a

"possunt quia posse videntur."
We have all seen the advertisement of one "whose sands of life have nearly run out," and as we marvel at the length of time during which those sands have been just on the verge of their final down-flow, we are led to ask if, for the sake of that world upon which an incalculable benefit in cases of consumption may be conferred for the price of one shilling, the benevolent possessor of the recipe may not occasionally have tipped up his hour-glass or diminished its aperture.

We all know the quack in medicine. We are not blind to the thousand astonishing cures of as many desperate maladies, to the placards on the highways, the columns of the press, the almanacs, the guides, the angels that come down in a hurry from heaven, calling through a trumpet to the moribund to hold on till they get there, with a bottle of sirup under each arm which shall restore peace to his afflicted family.

All these things we know; yet are there no other quacks than quacks in medicine? Are there no quacks of divinity? no quacks at law? no political quacks, that dose a diseased nation? no literary quacks, who break down the æsthetic constitution of the people? But, because Brigham Young points out the road to future blessedness through a phalanstery of wives, shall we no more go to church? Because Jeffreys was a villain, must no more causes be adjudicated? And are we to abjure all faith in the science of government inasmuch as some placeman theorizes to the mob in fustian during a campaign, or anathematize all authors in that somebody has befouled the pool of reading-mind by a volume of the Rag-picker's Nephew?

If we hold faith in gold, notwithstanding base metal, let us be assured that nowhere is that gold found at a higher percentage of purity than among doctors. Where one Faun hath stolen the mantle of Esculapius, as the good sire lay sleeping, there are a hundred upon whom he has dropped it as upon worthy children.

Of all men, the doctor is to be peculiarly cherished. Let us not forget that there was one season, very early in all our lives, when without him we might not have been. Let us remember how often, uncomplainingly, he has deprived himself of sleep, of meat and drink, of all those social endearments which beautify the world to us, that we might be set at ease upon some whimsical ailment, some pulse too little or too much. When the hour of a real need calls for him, with what anxiety he watches every flush of cheek and wandering of eye, with what strategic skill he brings to an issue the battle between the forces of life and death, with what calm earnestness he throws his own energy upon our side, how with the very parental anxiety he watches hour after hour at the painful bed, with what eye of suspense he beholds the crisis come, and now, when he knows that a Greater than he has come silently into the consultation, waits until an unseen finger has touched the clogged fount of life, and given him reason to rejoice with them that do rejoice.

In a deep sympathy, in tenderness, in allowance for human frailties, there is no man who meets us on the ways of life that more resembles that mightier Physician whose cures are felt in all the arteries of the world. Like Him, the doctor is compassionate, because, measurably with Him, "he knoweth our frame, he remembereth that we are dust." And, last of all, yet not least, be it not forgotten that there is waiting for us an hour of shadow in the Hereafter, when, all medicine failing us, save that grand one which is to cure us of the body which hath afflicted for years, the voices of farewell, mixed with weeping, that shall be heard around our pillow, will not lack one tone which hath cheered us on through so many remediable distresses, but among the last whom our closing eye shall gather in before it looks on the grand mysteries will be he who, yielding us up unwillingly to the Stronger, remains to help the beloved whom we can help no more -- the doctor.

It is hard to understand how any man who, like the physician, from morning till night, and often from night till morning again, is occupied with enginery and the repair of this complicated system of forces, the body, should rest contented with a mere external survey of the levers and pulleys of its machine, or the chemical phenomena of its laboratory. If he be the true man of science which his profession imperatively demands, he can not help perceiving, in a multitude of instances, that some intangible agent is working out processes for good or ill which do not array themselves under any material classification. Changes are taking place which do not seem to originate in the specific function operated upon; new elements enter the consideration of death or cure which can not be referred to food or medicine. The true physician will not be contented until he has gone back of the wheels, and investigated the nature of that strange imponderable force which is energizing them. To him the spiritual in his art is of even more importance than the bodily.

I have not, after all, been making a very wide digression, since it has just led me into the description of my friend the doctor -- to me, the doctor by eminence, since, spiritually, he did for my recovery that which none else could, in a life-time, have accomplished for it corporeally.

All his life he had been communing with the great and beautiful thinkers to whom our mysterious double nature was a beloved study. Yet no man perfected in mere book-lore was he. Without seeking apologies wherewith to excuse himself from following in the train of the dogmatists of any age, he had thought for himself, and, in the possession of an inner world thus acquired, he was independent of other resources to an extent which was equaled only by my hasheesh kingship, and by that only in degree and not in permanency. With him the spirit of all things was as much a felt presence as their gross embodiment is to material men.

From the commencement of our acquaintance I was as much with him as the pressure of cares would allow me to be, and, when my own life had become to me a vague and meaningless abstraction, by participation with his thought and sympathy I somehow gradually drew into it an injected energy which made its juiceless pulses throb again, and awoke me out of the lethargy into which I was sinking deeper with every day. For months, but for him, the allotted course of my duties had been a mechanical round; a galley-slave, a mill-horse, could not have labored with less interest or more weariness.

As the mountain of exercises and compositions grew gradually more and more level with the plane of my table, and the evening wore on toward night, I was wont to soliloquize, "One hour more, and I will go to see the Doctor." Once at his rooms, and the iron mantle of pedagogic restraint fell off; I was in the human character again; nay, more, I seemed to take off my body and sit in my soul. This very resumption of naturalness and freedom by one whose position demanded all day a peculiar self-control and reticence, will be understood by those whom fortune (or misfortune) has placed in like circumstances to be the most delicious privilege for which the tired mind can yearn. The ceasing to seem to be what he is not must always be an untold relief to any one who has not, by long training in the necessary caution of a responsible place, utterly ceased to be what he was.

Yet the benefit conferred upon me by my acquaintance with the doctor was something more than could be comprehended in this mere exchange of the technical for the natural, the life of a profession for the life of humanity. A most kind and lively interest did he bestow upon all that pertained to my past enchanted existence, and never with more gentleness and care than he did could an own brother have supported me through the horrors wherein I was painfully journeying on my way to complete disenthrallment. By condolence, by congenial converse, by suggestion of brighter things, by indication of a certain hope in the distance if I would but press on, in a thousand ways did this friend nerve me to persistent effort, and close more tightly behind me the gates of return.

It was through his labors chiefly that I began once more to take an interest in the world, not through any renewed affection for its mere hollow forms, but for the sake of that inner essence which they embodied. Henceforth forever, after abandoning hasheesh, was all endurance with the external creation to be denied me unless I could penetrate deeper than its mere outside. I had known the living spirit of nature; in its husks I no longer found any nourishment, but rather the material for a certain painful loathing to expend itself upon. In my then present condition, I beheld as little beauty in the best of external things, I granted as little admiration, as any old Athenian whose eyes last fell on the divine and spirit-breathing master-pieces of Phidias, revivified to pass judgment upon some elaborately-carven gatepost.

Through the aid of the doctor I began slowly to perceive the possibility of penetrating deeper than the shard of things without the help, so dearly bought, of hasheesh. Taking up, for instance, the subject of a spirit which works throughout all creation, by which the most microscopic plant-filament, no less than the grandest mountain, is inwrought and informed, we often talked together in parables, which, however, were never obscure to us, since we possessed that best dictionary of meanings, the bond of a close, congenial sympathy.

Let no one accuse us rashly of Pantheism, since it is not affirmed that we ascribed to that spirit of things divine, or in any way self-conscious attributes. Thus, as we were one day standing side by side before a window exquisitely arabesqued with trees by the noiseless graver of the frost, did the doctor discourse upon its process and its reasons:

"That the thing which men call dead matter has not wrought out this beauty is evident. The matter is here, but a more subtle force has moulded it according to hidden laws. The very necessary and primordial condition of matter is inertia, and without the touch of human hands inertia has here been overcome. Look at that palm-tree. We might shut out from our eyes its artificial frame, and all the other surroundings which connect it with man's workmanship, and, as we gazed upon its articulate trunk, and the plumy shoots spreading from the expanded bud which forms the capital of the shaft, believe ourselves upon an oasis of Araby.

"Wherein differs this palm-tree from its brothers of the desert, the tropical garden, and the bank of Nile? In this only. The spirit of a palm has been viewlessly wandering from zone to zone in search of a body. It reaches a warm land, and there, from ammoniacal soils, from water-atoms, from numberless elements, it slowly builds about itself, in conformance to its inner laws, roots, trunk, and branches, until some way-worn Howadji throws himself down under its shadow, saying, 'Blessed be Allah! another palm-tree.'

"A second palm-spirit, in its ethereal journeyings, comes not to the earth, but hither to this window-pane. Here it finds no soils, but only the water-drops, which all day long have been collecting from the atmosphere. Its visit is by night, and when we draw near the window in the morning, lo! the spirit has erected for itself a body of purest crystal, shaping it faultlessly, by its own unerring law, into the palm-tree which we see here.

"To-morrow the spirit of the Alga may float hither for its incarnation, and on the day after the spirit of the Fern."

Had I possessed any part in the origination of this idea, I should not venture to characterize it as I now do, singularly beautiful; yet I believe that I shall not speak without hope of sympathy in saying that such it did certainly seem to me. It chanced that in the long and severe winter which we passed together at W----, my friend and I had many opportunities of beholding the verification of his prophecy, for to our windows did come frequently both Fern and Alga, with many another spirit from the universal Flora, whose filaments and petals bitter blasts only breathed into more finished perfectness, and whose fragrance was a better, a more enduring one than that of odor, since it was exhaled to the soul without mediation of corruptible organs.

As we looked upon the frost-glorified panes, our minds meanwhile tinged with this poetic theory, it was impossible to refrain from carrying up the analogy into a field which is vaster, and orbed by higher destinies than those of the unconscious creation. To a certain body of the palm alone is the breath of winter fatal. In the higher zones an incarnation reared of soils and earthy juices perishes and droops away; yet the spirit of the palm is not dead. Wafted away, it collects for itself other materials to dwell in, and crystallizes around itself a form which shall only be beautified and confirmed by that very power which destroys its other embodiment.

There is another wind in Araby, called Sarsar, the icy wind of death, which blows not upon the tree, but on the man. At its chill the bodily drops off, but the soul has never felt it. Set free by the same breath which was lethal to its shell, it voyages into another region, it crystallizes around itself "a more glorious body." Who shall say that, to this new creation which it has informed, those very influences which worked the dismemberment of its ancient covering -- labor, pain, attrition, and all the thousand forces of decay, shall not the more through all the ages act to ennoble the soul, to make it a grander, better, and more harmonious being? Shall he who so clothes the grass of the field, and much rather clothes us, though of little faith, grant good uses of ill destiny to unconscious and not to conscious being?

As a legitimate and by no means unexpected consequence of our living somewhat in seclusion, and holding both opinions and converse which were not absolutely universal, there were not wanting those who dubbed us visionary, the severest epithet of reproach which can be hurled by A., whose horizon of interests is bounded by beef and clothes, at B., who inquires within a wider scope. I do not remember that we ever writhed very convulsively under this fearful thunderbolt, but bore it as became not altogether annihilated, good-humored martyrs.

As we talked of this subject upon a certain evening, thus spake the doctor in parable:

"Once upon a time there abode in a bar of iron two particles of electricity. Now one of these particles, being of an investigating temperament, to the great discredit of his family, and the shame and confusion of face of all who held high seats in the electric synagogue, set out upon a wild voyage of discovery. For a long time he was absent, and, as no tidings came from him, it was supposed he had perished ignominiously at the negative pole. In the mean while, the other particle of electricity, who staid at home and minded his own business, by gradual accretions had secured to himself size and dynamic consideration in the community. After the lapse of several seconds (which must be known is a long period to individualities which travel as rapidly as the electric) the erratic particle returned, and visiting his friend, the particle who had attained a position of high respectability, happened to let fall in conversation this remark: 'I have discovered in my journeyings that we are not the only beings extant, but that, in fact, we live in and are surrounded by a body called iron, which, from our difference of state, it possessing a far greater density than we, we do not perceive.'

"Thereat the other particle waxed wroth, and muttered something like 'humbug!' But the traveler, pressing the claim of his new fact, did so excite his respectable friend that he broke forth thus: 'Do you pretend to belie the evidence of my senses? All my life I have been going up and down about my business, and have never yet seen, heard, smelt, tasted, or felt such a thing as iron in the whole time. Why don't I run my head against it?' Since that day, it is credibly stated that whenever the practical particle stands on 'Change talking with other practical particles, and the inquiring particle comes along, the former shakes his head, and says to his friends, 'Unreliable -- talks nonsense about a crotchet which he calls iron -- visionary, very visionary.'"

XXII. Grand Divertissement.

As the months went on, the fervor of my longing toward the former hasheesh life in some measure passed away, and in general the fascination to return did not present itself so much in the form of pining for an affirmative as loathing of a negative state. It was not the ecstasy of the drug which so much attracted me, as its power of disenthrallment from an apathy which no human aid could utterly take away. Yet even now there were seasons of absolute struggle in which I fought as against a giant, or more truly to the nature of things should I say, in which I resisted as against a demon houri, for my tempter was more passing lovely than any thing on earth.

As in the earlier period of my warfare, I now and then caught glimpses of ravishing delight, which, through some rift in the thick cloud elsewhere completely enveloping my daily life, broke in upon me for a moment, yet lasted long enough to prove that I could not yet write myself secure, that my integrity was not yet beyond corruption.

Some of my readers will doubtless be amused, others pained, and a few disgusted at the childlike expedients to which I found it necessary to resort for the purpose of appeasing this renewed appetite for visions without a return to hasheesh. There were three different sets of circumstances which almost infallibly brought on the longing. It was never suggested by dark and stormy weather, since this was too much in consonance with my habitual mood to demand more than a passing notice. The man who has lost an intimate friend does not pay much attention to murk and mist; it is sunshine which seems to mock his melancholy. So in my own case did it happen. The season of most intense longing was a day of clear sky and brilliant light. That beauty which filled the heart of every other living thing with gladness, only spoke of other suns more wondrous rolling through other heavens of a more matchless dye. I looked into the sky, and missed its former unutterable rose and sapphire; no longer did the whole dome of the firmament sound with grand unwritten music.

It was a pain to look into that desert wilderness of blue which of old my sorcery had peopled for me with innumerable celestial riders, with cities of pearl and symphony-haunted streams of silver. I shut my eyes, and in a moment saw all that I had lost.

A night of brilliant moonlight brought me other repentings after my enchanted life, whose tone was not so high as those of the sunshine, but deeper and more enduring. Wrapped in a melancholy which could not be imparted, I wandered by the hour through the beaming streets, and looked sadly around me to see the meanest object by the wayside

"Change
Into something rich and strange."

The stones beneath my feet gleamed like unhewn crystals. The frosty fretwork on the panels of doors which I passed, at the touch of the divine Moon-Alchemist became exquisite filigrees of silver. The elm-trees and the locust, shedding sparkles of radiance from their ice-incased twigs, might well have been those trees of gleamy ore which Allah buried when man was cast out of Paradise.

Yet mournfully I thought of the old days, when I would have walked down these shining ways as through an ever-lengthening vista of glories, when the moon-light would have fallen on me mysteriously empurpled, when over all the wondrous domain I had felt myself unquestioned sovereign, and out of the beauteous recesses of earth and sky sprite voices had musically hailed me to my kingdom.

As I thought upon these things, now forever irretrievably abandoned to the past, I have wept -- yes, though it be unmanly, I have wept to find myself a discrowned king, a sorcerer ravished of his wand, a god shorn of his glories. I am not ashamed to remember that I did this; for if there be any ecstasy possible which we do not now feel imparted to us, if any excellency in things which does not now make itself tangible, it is no more ignominious to lament over it perished than to sigh after it tarrying.

There was another, a bodily condition, which I always found it necessary to avoid if I would not be smitten with repinings after the hasheesh life. It was the nervous sensitiveness induced by deprivation of tobacco.

In smoking, if in nothing else, could I boast regularity of habit. To be sure, for this regularity neither an unusually developed organ of order nor the possibility of any thing like a systematic arrangement in my multiplicity of labors was to be pre-eminently thanked. To defer for an hour the nicotine indulgence was to bring on a longing for the cannabine which was actual pain. When circumstances have occurred which made it impossible to smoke before entering my daily round of duties, until they closed I have hardly dared to shut my eyes, lest I should be borne incontinently out of the actual life into which necessity called me to a land of colossal visions. If for a moment I yielded to the impulse, I was straightway in the midst of sky and landscape whose splendors were only less vivid than the perfect hallucinations of the fantasia.

But I have not yet spoken of those expedients to which I resorted for relief and to avoid the necessity of resuming the use of hasheesh. Certainly, in them ingenuity, so far as I possessed any, was tortured to its utmost endurance.

Sometimes I spent the few moments of leisure which during the day could be snatched from business in -- mention it not confidently in Gath, breathe it not to the friend of thy bosom in Askelon -- blowing soap-bubbles. Not that there is aught deserving of contempt in the enjoyment of that which has been made a philosophic toy by one of the greatest of Anglo-Saxon sages -- not that the pleasure of rare beauties from humble elements is of necessity an æsthetic heresy, but because the hasheesh-eater is well aware of the existence of critics, to whom all that is childlike is also childish, who quarrel with men for being perversely happy on moderate means, and with their Creator because he has not made all the little hills as high as Cotopaxi.

Yes, throwing down the wand of professional majesty, degrading myself to the level of the most callow neophyte of an infant class, did I take up the pipe, and, going into the presence of the nearest sunbeam (a course which, by the way, might well be followed by those who for their light go farther and fare worse), did I create sphere after sphere, not, as the grotesquely but unintentionally blasphemous old poet hath it, snapping them off my fingers into space, but with careful hand taking rest over the back of a chair to counteract the tremulousness of over-anxiety not to tremble, did I inflate them to the maximum, and then sit wrapped up in gazing at their luxuriant sheen until they broke.

There I found some faint actualization of my remembered hasheesh-sky, and where the actual failed there did the ideal, thus stimulated, come in to complete the vision. Had time allowed me, I could have consumed hours in watching the sliding, the rich intermingling, the changes by origination, and the changes by reaction of those matchless hues, or hues at least so matchless in the real world that to find their parallel we must leave the glories of a waking life, and go floating through the firmament of some iridescent dream. Verily, he who would be meet for the participation in any joys must robe himself in humility and become as a little child.

There was one other way in which I measurably reproduced the past for my innocent satisfaction. Had I permitted, at certain seasons, any foreign eye to invade the sanctity of my room, it would have fallen, possibly with some surprise, upon a singular arrangement of the books upon my table into a form somewhat resembling those houses which children build at their play. Yet the stranger would have very little suspected a clew to the mystery in the fact that I had thus been embodying to myself the ideal of the ancient cavern or the resplendent temple in which many a day ago I had exulted through a whole evening, while the rocks echoed with strange music, or oracular voices spoke to me out of the inner shrine. Had he asked me the secret, he had probably not been much the wiser for my answer.

There is still another method, and by far the most efficient of all, by which I gratified the visionary propensity without returning to the old indulgence. I had been advised by the counselor to whose article I originally owed my emancipation, whenever the fascination of the drug came upon me with peculiar power, to evade it by re-enacting some former vision upon paper. A truly wise and well-considered counsel did I find this, and one which, whenever the possibility existed from any gap in my daily occupation, I followed scrupulously. As would have resulted from once more superinducing the hasheesh delirium, my visions, marshaled out of memory, marched past beneath varying banners; some of them banded under hell-black flags, and others carrying the colors of a rainbow of the seventh heaven.

From this reproduction of the past in the order in which it had occurred, I gained a double benefit, the pleasure of appeasing the fascination without increasing it, and the salutary review of abominable horrors without any more than the echo of a pang. In this way some portion of the present narrative was sketched at first, but of necessity a very small one, since the pressure of business made my abode, even in the most innoxious dream-land, that only of a wayfaring man who turneth aside but for a night.

XXIII. The Hell of Waters and the Hell of Treachery.

It is not to be supposed, however, that, with all these expedients, I was now leading a life of quite tolerable calm; on the whole, rather enviable for its ideal diversions, and free from most of those sufferings which, at its abandonment, if not before, Nature sets as her unmistakable seal of disapprobation upon the use of any unnatural stimulus. If, from a human distaste of dwelling too long upon the horrible, I have been led to speak so lightly of the facts of this part of my experience that any man may think the returning way of ascent an easy one, and dare the downward road of ingress, I would repair the fault with whatever of painfully-elaborated prophecy of wretchedness may be in my power, for through all this time I was indeed a greater sufferer than any bodily pain could possibly make me.

For many a month my nights, or whatever portion of them was given to sleep, were tormented with terrific visitations. After a time Niagara began again especially to haunt me. In every variety of dangerous posture, helpless, friendless, frequently deserted utterly of every living being, I hung suspended over the bellowing chasm, or slid down crumbling cliffs toward the treacherous pavement of ever-shifting emerald. But one consolation ever broke in upon my distress; it was that stony face, which mutely shared with me, beneath its everlasting veil, the terror of the waters. Could I but crouch beside it in my dream, one element was wanting to my utter isolation.

Yet it was not invariably for myself alone that I feared. Sometimes a tremendous ship came floating up the river without a sign of life upon its decks of man or beast. Against the current it made headway without wheels or sails, but on coming to a certain place always stood still. I soon learned to foretell what was next coming, so that I groaned in the consciousness of an infallible prophecy of evil. A shudder shook the river, as if some dire convulsion was breaking up from its measureless abysses, and then slowly did the giant vessel begin to sink, bow foremost. Slowly she settled till her fore-chains were out of sight; then came a tumultuous surging outcry of despair; the decks, the shrouds, the stays were populous with human beings, unseen until that moment of ruin, and still clinging with iron clutch to those vain supports for the life which could not last. I saw them, one by one, lapped in as the green water mounted, and with the last bubble of their dying breath the main truck disappeared, and a moment more saw the river sliding onward as before.

I have no idea how many times sleep rang changes of horror upon that dreadful dream, but often enough, indeed, to make me shudder with a speechless pang whenever water flowed or a ship drifted into the vast area of my nightly vision.

Gradually it grew the habitual tendency of my dreaming state to bring all its scenes, whether of pleasure or of pain, to a crisis through some catastrophe by water. Earlier in the state which ensued upon my abandonment of hasheesh I had been affrighted particularly by seeing men tumble down the shafts of mines, or, as I have before detailed, either dreading or suffering some fall into abysses on my own part; yet now, upon whatever journey I set out, to cross the Atlantic or to travel inland, sooner or later I inevitably came to an end by drowning, or in the imminent peril of it. It seemed singular to me, in the waking state, that I never made use of past experience, during terrific dreams, to assure myself that a certain danger was only imaginary. Before abandoning hasheesh, in natural dreams I had frequently employed the power of logical deduction -- which, in the case of many persons, remains tolerably active during sleep -- saying to myself, "You were frightened by this same danger before, and it turned out to be only ideal after all;" upon which I immediately awoke, or beheld the danger pass away.

Aware of this fact, I often determined, in the daytime, to rouse myself from the distresses of the night by the same expedient, but when they came it was never once thought of. That law of hasheesh operation by which all existence is merged in the present, and there is no memory of having ever lived in a previous state, was most consistently obeyed by the sleeping horrors of abandonment. There was no way so much as conjectured by which the spell of reality might be broken, and the determination of the day being thoroughly ignored, the only remedy was to endure unto the end.

Yet there was one most agonizing vision, whose close proved an exception to the ordinary watery catastrophe, and which stamped itself upon my mind with a vividness lingering, even while I was awake, for many days. It also, like so many of the rest, was connected with Niagara.

On a cliff below the Fall, elevated to a height above the water such as only hasheesh can give, I found myself seated upon a broad flat stone.

Beside me, and resting her hand upon my own, sat a person whom I well knew, when awake, as a queenly woman of the world, who caressed society and was caressed by it in return. So far as man has a right to weigh his neighbor in the scales of private judgment, she was utterly hollow, selfish, and politic almost for policy's sake. Indeed, I felt this, when awake, acting so powerfully as a repulsion, that had I, in actual life, found her so near me, I should have arisen and walked away for fear of showing her my true dislike. Now, however, I did not stir, for a singular fascination held me.

Presently she spoke, and called my attention to some object which was going down the river. I turned to look, but almost immediately heard a grinding sound beneath me, and felt the stone on which I sat slowly sliding toward the edge of the cliff. Facing about in an instant, I saw the woman gazing earnestly in another direction. Soon again she called me to look at some appearance in the river. Strangely reckless, I obeyed her. The stone slipped forward once more. This time I turned quick enough to detect her hand just moving away from the side. I sprang up; I caught her by the arm; I glared into her beautiful icy eyes; I cried out, "Woman! accursed woman! is this your faith?" Now, casting off all disguise, she gave a hollow laugh, and spoke: "Faith! do you look for faith in hell? I would have cast you to the fishes." My eyes were opened. She said truly. We were indeed in hell, and I had not known it until now. Wearing the same features, with the demoniac instead of the human soul speaking through them -- wandering about the same earth, yet aware of no presence but demons like ourselves -- lit by the same sky, but hope spoke down from it no more.

I left the she-fiend by the river-brink, and met another as well known to me in the former life. Blandly she wound to my side as if she would entrap me, thinking that I was a new-comer into hell. Knowing her treachery, as if to embrace her I caught her in my arms, and, knitting them about her, strove to crush her out of being. With a look of awful malignity, she loosed one hand, and, tearing open her bosom, disclosed her heart, hissing hot, and pressed it upon my own. "The seal of love I bear thee, my chosen fiend!" she cried. Beneath that flaming signet my heart caught fire; I dashed her away, and then, thank God, awoke.

XXIV. The Visionary; to which Chapter there is no Admittance upon Business

There are those philosophers who, in running the boundary-line between the healthful and depraved propensities of our nature, have left the longing for stimulus on the condemned side. Notwithstanding all that I have suffered from the most powerful stimulant that the world possesses, I can not bring myself to agree with them. Not because the propensity is defensible on the ground of being universal. True, the Syrian has his hasheesh, the Chinaman his opium; he must be a poverty-stricken Siberian who lacks his ball of narcotic fungus, an impossible American who goes without tobacco, and over all the world liquor travels and domesticates itself, being of all stimulants the most thoroughly cosmopolitan. Yet, if we make this fact our basis, we are equally committed to the defense of the quite as catholic propensities toward lying, swearing, and hating one's rival.

But there is one ground upon which the righteousness of the tendency toward stimulants may be upheld without the fear of any dangerous side-issues, namely, the fact that it proves, almost as powerfully as any thing lower than direct revelation, man's fitness by constitution and destiny by choice, for a higher set of circumstances than the present. Let it, however, be understood what, in this instance, is meant by the tendency to stimulus.

We do not mean that mere bodily craving which, shared equally in common by the most bestial and the most spiritual of men not disembodied, urges them alike to some expedient which will send their blood throbbing with a livelier thrill of physical well-being, blind them to the consideration of disagreeable truths, and eclipse all thought by the dense shadow of the Animal.

That of which we speak is something far higher -- the perception of the soul's capacity for a broader being, deeper insight, grander views of Beauty, Truth, and Good than she now gains through the chinks of her cell. It is true that there are not many stimuli which possess the power in any degree to satisfy such yearnings. The whole catalogue, so far as research has written it, will probably embrace only opium, hasheesh, and, acting upon some rarely-found combinations of temperament, liquors.

Ether, chloroform, and the exhilarant gases may be left out of the consideration, since but a few people are enthusiastic or reckless enough in the pursuit of remarkable emotions to tamper with agents so evanescent in their immediate, so fatal in their prolonged effects.

But, wherever the yearning of the mind is toward gratifications of this nature -- where it is calling earnestly for a nobler excellence in all its objects, nay, even wearied, discontented with those it now has, shall we pronounce this state a right or a wrong one?

Let us see what verdict we would give upon certain other yearnings. When the poor man fences in for himself a little spot of waste land, he first erects a dark and low cabin, that his household gods may not be shelterless. Pleased for a while by the hovel life, greatly better as it is than camping out upon the roofless moor, he feels all his aim satisfied, and insphered within the attainment of Nature's response to sheer physical necessities.

By-and-by, after the pleasures of not being cold, wet, exposed to suspicious eyesight, nor hungry (since he has a little potato-patch behind the cabin), have become somewhat odd to him, he happens to think, "How would a few flowers look before my door? There is something inside of me which seems to approve of flowers; I think they would do me good." So the poor man wanders out into the wood, and there, in that most ancient and incense-breathing temple of our God, he kneels down on the turfy hassock, which Spring, that ever-young opener of the cathedral doors, has laid for him, and gently, without unearthing a fibre of their roots, lifts a clump of violets.

When, a day or two afterward, we come along past the rude cabin, and as we lean over the fence to ask the tenant how he fares, what do we do when our eyes fall upon a little dot here and there of something more than ground, or grass, or vegetables -- azure faces looking brotherly up at the same-colored heaven? Do we shake our heads, draw down our brows, purse our mouths, and say, "Ah! dissatisfied with your circumstances, I see. Restless where Providence has placed you; grasping after visionary happiness; morbidly craving for what you have not; depraved taste!" and all that sort of thing?

I had really flattered myself that I was going to make a pretty cogent combination out of this, of the à fortiori and reductio ad absurdum arguments, but I am afraid I have failed. I fear that there are some people who would say exactly this.

204

Yet I will restrict the "we" to you and to myself, my reader, since I know that you have not the ability nor I the will to be guilty of so gross a speech. We, then, certainly shall not say it.

Let us finish the analogy. A man who, during his childish (not his childlike) years, was growing up into all that compacts, rounds out, and confirms the animal, has in that time attended solely to those claims of nature which have a reference to assimilation and secretion. With meat, drink, and raiment he was satisfied. Practical men cherished him as a sort of typical fact of that other broader fact, the respectable community.

Just at the moment that hopes of his "making something of himself" are at their widest (I will not say "highest," since there is no height to hopes of this kind, as ordinarily understood), he discovers that he has some other need hitherto unsuspected, and not coming under any caption in the catalogue of bodily well-being. His soul wants beauty; its yearning will not be repressed. For a while he is content with the discovery of that which springs up between his feet in this really very beautiful world. Absorbed in other aims, he had never noticed it before, and now it breaks upon him as from a new heaven and a new earth.

By-and-by he thinks that, since all this loveliness is transitory, liable to be obscured by clouds and bedraggled by storms, uprooted utterly or made distasteful by the presence of a bad association which will not be exiled, his soul, as immortal and expansive, may find grander views in another region.

This other is the region of stimulus. What shall we say to this man? "You are morbid; you are depraved; your yearnings are unnatural and sinful; you must contract your wishes, or, at least, extend your arms sideways farther into the dark, not upward higher into the light?"

No; a thousand times no! Let us rather say thus: "Man, in this your longing, you have the noblest testimony to the endless capacity for growth of that germ, your soul. You can not believe more of her than she is, for you can not believe more of her than God believes, and He was assured that He had made her in His own image. You do not, therefore, flatter yourself with the privilege of looking into things too high for you; there is nothing which you can conceive of as possible to your view which shall not be actual. Your wish is approved by Heaven, for from Heaven came the constitution which made you capable of such a wish. Your Creator does not condemn you, neither do we condemn you."

If that man therefore departs, and becomes addicted to the indulgence in opium, hasheesh, or whatever other spell may in his case possess the power of prying open for him the gates to more wondrous glories, shall not the blood of the man and the tears of ruined or bitterly sympathizing friends be upon our skirts?

Nay, most just and noble-hearted reader, for that which we have said to him should be only the exordium to another, a longer address. It is not the author's will more than his province to be dictative, yet be indulgent if he shortly sketches it here.

"You sin not in your yearnings. Yet may you sin grievously, even against the grand aim of those yearnings, by a certain suicidal gratification of them. Were hasheesh, or opium, or aught else of kindred nature between the poles the only alternative to your former gross life in mere meat and drink, the only alternative even to remaining within the limits of your first acquired beauty, it were better indeed to use them than to dishonor your soul by following mere material aims, or by crippling her energies of expansion.

"Yet this is not the alternative. In Nature there is yet undiscovered glory, a spirit which gradually will interpenetrate you as you commune with her. She is not a mockery, a sham, for a truthful essence indwells, informs her. Be this communing one stimulus to you!

"In Art there is also a spirit which you have not yet read. As the spirit of Nature is the ideal of God, so is the spirit of Art the ideal of man, the mind which God has made. With this also commune. In your actions upon it, in its reactions upon you, you will rejoice in perceptions of a meaning in life which you never felt; you will have one more stimulus.

"Around you are the starving to be fed, the naked to be clothed, the captive to be set free, the persecuted to be overshadowed by your wing, the benighted to be enlightened, the vile to be cleansed. Do good as you have opportunity, and find one more stimulus in that.

"The Infinite One is communing with this illimitable soul of yours to lift it higher. At a hundred doors he comes in to you continually. There are breathings within you which are not of yourself. Do you find yourself lower than you would be? Straightway the standard of true height is shown to you, held in a hand which can help you up to it. Are you obscured by the shadow of a misused past? To you, when you muse in the twilight, come angels, like the two who came even to Sodom at evening. There is hope of a better growth, a grander life; the light of a resurrection which shoots in from the time to come through the chinks of that sepulchre, your body. Wait patiently -- ah! for how few moments, and that sepulchre shall be a cenotaph. Let that hope of an advancing future, with all its unveiling of mysteries, its impulse along the path of an ever more and more glorious career, its exhaustless Beauty, and Truth, and Good, be your last, your noblest, your unfailing stimulus, until the Ideal and the Actual become the same, and it be needed no longer.

"But of the stimulus of drugs, of potions, beware. For the sake of that very majesty with which you justly wish to aggrandize your soul, beware. Their fountains will be presently exhausted, and then you shall helplessly beat your breast, as without possibility of arising from the brink you draw in their foul, their maddening lees, and curse yourself for slaying those noble powers which it was your longing to strengthen, to nourish, and to clarify."

Let this illustration be pardoned if, in spite of other intentions, it has become a sermon. The hasheesh-eater knows full well that not only in the world, but in our own country, shamelessly vilified as it is by the ignorant of other lands with the opprobrium of an all-absorbing aim at gain, there are many of those spirits who can not steep themselves in oblivion of all but physical ends, who can not rest in the mere knowledge that they are getting so many houses, so many acres of land, so much respectable consideration, to be possessed while a wind is passing by, while a twilight is fading. There are men who pine restlessly for riches which shall satisfy higher obligations of their being, shall endure longer, shall in themselves possess a nobler and more expansive essence. They are right in this pining. Yet if there be one voice which can speak from the gateway of a dangerous avenue to its satisfaction, that can say, "Ho there! pass by; I have tried this way; it leads at last into poisonous wildernesses," in the name of Heaven let it be raised.

And thus I excuse my sermon.

There are those, no doubt, who in reading it will say, "Is it not inconsistent to advise this possible hasheesh-eater to 'feed the hungry and clothe the naked' after inveighing so much against practical aims just before?" With a desire to anticipate this objection, I would here say that it is not against practical aims, but the making them the chief, the controlling ones. Or, rather, even more boldly, not against practical aims at all, but against pseudo-practical. Paradoxical as it may be, there is no man more thoroughly, more purely practical than he who is most truly ideal. It is needless to suggest that the word "practical" is a derivative from the Greek verb "to do," and is therefore most properly applied to the man who "does" the best for himself. Now which of two beings thus does the best for himself, he who does it particularly for that part of him which, in a few days, he is to abandon forever, or he who does it to the part which is eternally to abide by him? O practical men, judge ye.

The most perfect spirituality of aim, moreover, is not violated by any decent and orderly attention to the claims of the body. Only let the house be not more beautified than the tenant, the servant fed and adorned above his master, and then no one in his senses can quarrel because either the servant or the house is well sustained for the master's highest good.

It is, no doubt, the perversion of this principle which has caused the word "visionary," most righteously belonging, by its first title, to souls of the grandest insight, to be held, together with the idea which it conveys, in contempt even by serious and thoughtful men. Shallow persons, urging that claim to notoriety through extravagance, which they were aware they could not press to celebrity by greatness, have been disgusting humanity with their absurdities from the time that Diogenes coiled himself in his tub down to the era of the last apostle who blew his trumpet through Broadway. They have all glorified themselves with the name "visionary;" when the radiant mantle fell from the shoulders of the last ascending prophet who had worn it in reverence, it was snatched by the ancestor of all the unseemly clan -- it cloaked the rags of his spiritual beggary during his lifetime, and at his decession it was handed down through every succeeding generation of impostors. No better proof could be adduced for its primeval authentic dignity than the fact that there has never, within the memory of man, been a pseudo-poet, pseudo-philanthropist, or a pseudo- with any other termination, who has not tenaciously clung to the epithet as his birthright, his mark of the elect, his cross of the Legion of Honor.

We can not wonder at the astonishment expressed by Rogers, that most substantial banker of a most substantial country, when, after Byron had dined with him, for the sake of the spiritual man, upon one potato and a glass of water, refusing all the English cheer set prodigally before him, the moneyed man finds that, within the next hour, his brother bard has dispatched a steak and a bottle of Port at his club-house!

Yet this assumption of the spiritual where it does not exist -- this counterfeit presentment of the true visionary, certainly ought not, among thinking men at least, to discredit the real fact.

There are, doubtless, more than one who, when they have heard this fine word rung mournfully from some old watch-tower of conventional respectability, as the knell of all confidence, all position, all esteem among men, or echoing portentously from the tripod of Sir Oracle, big with evil omen to an unendorsed theory, have sighed for the ancient days when it beautified the threnody over a dead seer, or pealed from the lips of harpers as they sang the forecast of a living sage.

To its old place the "visionary" will never be restored until knaves cease to make it their claim to spurious reverence, or good men refrain from looking at every theory as unsafe which does not base its request for their attention upon some tendency to promote a bodily good or explain a bodily fact. If the former can not, is it possible that the latter may not be?

For him who shall reinstate that word there is a noble meed waiting in the future. The man who leaps into a stream and brings his drowning brother safe to shore is rewarded by the Humane Society with a medal, which he is proud to hand down to his children as their best inheritance. If we are true men, Truth is brother to us all, and the representative of a great and good idea is Truth. Help! then, help! until some one comes who shall place in the reverence of just thinkers. Verily he shall not lose his reward. But he must be a man of calm nerve as well as bold stroke; as able to take full in his face the outrageous pelting of the spray, as to wear the medal when he has wiped off the drops.

Then shall the soul be held worthier than the body, not only in-, but outside of the pale of speculative theology, and

"Then comes the statelier Eden back to man;
Then springs the crowning race of human kind.
May these things be!"

XXV. Cave Succedanea.

I am not aware of the existence of any in this part of the world who are now in the habit of using hasheesh. Those persons to whom, at their request, I formerly administered it, for experiment's sake, were satisfied with the one trial, upon my assuring them that any prolonged indulgence would infallibly lead to horrors.

Yet, since it is not at all impossible that these pages may meet the eye of those who, unknown to me, are incipient hasheesh-eaters, or who, having tested to the full the powers of the drug, now find its influence a slavery, yet are ignorant of the proper means of emancipation, I will not let this opportunity pass for suggesting, through a somewhat further narrative of my own case, a counsel which may chance to be salutary.

The hasheesh-eater needs particularly to resist the temptation of retreating, in the trials of his slow disenthrallment, to some other stimulus, such as liquors or opium. Against such a retreat I was warned by the same adviser whose article in the Magazine had been my prime motor to escape.

As in an early part of this narrative it has been mentioned, strong experimental tendencies had led me, long before the first acquaintance with hasheesh, to investigate the effect of all narcotics and stimulants, not so much with a view to pleasure as to the discovery of new phases of mental life. Among these researches had been opium. This drug never affected me very powerfully, not in one instance producing any thing like hallucination, but operating principally through a quiet which no external circumstances could disturb -- slightly tinged, when my eyes were shut, with pleasing images of scenery. Its mild effect was probably owing to some resistant peculiarity of constitution, since I remember having once taken a dose, which I afterward learned, upon good authority, to have been sufficient to kill three healthy men, without any remarkable phenomena ensuing. Several considerations operated with me to prevent my making opium an habitual indulgence, besides this fact of its moderate potency. This, of itself, might not have been sufficient, since the capability which I acquired in its use of sustaining the most prolonged and severe fatigue was in my case unexampled.

In the first place, I was secured from enslavement by the terrors of De Quincey's suffering. I felt assured that he had not unmasked the half of it, since his exquisite sense of the refined and the appropriate in all communion with the public, showing itself in a thousand places throughout his works, had evidently withheld him, in his confessions, from giving to the painful intaglio that deep stroke of the graver which he thought that good taste would not permit, even under sanction of truth.

Again, a consideration of more narrow prejudice withheld me -- the impossibility, if I should use opium, of concealing the fact from my associates, some of whom were physicians, and hardly any of them so unobserving as not to be attracted curiously to the peculiarities of the opium eye, complexion, and manner.

At this time the reputation of being an opium-eater was one very little desirable in the community which included me, had its further abominable consequences been recklessly put aside. It was impossible for any one known to have used the drug to make any intellectual effort whatever, speech, published article, or brilliant conversation, without being hailed satirically as Coleridge le petit, or De Quincey in the second edition. That this was not altogether a morbid condition of public sentiment in the microcosm where I dwelt, may be inferred from a fact which, occurring a few months before I entered it, had no doubt acted to tinge general opinion.

A certain person, in reading "The Confessions," had gathered from them (it would be hard to say how, since their author every where expresses the opium state as one whose serenity is repulsive to all action for the time being) that he should be able to excel De Quincey upon his own field if he wrote while at the height of the effect. Setting apart one evening for the English opium-eater's literary discomfiture, he drank his laudanum, and locked himself into his room alone with the awful presence of a quire of foolscap. On the following morning, his friends, knocking at the door repeatedly, received no answer, and, fearful of some accident, broke in the lock. Lo! our De Quincey in petto was seated in his chair, with pen in hand, and his forehead resting on a blank mass of paper, in all the abandon of innocent repose!

After the final abandonment of hasheesh, however, at times, when distress had reduced me to the willingness to test any relief save that of return, I once or twice tried the effect of opium. It was invariably bad, not operating, as a renewal of the hasheesh indulgence would have done, to lift me into the former plane of pleasurable activity and interest in things about me, but singularly combining with whatever of the hasheesh force might be remaining in my system to cover me once more with the pall which made the worst parts of the old life so painful. Insane faces glared at me; dire voices of prophecy spoke to me even when wide awake; I was filled with foreboding of some impending wrathful visitation, and learned to my sorrow that I was only exchanging one bitter cup for another. As the opium-influence never approximated the authority of a fascination over me, I willingly and finally abjured it as an impossible relief.

It was some time after this that my constitution, broken down by hard work, which, corporeally, to use an intensely idiomatic term, was much more "cruel on me" than hasheesh had been at its most nerve-racking stages, demanded not only rest, but something immediately tonic. The former was easily attained by closing my connection with the educational "Knight of the Rueful Countenance" -- a connection which all the while had not been chemical, like that of an acid with a base, but mechanical, like that of a force with a lever. The latter (the tonic) was to be found ultimately in exercise; but, for the sake of more instantaneous relief from debility, at the advice of a physician, I had recourse to spirits. A very short trial of their effect having convinced me that their stimulus was as dangerous as opium, I abandoned this also as a means of relief. The experiment made with it renewed, sometimes for two days together, the clarity, though not the exquisite beauty of the hasheesh visionary state, and repeated, in due succession, its ideal sufferings of night and daylight.

Thus taught that every possible stimulus of any power must invariably act as auxiliary to the partially routed forces of my foe, I called in no more treacherous helps from without, but went single-handed to the fight, armed only with patience and friendly sympathies.

Since learning this lesson, the progress into recovery has been by slow degrees, yet a progress after all. Ever and anon a return of the former suffering has made it necessary to spend half the night in walking; but the sense that every step forward was also a step, however infinitesimal, upward, is a greater relief than the possibility of once more journeying through the rosiest realms of the former hasheesh happiness. At least for the present -- as a proviso to the proposition let this be added -- for he who has once looked upon great glories can not but hope to behold them again, when nature is freed from all the grossness which makes them painful in the present state, and they shall come to him, not through walls which they must melt to make a passage-way, but like the sunlight, which, falling joyously and harmlessly, bathes the forehead of the little child asleep.

NOTES ON THE WAY UPWARD.

It is the author of "The Golden Dagon," one of our most original and interesting American books of travel, who gives to Boodh, as the deity of eternal absorption, the most appropriate title with which he has ever, to my knowledge, been glorified. He calls him "The Stagnant Calm." As I read it, such peculiar relevancy did this title seem to hold to one part of my own experience, that, but for occasional twinges of remaining humanity, remembered as having afflicted me about that time, I should have yielded to the conviction that I had myself then been an incarnation of Boodh. Hitherto my narrative has been of spell and counter-spell; of ecstasies bought on this side of Acheron, where the market was low, and paid for on the other side, where the rate of exchange is diabolic; of the checkered days of indulgence, and the one starless night of abandonment. It was during this latter period that the Boodhist state occurred. For many a month before I had been bathed in the springs of a fiery activity. I had lived in ether. Every sense had been worked at its highest power, the sense of the body, and the unspeakably more energetic sense of the imagination.

Now the exalting agency was removed. I have said how I suffered, affirmatively, from its lack in preternatural nightmares, in disgust at what seemed to me the lifeless forms of the outer world, in countless modes of pain and weariness, whose detail would be only less disagreeable to my reader than originally grievous to me. Far be it from me to recount these things again; indeed, for the past I have sometimes feared that I owed an apology, and might be expected to say, with him who had reduced courtliness to a science, "Pardon me, gentlemen, that I am so long in dying."

But, negatively, as the months of trial went on, I came into a state which, had it been pain, would have made me fear less for myself. Gradually, after having for a long time known what it was to say, "Now I am perfectly wretched," occurred seasons whose intervals constantly lessened when I said, "Now I am totally null." It was not happiness any more than the rolling of a ball is sustained motion; like it, I went on mechanically by the not utterly extinct momentum of a removed force.

This force, too, was an hourly retarded one. There was constantly less and less hope, less volition, less interest, and the only offset to this negation was the opposite negation of disagreeable emotions. I did not despair, because there seemed nothing to despair of.

What should I do? Often (for this state of non-entity was only occasional as yet) I was visited by stern self-reprovings, admonitions to bestir myself spiritually as well as mechanically, threatenings of a final absorption into utter listlessness unless I resorted to some immediate means for quickening the pulses of thought and action.

Good people told me to sleep; Nature was reading me a lesson upon the curative properties of quiet. Good people, I could not sleep. I should never wake up again. Moreover, I attended another church of Nature's, where the lesson for the day was, "He that will not work, neither let him eat;" and the margin was illuminated, not with cherubs like Raphael's, who have nothing to do except to rest their chins upon their palms, but with certain others, sitting in rows upon a bench, diversifying their hopeless stare at the topmost pippins of the tree of knowledge by the furtive conveyance, from pocket to pocket, of a baser variety of apple, smuggled into school for the stay and consolation of the outer man which perisheth with the using.

This being the exact state of things until I left behind me, with my fulfilled responsibilities, that portentous and uncomfortable ghost, in whom my previous relations had forced me to behold Duty most eccentrically making herself incarnate, there were strong reasons for activity, besides its necessity as an energy of existence. In dissolving my connection with the portent, the latter reason still remained, and the question was how to satisfy it.

There was no further possibility of seeking activity in a research through supernatural passages. Stimulus had been abjured; the accumulation of mental facts, to serve as food for wonder, under its influence, was finished. Reason, Right, Well, all asserted this. There remained for me but one expedient.

This was to take the facts already secured, and discover, if possible, their meaning, their relations to each other; to crystallize them around the axis of some hypothesis, and determine what they taught of the operations of their source, the mind.

It was in this way that I kept up the vital heat of thought for months, and battled against an all-benumbing lethargy. The results of this practice I now go on to give, without any pretension to group them into a system; not only lack of time, but of a sufficiently broad basis of experiment having prevented that. If I shall seem to have fixed the comparative positions of even a few outposts of a strange and rarely-visited realm, I shall think myself happy. To travel farther into the interior, even for the sake of science, would have required a heroism wearing the guise, as looked at in different directions, of the martyr or the suicide. Of the first of these titles I did not hold myself worthy, nor of the last desirous.

How far hasheesh throws light upon the most interior of the mental arcana is a question which will be dogmatically decided in two diametrically opposite ways. The man who believes in nothing which does not, in some way, become tangent to his bodily organs will instinctively withdraw himself into the fortress of what he supposes to be antique common sense, and cry "madman!" from within. He will reject all of experience under stimulus, and the facts which it has professedly evolved as truth, with the final and unanswerable verdict of insanity.

There is another class of men which has its type in him who, while acknowledging the corporeal senses as very important in the present nutriment and muniment of our being, is convinced that they give him appearances alone; not things as they are in their essence and their law, classified harmoniously with reference to their source, but only as they affect him through the different adits of the body. This man will be prone to believe that Mind, in its prerogative of the only self-conscious being in the universe, has the right and the capacity to turn inward to itself for an answer to the puzzling enigmas of the world. Mind, infinite Mind, to be sure, created them and must have known their law; as an inference, Mind, though finite, may still interrogate its own phenomena for the reasons of outer existences which, however grand, are far less majestic than itself, and may obtain a clew proportionally perfect.

Arguing thus, the man, albeit a visionary, will recognize the possibility of discovering from mind, in some of its extraordinarily awakened states, a truth, or a collection of truths, which do not become manifest in his every-day condition. From this man, a few such pages as these may hope for a candid reading, if not for total assent.

Nor am I anxious to repel the charge of insanity which may be brought against the facts evolved by a hasheesh delirium. Indeed, the exaltation, in this narrative, has been repeatedly called an insanity. I only wish to be understood as believing that into some subjects the insane man can look farther than the sane. Let not idiocy here be confounded with insanity. The former is the extinction of all faculties; the latter, the extraordinary development of one faculty or a group of faculties, while the others lie comparatively dormant.

In the same way, therefore, that the characteristics of the plant are sought, not in the microscopic filaments and tissues of the germ (although they truly exist there), but in the expanded individual of the species, we may, more legitimately and with much better hope of success, search out the law of a given mental organ in its unusually than its usually developed state.

Labyrinths and Guiding Threads.

Gentle reader -- not to make this one of my speculations more labyrinthine than nature, for I hate unnatural mysteries -- I will not, after the manner of an oracle, leave my title undefined until the sequel, but will here tell thee that the "labyrinths" are our bodily senses through which the outer world wanders in to commune with the soul. For a little while let us wander in together after the manner of the world, and if the clew of my speculation bring us not to the penetralia as surely as that of Ariadne, we may at least promise ourselves a safe-conduct out again. Let us try to discover the kind of communion which the world and the soul are holding together, and the manner in which they hold it.

Long before I had known hasheesh, and walked its weird uplands in pursuit of the secrets of mind, a revelation flashed upon me which, by its powers of amazement and perplexity, made the time and place of its occurrence forever memorial within me. It was a revelation in the same way that lightning is a revelation, clear in itself, yet showing hitherto unknown hills of unbroken midnight in the distance. While yet a mere boy, I was standing one afternoon by the side of two thinkers who talked metaphysics without taking me into their counsels, for they had no thought of my busying myself with any thing but the outside of nature as I met her laughing in my rambles.

"Yes, it is beyond dispute that our senses give us only appearances and not things -- certain qualities of the essence, not the essence out of which they rise."

In these words there was nothing to frighten a mind of ordinarily reflective habits; no barricade of "subjective" and "objective," or any thing else technical which I had not yet learned to scale. I was smitten with a sudden interest; I did not perfectly appreciate the meaning of the sentence, but wandered to a little distance to sit down and think it over till I had made it mine. There was a meaning there which held out the strongest fascinations to discovery.

"Our senses give us only appearances, qualities, and not things." Perhaps, thought I, this is only a sophism hurled down as a sort of challenge for argument. These metaphysicians love to argue.

Of course, I did not have to look far for a test. I was leaning against a tree, and Sense, in the support given me by its trunk, seemed to be triumphantly asserting her acquaintance with things -- stanch and stout things at that.

But hold! I said to myself; what do I find out in leaning here, which makes me think that I have found a thing? Why, resistance, hardness, to be sure. And it is a fact, these are qualities only. But this is nothing but feeling; let me try the senses of smell and taste. By applying nose and tongue to the tree, I perceived a fresh woody savor -- quality still! I put my ear to the tree and struck it: still nothing but quality resulted, the capability to beget sound. I began to be alarmed for the dignity of the Sense, as I saw her chance of proving herself worthy of my past consideration narrowed down to one single organ -- the eye. Alas for her! Quality still -- a brown tint, a faculty of transmitting certain rays of light, and absorbing others. It seems strange now, but it is true that, with my knife, I began blazing the side of the tree, with a sort of fond flattery of the Sense that, though the qualities lay in the bark, "the thing" was to be detected lurking underneath. In a moment, however, I laughed perplexedly, realizing that I could make the matter no better if I hacked the tree through.

Here ended my first lesson upon the domain of the senses. I know that this incident in itself can claim no such interest as to make it part of an experience which one man, without obtrusiveness, may press upon another's ear; but I have related it, believing that it may recall to some reader here and there the circumstances under which he made the same discovery. Still further, I mention it, since it may be a sort of common ground of sympathy between author and reader, upon which will be better understood something which I wish to say upon the philosophic sufferings of a great mind which it is our duty to appreciate as well as (and indeed in order to) pity.

David Hume, after having been fêted, buried, and reviewed, has been quietly laid upon the shelf by many serious men of the present century, in that especial niche devoted to "celebrated infidels." According to our different acceptance of the term, this verdict will be just or unjust. If just, a careful and discriminating generation ought to manifest their coincidence with it by permitting him to lie under the index of obloquy. If unjust, the sentence will, sooner or later, infallibly be reversed, and whatever light, however slight a pencil any man possesses for the illustration of the matter, is due no less to truth than to the shade of a philosopher.

Infidelity properly classifies itself under two divisions -- infidelity of the heart and infidelity of the intellect. The first of these is a malignant displeasure at truth for the obligations which it imposes upon life. It begins in a powerfully-felt repulsion between righteousness and the selfish will; it sometimes goes avowedly no farther, but leaves a man unjust, licentious, and in all respects, where the prudence of selfishness does not itself curb him, totally iniquitous.

In the case, however, of those who have carried on the offensive warfare of infidelity, one step farther has been taken, an utter and public rejection, namely, of the claims of truth upon self-interest. With this step has been conferred the degree, if I may so speak, of Grand Master of the Order of Heart Infidelity. It is not necessary that the man thus advanced should be pre-eminent, even above believers, in the prodigal gratification of passion and interest; temperament, society, a multiplicity of circumstances may serve as steering oars to his course, but circumstances only will direct him. The impelling force to any imaginable excess is present with him, and the certain compass of a felt obligation is gone. According to circumstances, he will go large before the wind with the graceful curvetings of a Bolingbroke, or stagger in a drunken sea like Paine.

The infidelity of the intellect is an entirely different thing. It arises, not from a hatred, but from an incorrect apprehension of truth.

When we remember how fundamental a part of human nature it is to systematize the dicta both of the written and the unwritten revelations, to build up the fragmentary formulas which express the manifold relations of our being into something like an orderly edifice, we must wonder, not so much that error infallibly vitiates to an extent more or less fatal some part of the workmanship, as that any structure so far resists gravity as not to tumble down. Not that this imperfection is to be ascribed to the habit of systematizing, but to the fact that it is human nature which systematizes — human nature, which never in any one age sweeps all truth in a comprehensive view and realizes at once the tendencies of opinions, but of necessity looks at half truths through a distorting medium, and sees only the present result of speculations. A corner-stone laid awry, some premise whose falsity is unnoticed because it has the sanction of antique opinion, may render the whole superstructure out of line and unstable, although it be reared by the most cautious workmen with unsparing scrutiny of square and plummet. In a former century, while men were contented merely with the foundation walls of a system, it mattered little whether every block was laid with perfect accuracy; there was as yet no edifice to be affected in its permanency by the error of the ground-work. But when, in the course of time, "other men builded thereon," accepting it with perfect faith as the careful structure of a master whose name was spoken reverently among men, what wonder that they pointed afterward to the marks of considerateness and caution with which they had built up their secondary walls of inference into a philosophy, as a proof that they must necessarily be stable and faultless, however much some of their compeers doubted it, though refusing to acknowledge any fault in the foundation?

The infidels of intellect have as often resulted from arguing logically upon some falsehood, hitherto universally accepted as a truism, as from any distortion of real truths of sophistical deductions from good grounds. That, if Hume was an infidel, he became one thus, we think it easy to show. Almost as easy is it to prove that, properly speaking, he was not an infidel at all.

As a central point for the consideration of Hume's infidelity, let us take the year 1746, the year in which he stood candidate for the Edinburgh chair of Moral Philosophy, and by the vote of the authorities (no doubt with the most perfect propriety) was defeated on account of his views of religion. Against the action which excluded him from a professorship so rigorously demanding an incumbent of Spartan principles upon the subject which was to be his speciality, certainly no thinking man can have aught to say. The fact of the exclusion is mentioned merely for the sake of determining some date when his bias was generally recognized among the people, who had treated with such neglect his "Treatise on Human Nature," published nine years before. In 1746, then, he had reaped the title of infidel.

For at least half a century previous, the speculative mind of the greater part of Europe (dynamically as well as numerically greater) had been under the dominion of John Locke, whose "Essay upon the Human Understanding" had been brought to light in 1690. It is perhaps rather an insincere compliment to speak of any mind as "speculative" which expatiated merely within his prescribed area. The system which bore his name is too well known to ask a statement, especially within these limits. Its parent he could hardly be called; certainly not with any more justice than we could ascribe to the man who casually remarks that it is a cloudy day the parentage of that meteorological phenomenon. His system consists mainly in the discovery that people generally get such and such ideas about their thinking faculty; that the said people have pretty nearly hit the nail on the head, and that he is glad to tell them so; all authenticated by John Locke, his mark. The majority of mankind attend to the knowledge secured through their bodily organs more closely than to any other; they elaborate truth by thinking upon this knowledge; and thus all truth comes to us through the organs, modified to a greater or less extent by reflection. In fine, sense, and reflection on its data, the sources of all knowledge, form the governing principle, the "articulum stantis aut cadentis ecclesiæ" of the Lockian philosophy.

Into this philosophy Hume, like all the other contemporary minds of his nation, was born as regularly as into the monarchical form of government. It was the nursery of his childhood and the school of his youth; his mind, when it wanted exercise, must run out and play in John Locke's small back yard, or not stretch its limbs at all.

Now there came a time when David Hume arrived at the very same point of speculation which I have previously mentioned as reached, on my supposition, by most of us who think. Let us see how he reasoned. Suppose him in soliloquy:

"I find that my senses give me nothing but the phenomena of things -- tell me merely how objects act upon me. My eye acquaints me with color and outline; my ear with vibrations of diverse intensities; and so on with all the rest of the organs. All give qualities of things, operations which things have a capability to perform on me, appearances of things, but never things themselves. How do I know that they do not? By reflection, certainly; reflection on the data afforded by sense. But why do we all believe, and act upon the belief, that we see, hear, feel, smell, and taste things? It must no doubt be sense that tells us so; that is the only conjoint source of knowledge with reflection. Then I have within me, and so has every one else, two exactly opposite verdicts. I do know things, and I do not know them. Now which is the lie?"

Hume did not decide. He did not pretend to stand arbiter between these two conflicting juries, which Locke fifty years before had impanneled to settle infallibly, and without appeal, all the questions of human science. He only hung in perfect equipoise between the reality and the nonentity of all being, himself necessarily included. He became, as a strictly logical consequence of that teaching which he had drunk with his mother's milk, and which he would have rejected as much in peril of being called an unnatural son by all his contemporaries, a Pyrrhonist, a universal doubter. And who, in the name of all candor, was the parent of his Pyrrhonism? Who but John Locke, who, while a believer himself, because he did not bowl far enough in his own direction, had nevertheless opened up an easy track to the most comprehensive system of skepticism in the universe.

There may be those who will think that we have made out no better case for Hume by proving him a skeptic than an infidel. What difference exists, they ask, between doubting and disbelieving? Every possible difference. Belief and unbelief are often wrongly taken as antipodes merely on account of their antagonistic sound, and doubting is often confounded with the latter. Unbelief is, in fact, the same mental act as belief, directed by evidence or passion to a different set of statements. Doubt recognizes an equiponderance of evidence, or a total lack of evidence on both sides. Now the impulses of hate, pride, and a thousand others may bear a man's belief one way or another, and so vitiate the sincerity of a judgment which ought to found itself calmly on proof. Doubt, where it is real, can never be thus produced by impulse. To sit upon the exact centre of the beam, it must be calm. Therefore, so far as any man is a sincere skeptic, so far is he proved guiltless of the charge of hostility to either side.

I do not assert this perfect calm for Hume. In the present imperfect condition of humanity we act so universally from intricately mixed motives, that it would not be safe to assert a purely ideal sincerity for any one. Doubtless Hume was influenced in the after maintenance of his Pyrrhonist principles by many of those partisan considerations which weigh with us all. But in the first susception of his doubt, acting, as he did, upon the every-where acknowledged basis that Locke was right, no man could have been more logical, more calmly, philosophically sincere. Ratiocination, and not hostility to religion, was the original cause of his skepticism.

It is particularly unfortunate for a man when he is thrown into the society of those who, by flattering that in him which his better nature feels to be a blemish and a disadvantage, if not a crime, lull his pain at its existence, and even persuade him to believe that it is his honor. We have to observe an exemplification of such misfortune in Hume, who, but for being lauded and fêted as the Coryphæus of infidels, for whom he felt no cordial attraction, might have outlived his skepticism through draughts of a better philosophy, or, at least, have kept it to himself as his most mournful secret.

Allowing himself to be applauded as the infidel which he was not, he fortified within himself the skeptic which he was; but that he never made a whole-hearted consecration of himself, as some would misrepresent him, to the cause of a malignant and offensive unbelief, is evident from many facts in its history; such, for instance was his indignant rebuff of the pert wife of the atheist Mallet, who took the liberty of introducing herself to him at a soirée: "We free-thinkers ought to know each other, Mr. Hume." "I am no free-thinker, madam;" and, turning on his heel, he strode angrily away.

There is a letter of his, also, which I only quote from memory, in which he exhibits the man he would have been if left alone, declaring that he never sat down to a game of chess with a friend, and thus threw off his logical panoply, without feeling his doubts vanish and the reality of things return. Yet this very letter has been quoted in evidence of his insincerity, because, it is said, he was forced to reason that he might support his doubts. But what if reasoning infallibly sustained them? Was he to trust in Hume playing chess or in Hume reasoning?

By his unnatural conjunction with infidels, he subjected himself to bear the obloquy of their praise. By their praise, an antagonist spirit of denunciation was excited in the society of believers. Denounced, he must reply, for the sake of his pride and his partisans. And thus, from the sincerely perplexed doubter, he came to be considered, and in a certain, though a far less degree to be, the sneering foe of Christianity.

I have dwelt thus long upon Hume and the circumstances which have tended to give him his present reputation, and to set upon the stamp of an odium in many respects unjust, because he is an example not less striking than painful of the evil which may be wrought for a man by some unnoticed error in his mental philosophy. How easily an error which is the germ of all things hurtful may escape the notice of men who accept without examining, can be seen from the fact that the good John Locke (for he was good) was never advised of the skeptical inference from his doctrine, but died as perfectly satisfied with it as he had lived.

Most gratefully do I remember that, at the time of my first discovery of the legitimate domain of the senses, I was not left, like many others in similar case, and Hume as the representative of them all, to retreat hopelessly into a negation of all knowledge.

It is the privilege and the glory of this day that its dominant philosophy is Transcendental. Much as this word, like its kindred visionary, is in the mouth of hawkers of theological small ware -- much as it has been applied, by a perversion, to all systems of error and nonsense -- much as it has been branded for a stigma upon the forehead of thinkers who would not travel in a go-cart, the idea which it represents has been the regeneration of speculative philosophy. The Transcendentalists are, indeed, climbers over, as their name signifies, yet not over sound reasoning nor the definite principles of truth, but over that ring-fence of knowledge brought in through mere physical passages, with which a tyrannous oligarchy of reasoners would circumscribe all our wanderings in search of facts and laws.

Older than its oldest historic supporting names, Transcendentalism still found champions in the more enfranchised minds of Greece, and from them we come per saltum to its German champions of the latter half of the last, and the elapsed half of the present century. Kant, awakened, as there is some reason to think, by the very perplexity which set boundaries to the mind of Hume, stands forth as the resurrectionist of the long-buried idea, and is followed, with more or less nonessential departure from his main track, by Fichte, Hegel, and Schelling; for, although the first of the trio may be styled a pure idealist, he follows Kant pre-eminently in the assertion of far higher grounds of knowledge than the sense. It is complained that these men, and chief of all Kant, are unintelligible; that their phraseology is cumbrous and obscure. It is not difficult, however, for any mind in charity with the direction of their efforts to see abundant reason why it should be so.

In the first place, while their language (when they did not write in Latin, and when they did their German modes of thought still went with them) is the most plastic in the world to all the moulds of mind, while it admits of endless word-compounding to give roundness or definiteness to ideas, still, from this very fact, it tends toward obscurity, for the reason that the compounds so lengthen a sentence as to make it very difficult to carry the meaning from beginning to end.

In the second place, it is to be remembered that the ideas which these men had to communicate were to a great extent new -- new even to one who looked at them fragmentarily -- new particularly in their combinations as a system. They who set them forth were the pioneers of Transcendentalism; they had nothing ready to their hand, nothing open or clear; and the first entrance into a territory is always of necessity by a rugged path; it is for those who enter into their labors, who come in upon the ground which they have opened, to attend to grading the causeway. First the military road, after that the turnpike. As well may we quarrel with Captain John Smith for not laying a railway through the forests of Virginia, as with Kant for not smoothing the passage into a philosophy through which he was the first traveler. It was enough for him that he had grappled with great ideas and fixed them; let his successors attend to polishing their surface.

Third, it has been put out of sight by the prevalence of a philosophy which calls itself that of common sense, but is much worthier of being named that of commonplace, that metaphysics is as true and distinct a science as chemistry, with its own peculiar and inalienable ideas, and in virtue of that prerogative demands, both as necessity and right, symbols to express its ideas which shall be its own exclusive property. Let the phrases of distinction, "objective" and "subjective," be an example. "Objective" is everything which, in the processes of mind, is not myself, but extraneous to me; "subjective," all that is myself and my own individual part of the operation. Now the sense philosophy could have no possible use for any such words as these, since it recognizes nothing but a paper distinction between a man and his objects for all purposes of perception, all his knowledge being gained through sense, and flowing into him as its passive receptacle. So sense philosophy sneers at such technical phraseology as pedantic. But, supposing it capable of requiring some symbols for such ideas, it would most likely adopt "outward" and "inward." For speculations, or rather assertions, so little analytic and accurate as its own, these might do well enough; but how inert, how useless, how vague would they be where any subtle mental fact was to be definitely expressed. We wish to give the idea of the mind as examined by itself. Transcendentalists call this treating the mind "objectively." Our sense men would be compelled to say, treating it "outwardly." How definite would be the idea conveyed in that!

When we complain of the sailor for speaking of his masts as spars, instead of calling them sticks, to meet the comprehension of some land-lubber who will not take the pains to learn practical navigation -- when the chemist is sneered at for saying crucible instead of pot -- when, in fine, public opinion shall compel all men to talk of the delicacies of their arts in street slang or boudoir twaddle, then, and not till then, will it be time to deride the science, wherein, more than all others, rigorous exactitude of expression is required, for having a peculiar, even though it be not a universally intelligible language. This talk about the pedantry of metaphysics is something which the age should be ashamed of as behind it, yet even now we occasionally light upon some reviewer who, in strains of touching pathos, laments to the public that he finds it impossible to read Hickok's Rational Psychology to his wife of an evening on account of the doctor's pedantic technicality, which makes him a sealed book even to that gifted woman.

In general, it is safe to lay down this proposition as a rule: first look cursorily over a book upon Mind, to see whether its general character for neatness and system proves that its author is neither fool nor sloven; and then, reading it through carefully and with candor, you will find that in proportion to its technicality is it the repository of new and deeper truths. This, of course, is to be understood of those books on Mind which, according to De Quincey's division in his critique on Pope, belong to the literature of knowledge, and not the literature of power. The same habit of mental indolence, which is loosening the cords of our American literature -- the loving such books as read themselves to us while we lie half asleep on a sofa; the greed for dainties which may be swallowed whole, and which tickle at a moment's warning -- this habit it is which has deprived of nine tenths of his legitimate number of readers such a man, for instance, as Hickok. Almost the only real metaphysician of America, perhaps the greatest now living any where, and worthy to be classed with the strongest and deepest thinkers of any age or land, he has, in his own country, about as many intelligent and appreciative readers as Pythagoras had of esoteric disciples. There is reason to fear that men love better to investigate how muslins, hay-rakes, and, above all and inclusive of all, money may be made, than how their own minds are constructed.

One might almost be content to leave them and their preference alone, on the ground that they are the best judges of the respective value of their own several commodities.

Great reason have I to be thankful, again I say, that I was suckled at the breast of Transcendentalism. I am doubtless not without sympathy in others when I say that the first moment when it flashed upon me how in the Reason might be found the laws and the essences of things, and that we were not confined for our knowledge to the mere ungrouped and unsettled appearances of the Sense, was like a revelation; it expanded and dignified the soul with a sudden access of glories such as no earthly kingship could give. At that moment spirit appeared to me for the first time something more than the hopeless bond-slave of matter. For the sake of experiencing that feeling again in its full force of grand joyousness, I would like to exchange places with Locke, at the instant of his disembodiment, when he found out that he was mistaken. In having gone astray as a philosopher, he suddenly had all the more glorious surprise as a soul.

There was one question, however, which for a long time troubled me, but to which I at length got a satisfactory, although, perhaps, most men may disagree with me in the belief that it is a true answer. This is the question, How does the outer world ever become apparent to the spirit? I could see very easily how in the Reason the law conditioning an outer world might be found, but how did the appearances themselves become known? The manner of intercourse between matter and matter, between spirit and spirit, or between any two individualities of the same kind, was plain enough, or at least such an intercourse was reasonable. But with our views of matter and spirit, two existences in their very essence utterly dissimilar, how could they ever become tangent?

Take, for instance, such a case as this: I am hit by a stone. The thrill conveyed along its appropriate nerve runs up the brain, and here we trace its ultimate footprint on the material organism. Yet an infinitesimal instant more, and my mind has learned it, is moved to anger, and reasons for revenge or remedy. I could not see the connection by which the fact of the blow, however refined by its passage, was prolonged from matter into spirit. The books said that, on reaching the brain, the fact became a tertium quid, a third something, neither matter nor spirit, but so etherealized that the mind could read it. What, however, was that tertium quid?

In the process of time, and by the aid of that ever to be blessed Transcendentalism which had helped me out of my earliest perplexity, I came to the conclusion that the tertium quid was a humbug, a metaphysical Mrs. Harris, upon whom the responsibility of all things impossible to be done or conceived was laid by psychological Mistresses Gamp. The answer which satisfied me was this: that there are only two kinds or modes of existence in the universe -- the one, self-conscious spirit; the other, the acts of such spirit. From these data arose such a theory of the universe as the following:

The Supreme Being, as Creator of all things, is ever in activity, according to certain eternal and universal laws of right and truth. Whatever else of self-conscious Being exists, came forth originally as an efflux from him, but is now in its will, though not for the continuance of its separate existence, independent of his direct action. As spirit, man is capable of communion with the supreme spirit. Since, however, spirit itself is in its very essence imperceptible to senses, the communion makes itself perceptible by appearances. These appearances, whose cause we call "matter," are therefore, in reality, but the effects of spirit's action upon spirit. In no sense, then, does any such thing as dead matter exist. It is God's thinking felt by us.

If it shall be said that there is no difference between this and Pantheism, let me be allowed to show how the two systems differ toto coelo. I do not assert that matter is God. I say that the actor is God, and the effects of his action upon other spirit, which we call matter, are neither God, nor in any sense self-conscious. To make it clear, let my reader suppose himself striking a blow. He here appears as the self-conscious actor; yet how great an absurdity would it appear to him to call the blow itself after his name, or to attribute self-consciousness to it. He would say, The act of striking is an abstract idea, to which the other idea of self-consciousness can not be pertinent.

To carry out the parallel for further illustration, let us suppose this blow to fall upon the cheek of a bystander. The man struck would gain, from the effect produced on him, a pretty correct idea of the state of the striker's feeling, notwithstanding he did not suppose that the blow was the striker, nor that it thought for itself.

Similarly in kind, let us suppose that the Deity is forever acting out through all the universe the principles of his infinite and righteous mind. By the effects of this action he becomes known to his spiritual creatures, and in reality manifests the state of his mind toward them. By such action, in its effect upon us known as matter, he attains the only incarnation of himself for reciprocal communion which could make him known.

I have said that this resolution of the problem of the Universe is the only one which ever satisfied me. The deductions which I made from it served to keep my own activity alive through many a day of suffering; and thus from it, in its satisfaction and its energizing, I received a double good. I will state some of the deductions.

Let me be permitted, for the sake of consonance with my theory, to speak, where accuracy is wanted, of matter, known in this light as the effect of the divine action, under the name of Force. I do not employ it in its mere mechanical sense, but as expressive of the manner of communion between two spiritual beings, to an extent metaphorically meaning something analogous to what in matter would be called the result of impingement.

1. In our bodily organism is one of the most cogent proofs of the Supreme good-will toward us. By his own act he has insphered us within a force, the body, which not only resists many other forces and preserves its own integrity, but, what is of much greater importance, modifies our reception of knowledge from without, and blunts the acuteness of our action within to such an extent that truth does not come to us with a fatal shock, but gradually and softened, until we are able to bear it. Viewed as a counteractive force, the body is thus one of the highest proofs of God's benignity, since, left in our present state of spiritual infancy without it, no lidless eyeball beneath a noonday sun might be more agonized. It is as much cause for thanksgiving as for aspiration to something clearer, that we now "see through a glass darkly." Let us not repine, for there is a reason in these half opaque and tinged panes. A sun as consuming as he is wondrously glorious is shining just outside.

2. We may here find a further illustration of that which in the previous pages has been said of the symbolization, by every existence of the world, of some spiritual fact. The incarnation is as the essence; the universe is as it is because God lives as he lives. He is making himself felt in the effects of his communion with us.

A thousand times in the year do we hear it said that every plant is an evidence of God's goodness; yet how much more amply, more nobly is this true than men generally suppose! Whatever of horror or deformity exists in the unconscious creation, is but the manifestation of Creative displeasure at our wrong; whatever of beauty (and how prodigally it is spread abroad!) is a testimony, rich with meaning, of that benevolence which mixes its displeasure with pity, and the return of wondrous good for an evil which is only less boundless. The continuance of Niagara, with its wealth of ennobling influences, is as speaking a proof to every man of God's good feeling to him as the continuance of his life. In the millennium to which men are looking forward, how easily conceivable is it that by the literal fulfillment of our grandest prophecies and hopes; that an unblemished scenery, an illimitable luxuriance of greenness in the fields, an inspiration of beauty by every visible thing, may be the exponent of the gladness in the Great Heart above us at the restoration into perfectness of his filial race.

But our philosophy does not limit us to an analytic gaze upon the earth alone. The firmament, from our eyes onward in all directions forever, is full of stars. Some of these, perhaps all of them, there is reason to believe are peopled; but, granting that they roll on in utter loneliness, what of that? They are there, and as they are, because God is acting grandly, wisely, and righteously, and that it is all-satisfying to know. Even now they teach us lessons nightly, speaking both of Beauty and Truth. But what if they may be, also, carrying on their far-off orbits some incarnation of an attribute of God, which in our present state, we are not sufficiently strong to bear?

It is the characteristic of the written revelation to be comprehensive. Doubtless all of God is there in the germ; yet how many a line is drawn purposely in deep shadow! We are not ready for it yet.

The natural revelation, the universe, is in itself as comprehensive; but, since we can never see it all at once, to us it must necessarily be fragmentary. Thus we now have Earth to read from; yet when we are disembodied and purified — when the incarnation through which the Divine is to come to us may with safety be made less gross than its form in the present matter, we shall learn through the stars, which have been kept waiting for us, sublimer and still sublimer truths of spirit throughout an ascending life.

Well may the man who, while his utmost gaze now catches them only as gleaming points, yet rejoices in the assurance of their significant harmony, break forth,

"O yet uninterrupted symbols, from afar I hail you as the promise of a truth which it is for Immortality to drink in! Beautiful, strange, yet not inexplicable; even now are ye beaming links of that chain which binds me to Deity; ye shall hereafter draw me close to his presence in a grander communion. Await me brightly while I calmly long for you."

In the closest circle of earthly fellowship wherein I have known what it is for heart to be knit with heart, it has ever been the beautiful custom to write the dead, who, though absent, were still one with the living brotherhood, under this title,

"Qui fuerunt, sed nunc ad astra."
How grand a meaning may there be in this!

3. Upon the ground that all knowledge through sense may be resolved into the idea of force, there are some reasons for supposing that this force may in itself be simple, and only varied by its approach to the soul through the differently modifying organs. In fine, that sight, hearing, touch, taste, and smell may be effects, to speak after the common nomenclature, of the same object, or one grand effect divided into several by transmission.

An inspection of the analogies of science must convince us that this proposition, if not à priori necessarily true, is, at any rate, extremely probable. The progress of philosophical research is invariably from the complex to the simple. The myriad phenomena of chemistry are all traceable to the action and reaction in various combinations of a very limited number of elements; these elements are still farther resolvable in their composition into still fewer and more ethereal bodies. In the same way, all the mechanical operations are due to differing applications of six motors; and these, by still further analysis, arrange themselves under the head of physical force. These are but two instances out of the multitude which prove the great law of simplification by research.

234

In many a field of inquiry the philosopher has reduced the agents effective for a given result to two or three; the next step would bring him to the all-comprehensive unity; but no, that step can not be taken, for nature here so suddenly subtilizes the springs of her activity, that she may float just before the face of her hierophant, and laugh invisibly at baffled microscope and hypothesis. Yet enough is known in all departments of investigation to prove that the tendency of discovery is invariably from the vast periphery of facts inward to one single central law.

Yet let us not leave the theory of the all-comprehensive oneness of sense to base its plausibility upon a general analogy. We are able to particularize. What reason, then, have we, from known facts, to suppose all the senses directly referable to force? A brief analysis will discover most of the evidence we have.

And, 1st. Touch, simply considered as the organ for determining the hardness, weight, and form of bodies. The two former will be seen to be directly resolvable into force, viz., the force of resistance, in the one case particularized as cohesion, in the other as gravitation. The distinction of form may be also comprehended as an idea of force by the following statement. I move my hand in all directions in the plane of the horizon, and, finding it every where resisted by an equal force from below, say, "This is a flat surface."

The resistance, in another instance, occurs in a different direction, and I express this fact by saying sphere, cone, ellipsoid, etc., as the case may be.

2d. Sight. It is, no doubt, well known to many of my readers that, in modern times, two theories have obtained upon the action of light, or, more properly, its origination. Both of them arose or were resuscitated from antiquity in the seventeenth century, but that which bears the name of Huygens is by a few years the earlier. This philosopher held that all luminous bodies are in a state of almost infinitely rapid, though infinitesimally small vibration; that this vibration propagates itself in all directions with an undulatory motion through an exceedingly subtle and elastic fluid, known as ether, which fills all space; that these undulations, impinging against any material body, bound back, or, in usual parlance, are reflected to the eye, and, striking upon the retina, give through the optic nerve, of which it is an expansion, the sensation of sight.

The second theory is that of Newton, who supposed that luminous bodies are continually giving off infinitesimal radiant particles, which, through the ethereal medium, impinge upon the eye in the same manner and with the same effect as the light-waves of Huygens' theory.

The former hypothesis (viz., Huygens') is that at this day entertained by the majority of savans, but the discovered laws of optics accord equally well with either. No further dissertation is necessary to show that in either case the conception of sight is resolvable into the idea of a perceived force.

3d. Hearing. Upon this sense there is certainly no need of enlarging, it being universally known that sound is the offspring of vibration, and therefore a force, subject in its transmission, reflection, etc., to laws precisely analogous to those of light, modified merely by the nature of the medium, viz., air or grosser bodies, through which it travels, in contradistinction to the infinitely subtle ether which propagates light. There is, however, one analogy upon which we may dwell for a short time, which would seem greatly to strengthen the general theory that all sensations are, in their essential agency, one.

The relationship between light and sound does not terminate in the fact, of itself sufficiently striking, that they both obey similar conditions of transmission and reflection. True, they each pass to the human organ, not by one unbroken leap, but by a series of waves. Literally, lightning no more darts upon the eye than the faintest beam of dawn; thunder comes undulating to the ear as truly as the softest sigh; and the light cast upon us from a mirror is only an echo through ether instead of air.

But there is a far more intricate affiliation between them. In the very possibilities of their existence they are the same. Every ray of light can be comprehended within the range of seven radical colors and the combinations of them. This law of but seven possible colors is not an accident, but a primeval and necessary accompaniment of the manner of transmission.

Every possible sound likewise lies between the two termini of a gamut whose number of root sounds is seven, and this septenary law of sound is as necessary as that of light.

The universality with which these laws are practically known by means of the prism and the octave, take off, as is the case in so many other habitual mysteries, the edge of our legitimate wonder. Yet when, for a moment, we reflect calmly upon the fact that we may analyze light of any possible kind with the most rigid scrutiny without adding a single principal color to a fixed range of seven; that we may utter any conceivable sound without escaping from the same mystic boundaries; that in both cases our only changes must be rung by reduplication or blending within those adamantine gamut walls; when we reflect, I say, on these two truths, each fit food in itself for wonder, and find that in fact they are but one truth, and that a characteristic of sensations which we have always treated as essentially different, we shall have reason to confess, with amazement, a far more intimate union between sight and hearing than any of outer coincidence. Indeed, excepting the before-mentioned difference, which their several media of travel impress upon them, philosophy can not find a mark of distinction between sight and sound.

How strong a claim to interior oneness this law of seven bestows can be fully felt only by realizing how essential a law it is. So essential is it that probably, in the whole universe, it may be impossible to find a complete range of any operations which does not, in its internal nature, submit to it. I say this perfectly aware that there are insuperable obstacles, while we enjoy no more than our present development of mind, to proving this to a logical certainty. Yet the vast probability which appears to me in the proposition rests upon one fact which I have never seen noticed in connection with these senses. Doubtless it has been noticed, however, for from time immemorial the significancy of the number seven has employed the researches of philosophers and theologians. The fact is this: In the Divine philosophy of Creation, which is, at the same time, the most reverend also for age, there is a stress laid upon the importance of this number as exponent of some law of completion, of perfectness, which, unless it be granted deeply significant, can be treated upon no middle ground between that and a puerility partaking of imposture. The seventh day as the one whose advent expressly witnessed the completion of the Kosmos (whatever of length we may give to the days of the creation); the impress of some secret import upon seven, by countless ceremonial symbols, inculcated to that people who, during the whole period of the Theocracy, held more direct communion with the Divine source of all Truth than any nation before or since; the constant recurrence, in the Word, of prophetic uses of the number, and such a phrase as this: "Wisdom hath builded her house; she hath hewn out her seven pillars:" all these seem to indicate, beyond the possibility, in my mind at least, of conceiving the contrary possible, that this number is a fundamental law of perfectness in the Universe.

As such, therefore, and comprehending under its rule the two senses of sight and hearing, it proves a oneness in their essential conditions which seems irrefutable. In some of the more intensely awakened hasheesh states, there was a great light thrown upon this subject, but, with many other views gained like it, through symbolization, on my return to the natural state it passed away from my mind forever.

4. Smell. Within the last ten years an attempt has been made by some Frenchman of speculative mind, whose name I forget, to determine if this sense a septenary gamut also, in which the only two tones that have not escaped me, to the best of my knowledge, were citron and rose. If the natural existence of such a gamut could be accurately determined, it would be a great auxiliary, certainly, to our argument; but I fear that our knowledge of the catalogue and relations of all possible odors is so very imperfect as to make the research only a fanciful recreation. From the great variety of the objects, and the lack of scientific delicacy of the sense of smell, it is a very difficult one to deal with. He who investigates it through its own instrumentality, which, of course, is the only possible method for an inductive science, is very much at the disadvantage of him who should try to dissect an animalcule with his finger nail.

Yet there is, even with such obstacles in the way, a possibility of proving odor ultimately resolvable into that force which we have discovered as the common idea of the preceding senses. I have held the opinion, whether original with me or not I can not say, that odor, like light and sound, may be propagated by undulations; if not as the only mode, at least as one of two modes, the other of which is immediate chemical action upon the organ. As an argument in favor of this, I would instance the grain of musk, which, without losing weight at all appreciably, will for years render the room in which it is kept intolerable to its enemies.

But, granting that the chemical action is its only one, this fact, so far from precluding the idea of force which we seek to make general, only illustrates it. The very chemical action is itself a force. As an example, notice the effect of some such odorous agent as makes its effect particularly marked; let us say hellebore, which, when smelled, causes odic action of the nerve, in some cases only less powerful than that appropriate to galvanism. The flower of the catalpa produces a similar effect upon myself, sufficiently severe to cause very troublesome bleeding; and I know several persons affected in like manner by the carnation pink and eglantine.

5. Taste. The theory supported by some physicists upon the operation of this very little scientifically understood sense is something such as this. The tongue, upon a foundation of muscular fibre, carries a nervous membrane, not wholly smooth even in the most delicate species, but bristling, more or less compactly, with highly sensitive minute nervous tufts, known to physiology under the name of "papillæ," literally, "little teats," from their peculiar form. Sapid substances being dissolved by the saliva, and thus resolved into their ultimate particles, in the form of these particles penetrate the papillæ. By something analogous to an exquisitely-refined sense of touch, these papillæ detect the peculiar form characteristic of every ultimate particle of the given sapid substance, and thus define it as a certain taste.

If this be the correct explanation of the taste-phenomena, they resolve themselves into a perceived force of form, and thus come within our law. But I imagine that the operation is still more subtle; and that in every substance possessing sapidity, there is, producing the sensation, a force by itself, possessing as true an individuality as the electric, and in each case bearing a specific characteristic which gives it its peculiar taste. Perhaps it may be akin to the galvanic fluid. This seems to be suggested by the result of an experiment very easily made, viz., placing a circle of zinc upon one side of the tongue and of copper on the other, when the curious possibility will be manifest of actually "tasting galvanism."

6. Feeling. I have made this distinction between feeling and touch for the reason that, although their sensations may be propagated along the same sets of nerves, the strongly-marked difference in nature between the facts which they separately apprehend renders it more philosophical to treat them apart. By feeling is meant here the sense of heat and its absence, pain of all kinds, and the sensuous pleasure not included under previously analyzed senses. In the latter part of this category, for instance, are included sexual gratification, the soothing effect of manipulation, whatever it may be styled, mesmeric or otherwise, and pre-eminently the exhilaration of narcotics and other stimuli.

The only argument which I shall adduce to prove the comprehension of the feeling-phenomena within the general idea of force will be simply to call to my reader's mind the fact that all such phenomena are spasmodic. Their idea is that of an injected energy of motion, manifest not only in the nerve, but in the brain, by contraction or relaxation or both, or the alternation of the two states of either.

Having endeavored, as briefly as an analysis at all satisfactory would permit, to test the truth of my theory with respect to each division of the sense, let me, in a few words, sum up the substance of that which has been sought to be proved.

It is this. That the soul in itself is capable of receiving all the impressions of all the senses from the action of the object which produces an impression upon a single sense; that in the bodily organs only and the media of transmission, which are relevant to the organs alone, lies the necessity for a divisory action; and, finally, as a consequence of these propositions, that the soul, either wholly freed from its present gross body, or so awakened, by any cause, as to be partially independent of the intervention of the corporeal organs, may behold the manifold impression from an object which now gives it only the fractional, thus seeing, hearing, smelling, tasting, and feeling in the most exquisite degree the thing which, in the state of bodily dominance, was the source of but one of these.

An opinion similar to this was held by Coleridge; and I can not but believe that it was suggested to him by some intimation of its truth which he received while in the exaltation of opium. Certainly there is no corroboration greater than he might have thus acquired for it, if the effect of that drug ever reached with him the intensity which hasheesh reached with me. By evidence of the most startling character was I repeatedly, while using the indulgence, put beyond all doubt upon the point. Indeed, at this day it lies before me in the light of as distinct a certainty as any fact of my being. Because, from the very nature of its source, I could not transfer that certainty, in kind, to the mind of my reader, I have made the attempt to approximate it by the preceding argument, not because I felt at all the need of strengthening myself in the faith.

As, some distance back, I have referred to my own experience upon the subject, asserting my ability at times to feel sights, see sounds, &c., I will not attempt to illustrate the present discussion by a narrative of additional portions of my own case. It might be replied to me, "Ah! yes, all very likely; but probably you are an exception to the general rule; nobody else might be affected so." This was said to me quite frequently when, early in the hasheesh life, I enthusiastically related the most singular phenomena of my fantasië.

But there is no such thing true of the hasheesh effects. Just as inevitably as two men taking the same direction, and equally favored by Providence, will arrive at the same place, will two persons of similar temperament come to the same territory in hasheesh, see the same mysteries of their being, and get the same hitherto unconceived facts. It is this characteristic which, beyond all gainsaying, proves the definite existence of the most wondrous of the hasheesh-disclosed states of mind. The realm of that stimulus is no vagary; it as much exists as England. We are never so absurd as to expect to see insane men by the dozen all holding to the same hallucination without having had any communication with each other.

As I said once previously, after my acquaintance with the realm of witchery had become, probably, about as universal as any body's, when I chanced to be called to take care of some one making the experiment for the first time (and I always was called), by the faintest word, often by a mere look, I could tell exactly the place that my patient had reached, and treat him accordingly. Many a time, by some expression which other by-standers thought ineffably puerile, have I recognized the landmark of a field of wonders wherein I had traveled in perfect ravishment. I understood the symbolization, which they did not.

Particularly was this the case in the hasheesh experiment of a friend of mine, made not three months ago, spontaneously on his part, and unknown to me until I was "sent for." Not only was it for ecstasy and wonderful phenomena the most remarkable I ever had the care of, but so clear a light did it shed on the investigation of the few preceding pages, that I will give it here in place of any thing additional of my own, which, as I have said, I will not give.

B----, this friend of mine, for four hours supposed that he was in heaven. Infinite leagues below him he heard the old, remembered bells of the world, and their sound, as it came floating, diminished up through the immense sky beneath him, seemed the only tie which bound him to any thing not celestial.

242

As I sat by the side of the sofa on which he was lying, and held his hand for a greater part of the time, I became a convert to all the most marvelous articles of the mesmeric creed. The connection which his peculiar state of sensitiveness had established between us, made us, for all purposes of sensation and perception, wholly one. I was able to follow him through all his ecstatic wanderings, to see what he saw, feel what he felt, as vividly as it is possible without myself having taken hasheesh. This, however, as you will say, was nothing wonderful. It might have happened, and no doubt, in part, did happen, from my former thorough acquaintance with all such states.

But the connection did not end here. I drank a glass of water, and B. felt it as distinctly as if he had taken it himself. He experienced the spasm of the muscles of the throat, which always accompanies drinking in the hasheesh state, so vividly that he really supposed he was drinking himself, and implored me to give him no more water.

For another person in the room he had always felt strong sympathies; they were now developed to an extent most surprising. This person had a habit, when in a brown study, of industriously rubbing his forehead after a fashion painful to look upon. Suddenly I heard B. exclaim, "Oh, Bob, stop thinking! stop thinking! you don't know how it distresses my head!" My eyes had been upon B. all the time; his own had not once been opened; how could he have known that his friend was thinking? I looked around, and lo! Bob, in medio brown-studio, polishing his forefront with the usual assiduity. Merely by the sympathy between them B. had known it all. This may be laughed at, but, if necessary, I would willingly file my affidavit that B., with his outer eyes, had seen nothing for half an hour previous. I had not taken my eyes from his face once during that time.

But I will go on to the facts which more immediately bear on my theory. While, as I have said, he had not the remotest consciousness of the place in which he really was, he still conversed freely with us on the basis of his celestial locale.

To him, we all seemed to be together "in excelsis." Naturally he was a loving and gentle spirit; this characteristic the upper atmosphere brought out more fully. In terms which it would not be modest for any of us to have repeated for ourselves, he expressed his sense of the congenialities which bound us together. But this sense, no less ethereal than in the ordinary state, was something far more visible.

"I feel," said he, "that we have many mutual ties of fellowship, but, more than that, I see them. I know you are feeling kindly to me now, for there are a thousand golden and azure cords which run between us, making a network so exquisite that it is unspeakable delight to look thereon."

"Are you not fancying it?" said somebody. "Fancying it? how can I fancy that which is immediately before my eyes? Besides that, I realize that it is true; it can not be false; it is a part of each of us delicately prolonged. I see all our characteristics blended in it -- oh, it is beautiful -- beautiful!"

Here was that inner sense, to which, as most intuitive, we have given by analogy the name of "feeling," shown to be reciprocal, or, rather, one with sight. But the oneness of the outer senses was also to receive corroboration.

B. looked at us, and as our countenances changed in the course of conversation, that change was embodied to him in tones. "Do you know," said he, "that all your faces, your forms, have a musical idea? I hear you distinctly, in harp-like notes; each one of you, as you look upon me, has his melody; together your appearance is a harmony. Do you yourselves hear the music which you are?"

While he lay with closed eyes we still talked to him. Now, every sound which we uttered had its being to him, not only in music, but in visible form. Indeed, as he afterward assured me, when in a state to philosophize upon the subject, he read in figures, while we were speaking, every idea as distinctly as from a book. Landscapes, temples, lakes, processions of all kinds of being, passed before him, borne with our voices, and impressed, not with the artificial letter-symbols of our meaning, but with the meaning itself, as in my own case I have expressed it, like an essence made incarnate.

The only sense which was not tested in this experience was that of odor. I have deeply regretted the deficiency ever since, for I am convinced that its oneness with all the others would have been exhibited as clearly as that of the others among themselves. Taste we did try with the fullest result. After much persuasion (for it seemed a degradation of his celestial nature), we prevailed upon him to eat a small piece of an apple. I took a piece of it myself, and if I, who was in heaven, could eat, he might also. Its taste he expressed as giving him likewise the idea of a tone. It was winter, and not a flower of any fragrance was within reach; but I know from my former experience, as well as the fullness of his own in every other respect, that he would have emblematized it in music immediately.

I would that every man whose eye is met by this recital, instead of reading it from my pen, and saying as coldly as is the custom at the present day, "marvelous, but doubtful," with a shake of the head, could have sat as I did by that sofa, and have learned the truth of this strange theory by an eye-witness as delightful as it was convincing. In not one single lineament of this case have I poetized; indeed, I feel deeply my most signal failure to satisfy my own ideal of what I there saw and felt. I am not aware of any recompense which would tempt me, if I could, to blot out the memory of that most exquisite lesson which I learned at the side of B.

Yet it may be said, "Your own experience had probably been pretty well known to him already, and these perceptions of his were but re-embodiments of things he had heard from you." I assure you, my dear reader, that of my own experience upon the subject of this unity of sense I had not said a word to him, not even to any person in the place where he lived. His views, from this fact, were perfectly spontaneous, as, indeed, any one present could have seen from the manner of their natural and irrepressible outflowing in his words. The only possible explanation of such perceptions, occurring as they have in several other cases besides his without any acquaintance with my experience, is that they apprehend real truths, common to all our humanity, and needing but some instrument of intense insight to bring them forth.

Within a few days of this literally clinical lecture upon my theory occurred another case, in some respects almost as singular. Another person, making the hasheesh experiment for the first time, showed the following strange characteristic in the effect of its influence. Though as perfectly conscious as in his natural state, and capable of apprehending all outer realities without hallucination, he still perceived every word which was spoken to him in the form of some visible symbol which most exquisitely embodied it. For hours every sound had its color and its form to him as truly as scenery could have them.

The fact, never witnessed by me before, of a mind in that state being able to give its phenomena to another and philosophize about them calmly, afforded me the means of a most clear investigation. I found that his case was exactly analogous to those of B. and myself; for, like us, he recognized in distinct inner types every possible sensation, our words making a visible emblematic procession before his eyes, and every perception, of whatever sense, becoming tangible to him as form, and audible as music.

There is something more than the mere fascinating activity of speculation in knowing such things as these. The excellency of their office consists in acquainting us with the fact that in our minds we possess a far greater wealth than we have ever conceived. Such a discovery may do much for us in every way, making material ends seem less valuable to us as ultimate aims, and encouraging us to live well for the sake of a spirit which possesses fathomless capacities for happiness no less than knowledge.

There is a condition in which the soul may exist, which is possible (and when we have proved any thing possible for a soul, we have, at the same time, proved it probable), in which every object of our perception shall infuse into us all the delight of whose modifications now but one alone trickles in parsimoniously through a single sense. With a more ethereal organization, the necessity for dividing our perception into the five or six modes now known may utterly pass away, and the full harmony of all qualities capable of teaching or delighting us may flow in at once to ravish the soul.

In the cases which I have mentioned, hasheesh had nearly perfected this etherealization already. Yet hasheesh must be forborne; we have no right to succeed to the inheritance till we come of age. In our longing for that spiritual majority which is to invest us with our title, we may stay ourselves on prophecies as well as patience.

Perchance we may listen to some such prophecy as this: There is a land, oh dreamer, on which the sun rises in music, and his rays are heard sounding symphony to the greeting of Memnon. The ever-shifting tints of cloudland forever rise into brightness and anthems, and fall back again to softness and lullabies. The fingers of the harper paint exquisite green fields with the pencil of a tone, and the child that sings by his side fills the soul with Claude Lorraine sunsets. The clasp of a brother's hand returning from over sea is felt in a rosy heaven, or the light of one more star and a thrill of glad-hearted song. The meaning of the brotherhood between wine and carols is known by a strain of music from the terraces of Rhine and the vineyards of Xeres, bathing the lips of the poet in added melody. With the fall of the sun upon empurpled cloud-banks of the west, the fragrance of the flowers floats to him in a hymn of good-night, and the wind from his portals rings a curfew upon lily and rose. Land twice blessed, where all things are manifold in their melodies, harmonious in difference!

Thus did I prophesy to myself, as, according to my wont, with closed eyes I sat listening to a sonata of Beethoven. Within me the prophecy was even now half fulfilled, for I was dreaming in a land of palaces builded of tones, a country whose rivers ebbed and flowed with the modulations of the outer music.

Are we persuaded of these things that we may be deceived? is our hope in vain? There is nothing too beautiful to believe of the soul. If its visions seem falsified by matter, it is only because they are above matter; because in prophetic gazings it mirrors a higher, a more ethereal incarnation of the Creative Spirit than yet communes with it through the passages of the fleshly sense.

Ideal Men and their Stimulants.

Of all the infinitely plastic shapes of language, perhaps the most Protean is that word "The World." Monosyllable as it is, it bears upon its back a load of incongruous meanings immense enough to have crushed into nothingness a dozen of the statelier sesquipedalia, which do not draw the marrow of their stubborn reality from so stanch a Saxon genealogy, nor plant their feet so firmly upon the usages of our hard, everyday life. In that word we see the triumph of Saxonism, for it is astonishing how any word which means so many things has not finally come to mean nothing definite at all, a "vox et præterea nihil." While it has held its place, many other words have been banished from the common parlance of men, or are allowed only when they can be explained by their context, or when vagueness itself is an especial desideratum.

Not to multiply instances, let the English "good" and the French "vertu" be examples. The first of these who ever thinks of using (we limit its reference to human attributes) when he wishes to express something defined of the character of another? The poets only, for they, indeed, from the picturesque necessities of their art, have preserved its original outlines clear, and give it always its noble, radical force; the good man, with them, is the man of developed heart as distinguished from his clever brother of the developed intellect. But in common conversation, to say that a man is good tells about as much of him as to ascribe to him the possession of a nose. He may be, for all we know, a sour Pharisee, held righteous in proportion to the number of things which he considers sins, an easy soul who does or does not pay his little bills, a kindly person of fluent sympathies, or

"A good-humored dunce with the best of intentions."

To the word "good," a man with the bump of Causality prominent must always reply "How?" and then come a host of particularizations on the other side to round out the idea.

In like manner has "vertu" passed utterly out of the universal sparkling Gallic mouth, not only for the reason that the idea which it embodies exists in a somewhat misty (as well as musty) state in the national brain, but because, very likely as a necessary outflow from this fact, it has been dissolved under the pressure of its numerous meanings into free vapor. The person who cultivates "la vertu" may be conceived of as a man who prefers reading the Constitutionnel of an evening to his wife, in slippers, to the society of Lorettes at the Bal au Masque; or again, for aught that we know, he may this moment be looking for medallions of Claudius in green spectacles and Pompeii.

But "the world," word as truly as thing, has held its course. We do not confound "the man of the world" with Humboldt, who has traveled all over it, nor "the ways of the world" with relations to its tumbling around from day to night, and from peri- into aph-elion. We understand every man in the speciality of meaning which he chooses to stamp upon the word, and pass on without further questioning.

With the Geographer it means -- no matter, we know what it means, not having in early youth blasphemed to no purpose the American idea of universal enlightenment over an Atlas. With the Ethnologist it is an affiliation of human manners; with the Philologist, a brotherhood of tongues. The man of society says "the world," and straightway it paints to him, if transatlantic, a vision of Almacks and the Clubs; if cisatlantic, a prodigality of entreés on the Avenue. A circle of spinsters whisper the mystic symbol over souchong, and lo! at uncontaminating distance, a dream of deluded souls dancing into inevitable destruction to a Redowa discoursed from Dodworth's balefully-fascinating tubes. Yet, by a more catholic appreciation than we give to any other word, in each case we catch the full force of the particular idea. O world, as word alone, truly there is no "transit" to thy "gloria."

Yet, from the very ease with which it carries its multiplicity of meaning, we are apt to forget how manifold they really are. We thus lose sight of a truth, than which there is none more actual, that, though we intermarry, walk, talk, and transact business together, we are each of us, this moment, living in a different world.

Even as a mere bald question of the bodily senses, this is beyond a doubt. A is a near sighted man, and has a very defective power of discriminating colors. Like several men whom I know, he may be utterly unable to distinguish the strawberry from its leaf, or, like certain others, to discriminate between the fly on his spectacles and the eagle in the firmament. B, on the other hand, sees ships in the offing before the signal-man has got the focus, and pronounces dogmatically, at a glance, between two shades of blue which do not differ from each other by a tenth. A and B live in two absolutely different sight-worlds.

Again, C perceives no difference between sounds or harmonies. He is, let us say, a celebrated divine whom I have the honor to know. Some years ago, when "Oh Susannah" was triumphantly ushering in the Ethiopian school of composition to popular favor, a roguish daughter of the gentleman happened to be playing that exquisite air upon the piano, and (much as I regret to state it) upon a Sunday morning also. Her father, struck with the novel beauty of the music, although he had heard it fifty times before, asked what it was, and was answered, with a sense of security which based itself upon his peculiar auricular failing, that it was "Greenland's icy mountains."

In the evening all the family were assembled in the parlor, and Dr. ---- asked the fair rogue to play the piece that had so much pleased him in the morning. Of course, by the family, "Oh Susannah" was reckoned among secular melodies, and, to speak popularly, would not "go down." Without a moment's hesitation, Miss ---- awoke the instrument to "Greenland," and the doctor was as perfectly satisfied as he had been ten hours before.

Such a one we will say is C. D, on the contrary, recognizes fifteen gradations between F and G of the natural scale, and whistles every air in Trovatore on his way home from its first performance at the Academy. If an itinerant miller of music, "knowing the wally of peace and quietness," refuses to move under a shilling, he makes over the additional sixpence and thinks it clear gain.

The sound-worlds of C and D are as truly twain as Mars and Jupiter.

But I will not consume the letters of the alphabet in any further analysis of a statement so apparent to the slightest thought. Just briefly, in their relations to the remaining senses, let me set the opposite types apart.

In Touch, on one side stands the artisan who, with his finger, can measure that convexity in a lens which few men could determine by the eye; on the other, the person who scarcely, by his hand, discovers any inequality in a board, provided it be planed. In connection with the former, I might mention such a case as that of Giovanni Gonelli, of Volterra, who, in the seventeenth century, gave to the world the spectacle of a man entirely blind, yet a most accurate sculptor, not alone of his own ideals, but of faces which he only knew by passing his hand over them. Among the likenesses which he left were those, both faithful and beautiful, of Cosmo di Medici, Pope Urban VIII., and the first Charles of England. Yet, though I have refrained, on account of the exceptional nature of this case, I might well adduce other instances of blind dexterity and delicacy of touch far from exceptional.

Again, in Smell, there are innumerable grades between the person in whom it is an absolute lack and the one to whom, our world being unfortunately not a universal spice-grove, it is a source of constant misery. At this moment I am writing but a few feet from a lady who, a day or two ago, assured me that if, by any operation, however painful, she could eradicate her sense of smell without danger, she would willingly submit to it, even though it cost her those rose and jasmine odors in which she delights with more intensity than practical people do in a good dinner.

In Taste we may shade off humanity between the two extremes of an Apicius, desolé on account of the one quarter grain of ambergris more than the receipt in his soup of flamingos' tongues, and the Scotchman who, outside of his herring and his bannocks, is at sea upon all delicate questions of gustative interest.

In Feeling, as defined in the preceding note, the sense, to speak in general terms, of pains and pleasures not comprehended by other organs, the grades are almost innumerable.

There is a case on record of a lady so exquisitely constituted in this respect that the recital of another's pain in any particular member immediately made her feel it acutely in her own. I might offset to this the instance of a person who avowed to me that the extraction of the largest molar give her as little suffering as the scratch of a pin, and she dreaded no possible operation to such an extent as to care to use an anæsthetic. Since she was at all times characteristically matter of fact, and never adorned the blank reality of her ideas with fiction, I had no reason to doubt that she rigorously meant what she said.

Here, then, we see both nature and cultivation making infinite variety in individual acuteness and range of all the senses. In the words of the great Chadband, "What does this teach us?"

There is, no doubt, an objective world, a something external to our perception, and outside of our originating energy, which produces the effects by us called collectively "the world." Yet, in order to become a thing perceived, that something must undergo a modification by our organs, which, after all, makes us as truly actors in the being of the world, for all purposes of perception, as if we had helped to create it. Accordingly as the senses vary, so also will the world vary, becoming all things to all men; and literally the same thing to no two men. So, not metaphorically at all, but in the most restricted sense, every human being of us has his own world which no other man has any conception of, and this, too, with all our senses wide open, and, if you please, looking in the same direction. Only upon abstract mathematical truths, or on the forum of axioms, do we ever come exactly together, and do business with each other by the same balances. Once off of this common ground, and, though we talk about things the same in words, we mean something which we see and feel very differently. The husband does not know exactly how his voice sounds to his wife, nor the wife whether to her husband her face looks precisely as it does to herself in the glass. All that they can be tolerably sure of in their intercourse with one another is that they hit the same general and necessary facts.

But if in the mere bodily senses we find such different worlds, how much more is it the case in our spiritual organism. From the characteristic of this variation we utterly exempt that faculty of direct insight which beholds truths that are necessary and therefore universal. This, which may be called the Intuition of Truth, is not only the same in its perceptions, but pretty nearly equal in its scope among all men. None but idiots, of whatever land or tribe, could fail to see that a straight line is the shortest distance between two points, and in the field of ideas to which that belongs there is at present a small harvest of similar facts, and none but men preternaturally exalted have reaped any more from richer heights.

Leave this plane, and we are all irreconcilable again. That which is one man's darling goal in life is the loathing or hatred of his neighbor. We are astonished at each other's attachments; and while we forget the old "de gustibus" aphorism, we forget also another thing whose remembrance would be much more apt to keep us calm than any dogmatic assertion of a fact without its reasons, like that of the proverb. My dear sir, the object of your friend's attachment you do not perceive in the slightest. With the index of a word out of your common dictionary he points in a certain direction. You look, and see something which does not please you. Do not growl for that fact; if he had your spiritual eyes, he would see something that did not please him; had you his, you would see an object as lovable as he himself sees.

The importance of a proposed measure, the value of a certain end to be secured, are utterly different with different individual judgments. The majority which wins the day must not be understood as a body of men who all think alike. Each individual mind composing it sees the question in a light varying by inexpressible shades from that which illuminates each of his colleagues. The majority is nothing more nor less than a collection of minds who, seeing one proposition in certain connections, varying in each case, think they all understand it as the same, and consent to let go their minor views with relation to it for the sake of carrying through that which on the whole they believe to be the best, though for very different ends.

There are philosophers who seriously lament over this infinite variance of perceptions, judgments, and feelings, as if it were the grand obstacle in the track of human perfection.

Deferentially, though candidly, I acknowledge that I think this a mistake. Indeed, the problem of our humanity standing as it does thus -- Given our present nature, and the necessity arising out of it that investigation should be the instrument of acquiring wisdom, what is the best possible contrivance for furthering the operation? I would reply, this very state of omnipresent variance. Supposing that suddenly, and just at the point in all science which we have now reached, the law of mind should change, and, a great average being struck, we should all, not to make an extreme case by saying throughout the world, but merely over its civilized area, henceforward see every thing precisely alike, and precisely alike be affected by every thing which we saw -- it seems to me that a worse calamity could not happen to mankind. The wheels of our spiritual progress now roll somewhat erratically, it is true, as the impulse of the hosts who urge on the chariot is stronger now on this side, now on that, but the resultant of all the forces is a rapid and a forward motion. The check which would ensue to that progress from the coming in of an entire uniformity would be sufficient to retard for centuries the millennium of mind. True, all would push in one direction, but the grand nisus, the energy of ambition, would be lost.

In the contests -- yes, even in the quarrels of opinion, we have a guarantee for the development of truth. Fertility is not the characteristic of unbroken plains; they become the torrid desert or the icy steppe; but it bestows itself upon a grouping of entire opposites; the peaks catch the clouds, and with them water the valleys. As the collision of flint and steel gives fire, so from the crashing together of many adverse views comes out Truth, the bright, the beautiful, the eternal. Let us thank God that human thought and human feeling are not one vast stagnant lake, but a sea whose ever-struggling and colliding waves keep their mass pure, and cleanse the intellectual atmosphere.

Our great need is not a reducing to uniformity, but a purging from all acrimony in our contests, the infusion of a willingness to permit and a readiness to appreciate all those differences of form, which, in every one of our neighbors, opinion must necessarily take. We have not all to bow down at the same shrine, but to respect those of all other men while we worship at our own; to put down the iconoclastic hammer, though not pretending to burn incense before one great average god of sentiment.

This tolerance is yet to be learned, for it is not a remarkably flourishing virtue even of the nineteenth century. Our great advance at this day has been made in the direction of refining our intolerance. For the stake and the dungeon have been substituted the taunt and the sneer, an invective which burns more lingeringly than the former, and a neglect which surpasses the latter in its fatal chill. We have yet to open our ears to the Past, which, up to our present summit of enlightenment and vision, is calling forever, in sad and earnest litany, "By Smithfield and the Lollards' Tower, by the poverty of confiscation and the weariness of banishment, by the blood of Savonarola, and Galileo shut up in prison from his stars, be merciful -- be tolerant!"

There is one excellent result of this great multiplicity of worlds which we seldom value as we ought. Who that of a morning walks up Broadway, in one of the two currents of that hurrying life, does not wonder that all the thousands who are rushing on, each for the sustenance or gratification of self, do not oftener jostle through that very selfishness, that the crowds do not interpenetrate each other with more friction? As a fact, we see them tolerably calm, obliging, and self-continent. As a problem, supposing it given to a philosopher who calculated only upon the data of our well-known human selfishness, could he solve it? Something else is requisite for the solution. We are none of us aiming at precisely the same mark. With no two men do the points on the target exactly coincide. The most similar of us still aim a hair's-breadth out of each other's way, and thus, in the great match, unless intentionally we tread on each others' kibes, there is room for us all.

If we wished to make a general distinctive classification which, in one way or another, would comprehend our whole humanity, living in its different worlds, there are perhaps no two divisions which would so nearly comprehend it all as those of Ideal and Non-Ideal. Each of these forms is a Kosmos by itself, which, from its great interior diversity, might, even as thus coaggregated, be properly translated rather system than world; but for our uses the narrower rendering will do, since all the grander laws of each Kosmos are the same for each of its inhabitants.

By these terms, Ideal and Non-Ideal, we mean very much the same ideas that a poet would get from "Visionary" and "Practical;" but these phrases are not of sufficiently catholic interpretation, the former not justly embodying that sneer, nor the latter that praise, which the language of conversation conveys in them.

We have spoken of the intuitional perception as a common ground for all men, limiting, however, the assertion to that branch of the intuitional which has its object in universal truth, and thus meaning that every body acknowledges an equal force in axioms; and, however we may dispute on other points, all agree that the whole, for instance, is equal to all its parts. Yet there are two other fields of the intuitional, which, so far from their being equally expatiated in by all men, are to some merely known by glimpses, to others, we might almost believe, entirely shut. These are Beauty and Good, higher than Truth, and therefore neither so much needed in our lower affairs, nor so much opened to all mankind by nature or cultivation.

Both the Good and the Beautiful forming each an ideal by itself, for our present purpose we need only treat with the latter. It is in relation to the Beautiful particularly that we wish to exemplify this classification of the Ideal and Non-Ideal.

That beauty is really an ideal, something of the thought inner to us, and not coming in through the passages of the sense from without, is too little perceived in our inaccurate every-day thought, and too little granted even in our moods of calmer philosophy. For this as for so many of our other perversions, we have to thank the sense-theories.

We may examine the matter without a very painful analysis. Treading reverently and softly, as becometh umbræ who intrude upon the privacy of great men, let us steal into Abbotsford, and stand by the chair of Walter Scott, who is looking at a sunset. By his side, upon the floor beneath us, lies that faithful companion of his strolls among the heather, Maida. Since the test we are about to institute demands fairness, we will free our comparison from all imputation of artifice by placing together with the noblest specimen of man the noblest specimen of beast.

Both the poet and the greyhound are looking westward. The same tints fall through the panes upon the faces of both; far up, toward the springs of Tweed, they see the same hills bathed in a dying light, and the clouds that shift above them. Does it surprise us to hear Sir Walter bursting forth in enrapturement; or, truer still, as a meed of the heart to beauty, see him silently gazing toward the sundown with a face which glows and changes, telling more than a thousand lips? But would we be astonished or not if Maida should suddenly give vent to a lyric bark of ecstasy, or even should she refuse to be wheedled from the glories of that view by the whistle of a keeper immemorially associated with dog-meat? Not in the least, you will say; and most people would agree with you; for a hound who appreciated sunsets would be as great a sensation, even in our most nil admirari world, as a cow, who, like Landor, should write feelingly upon green grass, and publish it. He would have the entreé of all literary circles; dinners would be pressed upon him; he would be presented with services of plate; not an album would be without the autograph of this veritable Prince di Canino. Eclipsed in the blinding glory of his eclat, the learned pig would commit suicide by surfeit, and the accomplished fleas end their mortification with their own poison.

But why? A cat may look at a king, why not a dog at a sunset? "Hath not a dog eyes? Hath not a dog paws, organs, dimensions, senses?" Yet, with quite as much astonishment as Shylock asked,

"Hath a dog money? is it possible
A cur can lend three thousand ducats?"
do we all inquire, "Can a dog see beauty in a sunset?"

Anatomically we dissect his eyes, and (especially if he be a gaze-hound) find them far better calculated than man's for length and breadth of vision. In all respects they will compare favorably with the same piece of human organism, granting the latter even at the rarest point of development.

Far deeper than any sense lies this subtle appreciation. There is a something in the outer world which does not impress itself on the retina, and of which the mere visual image is but a type. That which delights us is the peculiar essences of things, and the intangible relation of harmony which the essences, manifold in unity, bear to each other and ourselves. In lakes, and mountains, and sky there is beauty to us, because the same Creator lies behind and continues us all. Sprung from the same source, we have a fitness for each other, arising out of the very fact that in our own souls and the world also creative spirit is making itself manifest; in the tangency of the two there is a delightful communion between spirit and spirit, and for the beast this does not exist, since he is not spirit. This very capability which we possess of expressing this communion in language, shows that it is not through sense that the Beautiful flows in, for what can be conceived as more cruel, more in every way unnatural, than that the hound, with senses like our own, should still be dumbly shut up to an impossibility of expression, if, while standing by our side, he was overburdened with the same loveliness as we? The idea is indeed horrible.

Yet doubtless we may wrong the animal upon the other side. Few of us being willing to carry out the sense philosophy to its ultimate conclusions by giving the dog perception of Beauty equally with ourselves, we often go to the opposite extreme, and rather pity him as a being without gratifications beyond the present bone, hearth-rug, or exciting chase. He very likely enjoys contemplation as much, proportionally to his kind, as we do. Not the contemplation of the beautiful in nature indeed, but of some other characteristic, which has as true a fitness to his constitution as Beauty has to ours. What this is, of course, from the entire difference of our plane of being, we can only conjecture.

It may be something such as this: in the creation there is a capability of sustaining animal life through food, atmosphere, and a variety of means. To us this capability seldom appears except as a logical deduction, in the form of statistics or agricultural history. To the animal it may appear stamped upon all surrounding things; it may be for him the essential truth which they embody, and in trees, herbage, fruitage, he may feel the symbolized principle which prophesies the sustenance of his highest life as our ideals prophesy ours. The Creator, who careth even for sparrows, and will not let them feel themselves unsupported in this great lonely world, may on this lower basis commune with the beast, and by it give him a suggestion of His good-will toward him, which in his case may be the source of an enjoyment measurably keen with our own.

But through the Beautiful He talks with man only, and to him alone the fitness of the conscious and unconscious creations are expressed in this way. It is a memory of the elder time to be cherished, even though it be the memory of something heard only in dreams, that all men long ago, in ages however primeval, realized Beauty, and answered back its thrill with gladness and hymns. Such a remembrance -- yes, if you will say so, even such a dream -- is like some not yet extinguished echo of the Creation strophe and antistrophe, when, on the one side, "the morning stars sang together," and, on the other, "all the sons of God shouted for joy."

Sadly enough, many of the latter band of singers have been struck dumb since that day. It might be painful to read a census, could we get such a thing, of the persons who love or even recognize Beauty, by itself and for its own unmarketable sake. The bulk of such a document would probably depend upon the style of man who went around through humanity to compile it. A poet would make sad work. His best questions would be so analytic as either to render him unintelligible or obnoxious. At some houses he would be answered, "No, I am no visionary;" and at others, "Clear out! Do you mean to insult me? Can not I see Beauty? Isn't this a beautiful day, to be sure, with the sun shining so bright that I can get in all my hay?" At all events, he would come home, without having found it necessary to purchase another valise for the conveyance of his papers.

Whatever may be the reason, it can not be doubted that there is a great difference between men in the appreciation of the subtle characteristic, and in some it seems to be entirely lacking. There is one class of men who exult in beauty, who live in it, whose extreme representatives are willing even to commit all sorts of practical extravagances for its sake. There is another, whose members look at a statue of Phidias, and then at a gate-post, and in both see only something hard, white, and tall.

Yet they both have to live in what is geographically the same world. It is of the ideal man, as representative of the former class, and of some of his relations to that world, that we have to speak. A greater breadth of these relations than might at first sight be supposed is included in the question. Why do ideal men often use narcotics? Indisputably it is ideal men. The fact is there, however great a pity it may be. Let us seek, for a while, an answer to the question.

The wants of the ideal man, while in number less than those of his opposite, in degree are far greater. Dives, as the type of the pure worldly life, is as incapable as guiltless of those vague, unsatisfied longings which he so much censures in a neighbor and discourages in a dependent. All things out of which he can extort pleasure coin themselves for him in a perfectly tangible shape. He is fully satisfied, his wishes need no additional fulfillment to make a complete orb, if his balance strikes accurately at the counting-room, if he can go home behind his own horses when too tired to walk, his dinner is good, his wife handsome, his house comfortable, his daughters well settled, his sons imitating their father. All these requisitions he can lay his hand on; if he could not, his longings would not be vague; he would know what he wanted, and, under ordinary circumstances, could get it in time.

Ariel, on the other hand, is contented with a catalogue of enjoyments in numerical and money value far less. It was not he who originated that sneer upon love in a cottage. He was filled with infinitely more than the mere satisfaction of their material by the woodbine which clambered around his windows, the roses leading from the door-step to the gate, the lake below him, the mountains on the other side, the fruit and the loaf upon his table, and the other cleanly and kindly answers to his domestic needs.

But the tax-gatherer came to spy out the land, the insatiate genius of mill-building looked at the brook which ran by his garden, and pronounced it a "location."

Presently the waters began to run foul with dye and sawdust, gigantic band-wheels spun and hummed where birds had sung; there was a creaking, a dust, a baleful fire night and day, which invaded his library and his dreams. Provisions rose; the simplest fare upon which he had kept together soul and body now stood just where his labors could reach it upon tiptoe.

So strongly, while it does cling, does the body pull upon the soul, that, though we may be spiritually happy without being sumptuous, we can not, at the same time, be spiritual and hungry. At least most of us can not. Into what a glory, looked at through such a fact, does the Massinger tower who, with one hand stiffly holding the wolf at arm's length, with the other can indite the Virgin Martyr. Yes, there have been some such souls after all.

But our Ariel, being of less muscular make, is not among them. His "mind to him a kingdom is," but he is expatriated from it on a foraging expedition; through the jaws of Scylla and Charybdis, starvation on the one hand, and the premature old age of over-wrought energies, he is voyaging in a supply-ship. If even now he could sit still in an occasional lull, and grow better by drinking in beauty, and make other men happier by imparting it to them through words, writing, or kindly offices, he sees only money-utility stamped upon the rivers, and the whole face of nature is staked off into building-lots or manufactory-sites. The features of his goddess have become the "desirable features" for a paper-speculation town.

There are a thousand ways in which his neighbors can evaporate the essence which is all in all to him, while they at the same time give to his scenery a ponderable value which to them is worth far more.

Perhaps, like Southey, he now out and out curses the mills. But this is wrong; for Southey, though a noble poet in spite of the insolence of Byron, was still no great political economist, notwithstanding the opinion of himself. Perhaps, therefore, he only sighs, and moves his household gods to another hearth -- it may be where loneliness will better secure him from disturbance, it may be where labors of his particular kind yield fuller sustenance to the crying wants of life. The pangs of such a moving are little known to any one but himself, or, if he has God's crowning gift in a deep-feeling and congenial wife, to her alone beside him. The men of the world can not hear the groans of the uprooted mandrakes.

There is the hill-top, upon which, first of all visible things, his eyes for so many years have lighted in awaking. It has grown to be to him the only summit over which it could be conceived possible for the sun to rise. There is the lake along whose shores he has led his children, calling them to watch its hues and dimples at evening; along those same shores, mayhap, his father led him. Every tree, as far as the skirt of the horizon, is known to him; he has wandered over every slope; he has dreamed or written suggestions in his note-book upon every crag. The whole scenery has been to him his school, his gymnasium, his holiday-ground. He must leave it all.

And his house -- it was there that he felt upon his forehead, in blessing, the hands of the now long dead; here, many a year ago, he knew man's only peace except death, childhood -- knew it for a little time, while his locks were sunny and the grave shadows yet tarried from his face -- then vanished it away. Hither he led home his new-made wife; here, "into something rich and strange," blossomed that mystic, intangible relation of delights when a child was born to the bosoms which are twain, yet one; here, with his children, in the firelight gambols he kindled the dampened torch of the younger time, and for one evening was a child again.

Here, too, is his library -- that cave in the rock above the world's high tide, set farther in than the surges beat or the winds blow. The tide has reached it now. There are waves and sea-weed on the floor at flood -- they do not all go out at ebb. Where can he read but at that window? Where can he write but on that desk and against that wall? How can the old familiar animus of the place be left behind, unless his own soul, which had grown its twin, stays with it? Yet how can the animus be transported? No, no, it can not. It knows no luggage trains; it is not a thing of drays.

Every where the tentacles of his root must give way with a wrench; the necessity being granted, the pain is inevitable; the only remedy, a manly patience under the irremediable -- the

"Quicquid corrigere est nefas."

Now if he were to tell Dives all this, taking him into his confidence, would he not laugh? "What is the sense," would be the reply of that satisfied person, "in fashing your beard about one place or another? If you are going to town, you will probably take a far better house than this trumpery cottage -- four stories high, free-stone front, all the modern improvements, and eligible situation. Why, my dear sir, you must be mad! Think what an exchange -- gas instead of spermaceti; bathing apparatus, with warm, cold, and shower cocks, instead of this portable concern you have here, or perhaps instead of mere swim in your two-penny lake; the market within ten minutes' staging; shopping conveniences for your wife; a daily laid, still wet, on your door-step -- every thing imaginable, in place of this uncultivated, mountainous, windy, woody situation, out of call of express-wagons and solid respectability. Or, if you are going still farther into the woods (which, I own, is very foolish, since you might stay here and put up a saw-mill on your own part of the brook, which would make you one of our first manufacturers), there is still no such cause as you seem to think for sorrow at moving. Probably, where you will settle, vegetables and all provisions are far cheaper -- you can get your wood for almost nothing -- and certainly those are advantages that a man need not pull a long face over. Be a man. Satisfy yourself with the world, as I do."

Ah! unction not in Ariel's pharmacopoeia! He is hurt where such salves will not heal him.

In many a way may the sources of his enjoyment be dried up or imbittered which the world knows not of. The ideal nature is indeed a harp of many wondrous strings, but the airs that play upon it in this life are seldom of the gentlest. The one-stringed Hawaiian guitar of the non-ideal man is easily thrummed, and never lacks tone save when its proper backbone of material well-being is temporarily lax.

If any of us, even the most tender and spiritually appreciative, could understand the various intensity with which this law works out its office in other men of the same nature, we would be much kinder in our judgment of the man who runs to narcotics and other stimulants for relief, while we regarded the habit as no less grievous. Could we, for example, enter thoroughly into the constitution of such a one as Coleridge; could we realize his temptations to the full extent; understand his struggles, and weigh all the forces of the mind which gave him, from his very birth, a perilous tendency, how much oftener with tears than with denunciations of his indolence, his neglect of duties, would we read such memorials of him as have been published, much as the most of those seem directed to bias us in the contrary way.

For it seems as if there has never been a real "Life" of Coleridge. We have had, in abundance, sketches of what he himself might have called his "phenomenal existence." We have the changes of place which he made; the towns in which he lectured; the letters from home which he did not open, and the correspondences for aid in starvation which he did open; the worth, in pounds sterling, of the laudanum which he drank per week; the number of bottles of brandy which he emptied in the same time; the extravagances of his expenditure; his repentings, his concessions to Southey and Cottle. All these are phenomenal -- yea, even the last three. We have external events -- movements of which we do not see the motor. Perhaps it would be impossible to see it from any thing but an autobiography so full, so ab intra, that pain and humiliation would deter him from writing it, were he living. This would be a "Life" of Coleridge; the others are mere results of that life.

Perhaps the best substitute for such a work is to be found in his brief and fragmentary prose works; for, although they have almost nothing of that narrative style which is supposed to be necessary to the legitimate memoirs, they still show us, to a degree unequaled by any thing extant, Coleridge, the Man and the Mind.

A man he was to whom the world of his imagination and his reason was far more than that wherein he reaped his honors and his daily bread. Sensitive as a child to that intangible yet infinite meaning which is expressed in frowns and smiles, in love, scorn, and neglect; by nature gifted with an insight into her excellencies which cultivation and the other circumstances of his progressive being made at times even morbidly acute; living, by the very necessity of his particular inborn law of life, at the very summit of his energies, he had worn out nerve and elasticity at an age when, according to all ordinary judgments which base themselves on insurance averages and statistics of longevity, he should have been in the prime of his life, and battling his way with fortitude to a competency. He exhausted by mighty drafts all his credit at the bank of healthful life, and that is a corporation which never permits us to overdraw. Up to the very last deposit of blood and sinew, nerve and spirit, prompt payment will meet every demand; then comes the crash, and the bankrupt nature is no longer known on 'Change. If all that we know of Coleridge from without, the statement of himself and his contemporaries, did not intimate to us that such was the case with him, we might determine that it would necessarily happen so, à priori, from that which we know of the mental constitution of the man.

He tells us through his memorializer, Cottle, and the other who have written about him, that he first used opium as a remedy for disease -- a painful disease of the legs -- that he found its effects a delicious and perfect relief. Furthermore, that he abandoned it with the completion of his cure, but resumed it upon his finding, with the abandonment, the pains return. That he made several attempts to free himself with the same termination, and at last settled down into the opium-eater which he was for it is impossible to say how many years of his life.

All this we have no reason to doubt. As an alleviative to severe pain the narcotic first became known to him. Yet the secret of its excessive use, the rapidly increasing doses, beyond all the demands of the body for relief -- what was that? Ah! the poet himself would confess that to his mind the indulgence spoke with a fascination far greater than to his physical nature. It was, in fact, the very thing necessary for the replenishment of his exhausted capability of enjoyment.

How is it, we must ask, that opium acts upon the whole organism of a susceptible man? Physically the books of medicine tell us how -- that is, to a certain distance they mark its pathway through digestion, circulation, the sympathetic nerves, and, where it causes death, leave it in an engorgement of the brain.

Probably all these phenomena are the merely external ones; they do not at all give us the mode of its action, after all. At one time, in the course of some experiments, I thought I had reached a little deeper principle of its operation; some singular facts led me to form a theory upon the subject. I will not give it here, since there is not yet a basis of tests broad enough for it to rest upon philosophically. Of all specific actions, that of narcotics is conceded by physicists universally to be one of the most recondite. Hardly any thing is really known about it by the practitioner more than by his unscientific patient. We have mere facts ungrouped about their governing principle.

But mentally we know its working better. Opium supersedes, and, by long continuance in its indulgence, actually extirpates that vital force out of which arise hope, insight into excellencies, fortitude, volition, and volition made permanent in perseverance. It is an artificial energy destructive to all natural; men habituated to it live on when what is called the nervous life is perfectly extinct.

That Coleridge could not have continued to live at all without such energy in some form is evident from the whole constitution of the man. Without the ever-present sensitive perception of spiritual beauty for which such an energy was necessary, house, lands, comfortable family arrangements, the remunerative place in the Quarterly which his friends procured him would have seemed mere eidola. He hungered and thirsted for the spiritual. The world of dreams which he had built up in his "Pantisocracy" had been exhaled under the pressure of daily-bread necessities when to his fortuneless bosom he took a portionless wife. It is impossible that such a nature as his, emptied of the ideal Utopia, should be long void of something else as ideal. And so through all his life we see him forgetting hunger in dreams till it bites him to the heart. Then he starts up to spasmodic exertion, to sleep again in visions when the foe is driven to a respectful distance. Call this wrong, call it undutiful to relationships which he was bound to respect, yet you can not call it indolence. He was not fitted by nature to do the work of a material life, yet higher obligations called him to change his element, and he should have obeyed, against nature. In his own world he was a diligent, a glorious worker -- he was not indolent -- he only wrought out life according to his tendency, his constitutional fitness, and there he sinned.

Yet, oh man of the world! you who are so ready to sneer at Coleridge, let the comparison between him and yourself be put upon fair grounds before we join you in denunciation of the sin. The way in which you state the comparison is this: "Here am I, fighting the world in its roughest forms for a livelihood; there was Coleridge, who would not brace his muscles and fight like me." In another way let us state the case. Suppose yourself and Coleridge translated to that spiritual world where there are no actualities of the precise kind which you cope with. Grant that you each retained the same natural constitution as on earth, with how much ease or willingness would you change your element and labor in his province? It would then be his right to be called the actor; you would be the dreamer, and your dreams would be of things which as little suited his every-day activity as in this world his suited your own. You would be called with stentorian voices to awake to the reality of things -- to dismiss the visionary figments of commerce, manufactures, credit, and capital, and to strive boldly in the arena of thought and art, and other spiritual excellences.

Do you say, "But every man's business is with the world in which he is placed for the time being?" I acknowledge that; but it is a misfortune, an imperfection of the present state. The greatest harmony is that wherein every mind works out most fully its own office. Still, the higher obligation, the moral, called Coleridge to an uncongenial activity, and in not going he was wrong. Remember in an analogous case what you would do; think what a hard thing is the change of element, and then denounce if you can.

Interpreting the opium passage of Coleridge's life by marginal references from all the pages previous, we shall see him more justly, and therefore more gently than by any light thrown upon it as an isolated paragraph, from severe commentaries framed according to a personal and unappreciative standard.

We shall see him first as the boy. The child, as the cut-and-dried biographies have it, of poor but highly respectable parentage, that very strict economy which is so erroneously supposed to educate families into practical habits, cultivated his ideal tendency until it became exquisite. The necessity of a careful use of means in a household is the last of all things to rear its children practically. Extreme poverty, no doubt, from stimulating the very primitive activities of existence, may make a progeny which is intellectually too active to remain in the condition into which it was born, sharp-witted, cautious, provident, business-like in every respect. This fact is frequently to be observed in poor families, where sloth and viciousness do not prevent its occurrence. But the man with moderate means, who in his household affairs must be continually regulating expenditure, has reason to believe that his children, especially the more mentally active of them, will grow up, unless great care is taken, into very unpractical views. The reasoning is something like this:

From earliest consciousness they will be thrown upon their own resources for enjoyment. The expensive toy, the luxurious recreation, will be entirely out of their reach. Yet, as the outwelling child-life must have some outlet, they will not be without toys, without recreation of one kind or another, and they will invent them for themselves. Out of the imagination they will fashion for themselves a domain where the simplest things have some rich meaning, glorified by an ideal excellence, and where all the most extravagant wishes are realized. In their plays they will be kings and queens of a garden-spot, transact weighty diplomatic business on the backs of old letters, and make boundless purchases of territory with pebbles or shells. In this cheap kingdom they will live as all-absorbing a life as the dignitaries whom they counterfeit live in theirs; and, still more, they will contract a bias very difficult to alter as increased years make it necessary. The boy who suddenly awakes to find himself a man finds it hard to believe that his old ideal efforts and ideal pleasures can not, by an elevation of their plane, be made sufficient for the satisfaction of a life-time.

More particularly is this true when, as in the present age, the world of books offers an additional asylum to the active child, to which, unless, both in mind and money, he is very poor indeed, he may retreat for the enjoyment which an outer world does not supply. He is thus reared in an ideal atmosphere until it becomes the nutriment of his very being.

From such a state as this, and through his rough experience of human mercies at the hands of Dr. Bowyer, of Christ's Hospital, we may follow Coleridge on till we find him at Cambridge. How little he was fitted by nature to cope with the stern substantialities of an English University course is to be read in his final abandonment of its honors under the pressure of pecuniary difficulties, and the despair of an impossible attachment, and his enlistment into the Dragoons as a desperate indication of a desperate state of mind. Then succeed the Pantisocracy, marriage without the means of a livelihood, editorship without patrons, and without a single natural qualification for the office except the proverbially unremunerative one of out-speaking sincerity; literary labors of all kinds, from the volume of poems to the political leader, travels upon a pension, communion with German mind in books and men, of all ideal things the most ideal.

At length, by these steps, with here and there a repetition, we reach the period when his opium life commenced. In all fairness, what sort of a training had his whole previous existence been for a calm looking at the dangers of the fascinating indulgence, for a rejection of its temptation?

I dare to affirm that there is many a man who, when jaded by the day's labor, throws himself down to be refreshed by music, who in such an indulgence is committing no greater sin of intention than Coleridge committed when, coming weary from a life-time, he abandoned himself to the enjoyment of that dangerous beauty which absolute necessities and spent vitality forbade him to look for in the external world. You and I, my reader, should we abandon ourselves to the opium indulgence, would know fully the wrong we were committing; Coleridge had not any definite idea. Bitterly did he repent it afterward; but his sorrow arose rather out of the terrible results of his course than from any self-recrimination, even in his sensitive mind, of malice aforethought.

But whether, in the case of any opium-eater, the habit be or be not contracted with a full knowledge of its evil, there is but one view which we can take of the fruitlessness of struggles made for disenthrallment at a later period of his career. That fruitlessness is not to be treated with contempt as evidence of a cowardly lack of self-denial which prevents the man from breaking the meshes of a bondage grown delightful to him. We are called rather to look upon the agonies of one who, in a nightmare-dream of fearful precipices, has not the power of volition to draw himself from the edge; we must pity -- deeply pity. The protracted use of opium, not by any metaphor, but in a sense as rigorous as that of paralysis, utterly annihilates the power of will over action.

It is no mere cloak of apology which I would throw over those unfortunates who, after ineffectual attempts at being free, have subsided again into indulgence; it is actual fact that, in the horrors and the debility resulting from the disuse of the narcotic, its sufferers are no more responsible for their acts than the insane. When every man is a Scævola, and can hold his hand in the flames till it is consumed, then may we expect men to endure the unrelieved tortures of opium-abandonment to their end in enfranchisement. Who of us would hold himself responsible for withdrawing his hand from the fire? I fancy the best of our martyrs, willing as they were to die for their cause, would have leaped out if they had not been chained among the fagots.

270

So far from extenuating the wrong of narcotics and stimulants, I believe myself only proclaiming (and I would it were with a thousand tongues) the perils into which they lead, as the most striking exponent of that wrong. This very emasculation of the will itself, while it may not produce the sensation of a detail of horrible visions, is in reality the most terrible characteristic of the injury wrought by these agents. A spiritual unsexing as it is, it vitiates all relations of life which exist to its victim; by submitting to it he sows a harvest of degradation, which involves in its mildewed sheaves manly fortitude, hopefulness, faith of promises, all the list of high-toned principles which are the virile -- yes, still more broadly -- the human glory.

To this truth let a spirit so essentially noble as Coleridge witness, agonized by the shame of those subterfuges which were necessary sometimes to procure the indulgence that had become to him the very nutriment of his being.

It is vain for us to shut our eyes to the fact that opium-eating in all countries is an immense and growing evil. In America peculiarly it is so, from the constitution of our national mind. An intense devotion to worldly business in our representative man often coexists with a stifled craving for something higher. Beginning, for the sake of advancement, at an age when other nations are still in the playground or the schoolroom, he continues rising early and lying down late in the pursuit of his ambition to a period when they have retired to the ease of travel or a villa. Yet from the very fact that his fathers have done this before him, he inherits a constitution least of all fitted to bear those drafts upon it.

The question of his breaking down is only one of time. Sometimes it happens very early; and then not only does an exhausted vitality require to be replenished, but the long-pent-up craving for a beauty of which business activity has said, "It is not in me," rises from its bonds, and, with a sad imperativeness, asks satisfaction.

How hard is it now to unlearn that habit of hasty execution which had been the acquirement of his whole previous life! The demands of business had always met from him with rapid dispatch; this complex craving must be answered as rapidly. The self-denial of recreation, abandonment of care, well-regulated regimen, might gradually restore to him health, and, with it, the elastic capacity for receiving happiness. He can not wait; the process is too slow. And the only immediate infusion of energy must be the artificial; the devil stands at his ear, and suggests opium. From that moment begins the sad, old, inevitable tale of the opium-eater's life.

Alas! it is no rare one with us. The inhabitant of the smallest village need hardly go out of his own street to hear it, and the unknown wretched who hide their shame, first in sad family hearts, last in the unwhispering grave, are even more in number, doubtless, than the known.

The only effort which can be made by a man of good feeling to his race is to suggest some means of escape to those who feel their bondage. For the terror of beginners, enough both of precept and example has been diffused widely at the present day, if that would do any good. I would not be satisfying my convictions of right did I not add to any denunciation of the habit some index toward freedom; for I believe there are many men, perhaps some who will read these words, who would escape from the opium slavery at any expense of effort, provided that the lethal stupor of their energies could be removed. Where there is one man who, like De Quincey, can at last get free by his own unaided struggle, there are a thousand to whom help from without is an absolute necessity.

It was my happiness, very soon after breaking away from the hasheesh thraldom, to make the acquaintance of a gentleman whose experience of narcotics from eye-witness in their particular mother-countries, added to the capabilities which he possessed, as a medical man, for philosophizing upon such experience, interested me much in speaking with him. It had been his good fortune to meet with some singularly inordinate opium-eaters, who were in utter despair of recovery, and, still better, it was his blessing to effect a permanent and radical cure. In one case with which I became acquainted, the patient had reached a higher point of daily indulgence than De Quincey at his most desperate stage, and had seemingly lost all constitutional basis for restoration to work upon. Yet the restoration was effected. I owe it not less to a proper good-will to humanity than to gratitude on the part of men to say who this physician was. Sincerely desirous of being in some way instrumental in the cure of a bondage which, if not my own, was, at least, so near akin to it that I can deeply sympathize with its oppressed, I give a name whose betrayal in these pages violates no secrecy to the public, while it may do a great good -- Dr. J. W. Palmer, of Roslyn, Long Island, the author-surgeon, late of the Honorable East India Company's Service, and of "The Golden Dagon," to which I have referred. *

Appendix.

-

Note A

The work referred to is a monograph upon Trance and human Hybernation, by Dr. James Braid, of Edinburgh, and published by John Church, Princes Street, Soho, London. Besides the copy now in my hands, through the kindness of my friend Dr. Rosa, of Watertown, I have never seen any other, although it probably exists in medical libraries in this country. Aware, at any rate, that the book is inaccessible, except by considerable painstaking, to general readers, I will state the authority upon which the phenomenon of the fakeer's interment and trance is related, in order that it may rest upon a stronger basis of proof than the testimony of an exceedingly credulous and superstitious people like the natives of Lahore.

Sir Claude Wade, formerly of her majesty's service, and, at the date of Dr. Braid's writing, residing in Ryde, on the Isle of Wight, assures the doctor by letter that he was present at Lahore during the period of the fakeer's inhumation, and witnessed his disinterment. By this gentleman, Sir C. E. Tervelyan, and Captain Osborne, all that is stated of the fakeer by Dr. Braid is authenticated, and, indeed, through them did the doctor obtain the materials for his narrative.

By as strong a conjunction of testimony, therefore, as could be desired for the proof of the most startling assertion, is this recital put beyond the possibility of being an imposture.

-

Note B

274

Among a number of articles written at various times by this author upon the subject of the narcotic fascinations, is one, published some time ago over his own signature in the New York Tribune, relative to the employment of hasheesh in India both as a gratification and a remedy. My knowledge of his thorough acquaintance with the habits of the ultra Oriental people, among whom he so long dwelt, together with a number of astonishing cures of the opium bane which he effected when, as I have said, all hope of restoration seemed forever gone, makes me particularly desirous to give the article of which I speak in full, as supplementary, through its specific value, to that which I have written of my own experience of hasheesh. Except as an antispasmodic in a very limited number of diseases, the Cannabis is known and prized very little among our practitioners, and I am persuaded that its uses are far wider and more important than has yet been imagined.

Urged by this conviction, I have therefore transcribed the article of Dr. Palmer, and offer it here to the thoughtful attention which it deserves from all, whether professional or lay, who wish to add a most beneficial agent to their pharmacopoeia. It is entitled

HASHEESH IN HYDROPHOBIA.
To the Editor of the New York Tribune:
Sir, -- In your journal of Friday last appeared a timely paper on hydrophobia, from Dr. Griscom, of the New York Hospital, being a report of the interesting case of Edward Bransfield, with the inevitably fatal termination. Allow me to add to the communication of Dr. Grsicom another on the same subject, which may be deemed important. It is the result of medical observation in the East on the use and effects of hasheesh (Cannabis Indica). In thus writing for the public I shall avoid technicalities.

The Radda and Coolee bazars of the Black Town of Calcutta are the Borroboola-Ghas of heathendom -- the back slums of Budhism -- where the most abject of helots and a very Herod among cruel heathen are presented in the same person -- whither the flannel shirts and small-tooth combs of the Rev. Aminadab Sleek are sent every Friday night from Burton's Theatre, but never reach. It is there you must go to procure your hasheesh fresh from the fields, and see your living subject try experiments on himself. If you have a lively case of Rabies in your compound, and carry a copy of Monte Christo{1} in your pocket, so much the better -- you are posted in the phenomena. You will find dirty, dreadful-looking shops, redolent of petroleum and the hubble-bubble,{2} and prolific in Pariah dogs, ochre-colored urchins (which, as they flounder about on their bellies, always a shade or two lighter than the rest, oddly resemble young crocodiles), and every other living thing which should make those small-tooth combs lively in the market. And, amid these essentially Oriental surroundings, you will find a fat old gentleman, with the least possible clothing, to compromise between decency and the climate, who is either galvanic like Uriah Heep, or asleep like the Fat Boy, as you happen to catch him just before or after his pipe, and who is licensed to dispense to the denizens of that quarter churrus, gunjah, and bhang, in the name of Lord Dalhousie, the most noble the Governor General in Council.

At the season of flowering, a resinous substance exudes and concretes on the slender stalks, leaves, and tops of the hemp plant in India, a sticky gum which causes the young stems to adhere together tenaciously in the bundles of gunjah. Men, now dressed all in leather, are sent into the fields to run to and fro, sweeping the plants with their garments, from which afterward they diligently gather the resin that has adhered. This is the churrus, wherein is all the narcotic virtue of the herb, all the seventh heaven of hasheesh intoxication for the Hindoo and the Arab. The most potent of it comes from Nepaul. Bhang, or subjee, is the larger leaves and capsules of the Cannabis compressed in balls and sticky layers, with here and there some flowers between. Infused with water, it forms an intoxicating brew, to which, however, the Hindoos are not commonly addicted. Gunjah, mixed with tobacco and smoked in a pipe, is the shape of the drug which they popularly affect, and it is as gunjah that it is commonly sold in the shops. This comes in bundles, twenty-four of the plants entire, stalks, leaves, capsules, and tops undisturbed, and from which their resin has not been separated, adhering tenaciously. Gunjah, indeed, is the term proper to Hindostan, hasheesh being Arabic, and used to denote the tops and tenderest parts of the plant, sun-dried and powdered.

Romantic extravagances have been written and told about the magic and the marvels of hasheesh, and Indian Coleridges and De Quinceys have been pressed into service to furnish forth characteristic stories for Oriental annuals and spectacles of the Monte Christo kind. These are for the most part fictitious, though, to be sure, your kidmudgar, if he happens to be a gunjah-wallah, is apt at times to indulge in splendid fancies, to make you a grand salaam instead of a sandwich, and offer you a houri when you merely demanded a red herring. But Dr. O'Shaugnessy, the present distinguished superintendent of the Indian telegraph, who formerly administered a model system of discipline among the native hospitals, and from his Eastern look-out has added here and there a new light to the firmament of science, who was the first to pursue this subject with well-directed researches, and procure from it definite results, describes the uniform effect of this agent on the human economy as consisting in a prompt and complete alleviation of pain; a singular power of controlling inordinate muscular spasms, especially in hydrophobia and traumatic tetanus; "as a soporific or hypnotic in conciliating sleep;" inordinate augmentation of appetite; the decided promotion of aphrodisiac desire; and sudden cerebral exaltation, with perfect mental cheerfulness, is in no case followed by the painful nervous "unstringing," the constipation and suppression of secretions which attend the use of opium.

Having daily under his eyes, in the streets of Calcutta, examples of this marvelous power of the gunjah, Dr. O'Shaughnessy proceeded, in a succession of judicious experiments, to apply it in several diseases attended with much muscular convulsion. Its action he discovered to be primarily on the motor nerves, promptly inducing complete loss of power in almost all the muscles; hence its timeliness in the spasms of tetanus, in the cramp of Asiatic cholera, in the sharp constriction of the muscles of deglutition in hydrophobia. In tetanus especially he met with signal success, even in his earliest experiments perfectly restoring ten cases in fourteen, and since then, to my personal knowledge, a still larger proportion. In the summer of 1852 it was administered with convincing success in cases of Asiatic cholera among the Company's troops in Burmah, even in the collapsed stage, subduing cramp and restoring warmth to the surface. Under its influence alone, that peculiar blueness and shriveling of the nails and fingers, familiarly known as "washerwoman's hands," has been rapidly dispersed, the flesh plumping out rosily again, like a decayed apple under an air-pump.

Every intelligent physician will perceive that there is nothing in the kind of virtue manifested in these cases which has not a direct bearing, and by the same modus operandi, on the phenomena of hydrophobia, since it has been ably contended, especially in India, that the three diseases are of a kindred type; that their phenomena are purely nervous and functional, and that no local inflammations are necessary to their definition.

In an occasional contribution to the British and Foreign Medical Review, and in some excellent monographs published in Calcutta, Dr. O'Shaughnessy has given the results of his experiments since 1850, by which it appears that in almost every case, with the Cannabis alone, he has succeeded in procuring perfect alleviation of pain, complete control of the spasm, and its attendant apprehension and infernal imagination -- indeed, an utter routing of all the horrors of the disease; and claiming, with a saving clause, one or two cures, he makes it evident that in every instance a painless, tranquil, conscious termination is attainable. His patients have swallowed water with avidity, paddled in it and made merry with it, and been friendly with it to the end.

That it has thus overcome the horrors of Rabies and all the dreadfulness of such a death-bed, should procure for the Cannabis more consideration than it has met with at the hands of the profession in this country. The objection, hitherto valid, that its preparations are of unequal strength, and that the drug loses all its virtues by change of climate, is conclusively met and defeated at last by the admirable alcoholic extract of Mr. Robinson. The writer of this has seen a sepoy of the 40th Rifles, an hour before furiously hydrophobic, under the influence of the Cannabis not only drinking water freely, but pleasantly washing his face and hands.

In conclusion, I would invoke for the Cannabis Indica the interest of American writers and practitioners by research and experiment.

* * * * * * * * *

J. W. Palmer, M.D.

THE END.

1. For the benefit of those who have not read this novel of Dumas, let me say that in it quite a lively hasheesh vision is recorded.

2. Indice for water-pipe.

PUTNAM'S MONTHLY

A Magazine of Literature, Science, and Art

VOL. VIII. - DECEMBER, 1856. - NO. XLVIII.

THE APOCALYPSE OF HASHEESH

by Fitz Hugh Ludlow

In returning from the world of hasheesh, I bring with me many and diverse memories. The echoes of a sublime rapture which thrilled and vibrated on the very edge of pain; of Promethean agonies which wrapt the soul like a mantle of fire; of voluptuous delirium which suffused the body with a blush of exquisite languor -- all are mine. But in value far exceeding these, is the remembrance of my spell-bound life as an apocalyptic experience.

Not, indeed, valuable, when all things are considered. Ah no! The slave of the lamp who comes at the summons of the hasheesh Aladdin will not always cringe in the presence of his master. Presently he grows bold and for his service demands a guerdon as tremendous as the treasures he unlocked. Dismiss him, hurl your lamp into the jaws of some fathomless abyss, or take his place while he reigns over you, a tyrant of Gehenna!

The value of this experience to me consists in its having thrown open to my gaze many of those sublime avenues in the spiritual life, at whose gates the soul in its ordinary state is forever blindly groping, mystified, perplexed, yet earnest to the last in its search for that secret spring which, being touched, shall swing back the colossal barrier. In a single instant I have seen the vexed question of a lifetime settled, the mystery of some grand recondite process of mind laid bare, the last grim doubt that hung persistently on the sky of a sublime truth blown away.

How few facts can we trace up to their original reason! In all human speculations how inevitable is the recurrence of the ultimate "Why?" Our discoveries in this latter age but surpass the old-world philosophy in fanning this impenetrable mist but a few steps further up the path of thought, and deferring the distance of a few syllogisms the unanswerable question.

How is it that all the million drops of memory preserve their insulation, and do not run together in the brain into one fluid chaos of impression? How does the great hand of central force stretch on invisibly through ether till it grasps the last sphere that rolls on the boundaries of light-quickened space? How does spirit communicate with matter, and where is their point of tangency? Such are the mysteries which bristle like a harvest far and wide over the grand field of thought.

Problems like these, which had been the perplexity of all my previous life, have I seen unraveled by hasheesh, as in one breathless moment the rationale of inexplicable phenomena has burst upon me in a torrent of light. It may have puzzled me to account for some strange fact of mind; taking hypothesis after hypothesis, I have labored for a demonstration; at last I have given up the attempt in despair. During the progress of the next fantasia of hasheesh, the subject has again unexpectedly presented itself, and in an instant the solution has lain before me as an intuition, compelling my assent to its truth as imperatively as a mathematical axiom. At such a time I have stood trembling with awe at the sublimity of the apocalypse; for though this be not the legitimate way of reaching the explications of riddles which, if of any true utility at all, are intended to strengthen the argumentative faculty, there is still an unutterable sense of majesty in the view one thus discovers of the unimagined scope of the intuitive, which surpasses the loftiest emotions aroused by material grandeur.

I was once walking in the broad daylight of a summer afternoon in the full possession of hasheesh delirium. For an hour the tremendous expansion of all visible things had been growing toward its height; it now reached it, and to the fullest extent I realized the infinity of space. Vistas no longer converged, sight met no barrier; the world was horizonless, for earth and sky stretched endlessly onward in parallel planes. Above me the heavens were terrible with the glory of a fathomless depth. I looked up, but my eyes, unopposed, every moment penetrated further and further into the immensity, and I turned them downward lest they should presently intrude into the fatal splendors of the Great Presence. Joy itself became terrific, for it seemed the ecstasy of a soul stretching its cords and waiting in intense silence to hear them snap and free it from the enthrallment of the body. Unable to bear visible objects, I shut my eyes. In one moment a colossal music filled the whole hemisphere above me, and I thrilled upward through its environment on visionless wings. It was not song, it was not instruments, but the inexpressible spirit of sublime sound -- like nothing I had ever heard-impossible to be symbolized; intense, yet not loud; the ideal of harmony, yet distinguishable into a multiplicity of exquisite parts. I opened my eyes, yet it still continued. I sought around me to detect some natural sound which might be exaggerated into such a semblance, but no, it was of unearthly generation, and it thrilled through the universe an inexplicable, a beautiful yet an awful symphony.

Suddenly my mind grew solemn with the consciousness of a quickened perception. I looked abroad on fields, and water, and sky, and read in them all a most startling meaning. I wondered how I had ever regarded them in the light of dead matter, at the furthest only *suggesting* lessons. They were now grand symbols of the sublimest spiritual truths, truths never before even feebly grasped, utterly unsuspected.

Like a map, the arcana of the universe lay bare before me. I saw how every created thing not only typifies but springs forth from some mighty spiritual law as its offsping, its necessary external development; not the mere clothing of the essence, but the essence incarnate.

Nor did the view stop here. While that music from horizon to horizon was still filling the concave above me, I became conscious of a numerical order which ran through it, and in marking this order I beheld it transferred from the music to every movement of the universe. Every sphere wheeled on in its orbit, every emotion of the soul rose and fell, every smallest moss and fungus germinated and grew, according to some peculiar property of numbers which severally governed them and which was most admirably typified by them in return. An exquisite harmony of proportion reigned through space, and I seemed to realize that the music which I heard was but this numerical harmony making itself objective through the development of a grand harmony of tones.

The vividness with which this conception revealed itself to me made it a thing terrible to bear alone. An unutterable ecstasy was carrying me away, but I dared not abandon myself to it. I was no seer who could look on the unveiling of such glories face to face.

An irrepressible yearning came over me to impart what I beheld, to share with another soul the weight of this colossal revelation. With this purpose I scrutinized the vision; I sought in it for some characteristic which might make it translatable to another mind. There was none! In absolute incommunicableness it stood apart, a thought, a system of thought which as yet had no symbol in spoken language.

For a time, how long, a hasheesh-eater alone can know, I was in an agony. I searched every pocket for my pencil and note-book, that I might at least set down some representative mark which would afterwards recall to me the lineaments of my apocalypse. They were not with me. Jutting into the water of the brook along which I wandered lay a broad flat stone. "Glory in the Highest!" I shouted exultingly, "I will at least grave on this tablet some hieroglyph of what I feel!" Tremblingly I sought for my knife. That, too, was gone! It was then that in a frensy I threw myself prostrate on the stone, and with my nails sought to make some memorial scratch upon it. Hard, hard as flint! In despair I stood up.

Suddenly there came a sense as of some invisible presence walking the dread paths of the vision with me, yet at a distance as if separated from my side by a long flow of time. Taking courage, I cried, "Who has ever been here before me, who in years past has shared with me this unutterable view?" In tones which linger in my soul to this day, a grand, audible voice responded, "Pythagoras!" In an instant I was calm. I heard the footsteps of that sublime sage echoing upward through the ages, and in celestial light I read my vision unterrified, since it had burst upon his sight before me. For years previous I had been perplexed with his mysterious philosophy. I saw in him an isolation from universal contemporary mind for which I could not account. When the Ionic school was at the height of its dominance, he stood forth alone, the originator of a system as distinct from it as the antipodes of mind. The doctrine of Thales was built up by the uncertain processes of an obscure logic, that of Pythagoras seemed informed by intuition. In his assertions there had always appeared to me a grave conviction of truth, a consciousness of sincerity, which gave them a great weight with me, though seeing them through the dim refracting medium of tradition and grasping their meaning imperfectly. I now saw the truths which he set forth, in their own light. I also saw, as to this day I firmly believe, the source whence their revelation flowed. Tell me not that from Phoenicia he received the wand at whose signal the cohorts of the spheres came trooping up before him in review, unveiling the eternal law and itineracy of their evolutions, and pouring on his spiritual ear that tremendous music to which they marched through space. No! During half a lifetime spent in Egypt and in India, both motherlands of this nepenths, doubt not that he quaffed its apocalyptic draught, and awoke, through its terrific quickening, into the consciousness of that ever-present and all-pervading harmony "which we hear not always, because the coarseness of the daily life hath dulled our ear." The dim penetralia of the Theban Memnonium, or the silent spice groves of the upper Indua may have been the gymnasium of his wrestling with the mighty revealer; a priest or a gymnospohist may have been the first to annoint him with the palæstric oil, but he conquered alone. On the strange intuitive characteristics of his system, on the spheral music, on the government of all created things and their development according to the laws of number, yes, on the very use of symbols which could alone have force to the esoteric disciple, (and a terrible significancy, indeed, has the simplest form, to a mind hasheesh-quickened to read its meaning) -- on all these is the legible stamp of the hasheesh inspiration.

It would be no hard task to prove, to a strong probability, at least, that the initiation into the Pythagorean mysteries and the progressive instruction that succeeded it, to a considerable extent, consisted in the employment, judiciously, if we may use the word, of hasheesh, as giving a critical and analytic power to the mind which enabled the neophyte to roll up the murk and mist from beclouded truths, till they stood distinctly seen in the splendor of their own harmonious beauty as an intuition.

One thing related of Pythagoras and his friends has seemed very striking to me. There is a legend that, as he was passing over a river, its waters called up to him, in the presence of his followers, "Hail, Pythagoras!" Frequently, while in the power of the hasheesh delirium, have I heard inanimate things sonorous with such voices. On every side they have saluted me; from rocks, and trees, and waters, and sky; in my happiness, filling me with intense exultation, as I heard them welcoming their master; in my agony, heaping nameless curses on my head, as I went away into an eternal exile from all sympathy. Of this tradition on Iamblichus, I feel an appreciation which almost convinces me that the voice of the river was, indeed, heard, though only in the quickened mind of some hasheesh-glorified esoteric. Again, it may be that the doctrine of the Metempsychosis was first communicated to Pythagoras by Theban priests; but the astonishing illustration, which hasheesh would contribute to this tenet, should not be overlooked in our attempt to assign its first suggestion and succeeding spread to their proper causes.

A modern critic, in defending the hypothesis, that Pythagoras was an impostor, has triumphantly asked, "Why did he assume the character of Apollo at the Olympic games? why did he boast that his soul had lived in former bodies, and that he had been first Acthalides, the son of Mercury, then Euphorbus, then Pyrrhus of Delos, and at last Pythagoras, but that he might more easily impose upon the credulity of an ignorant and superstitious people!" To us these facts seem rather an evidence of his sincerity. Had he made these assertions without proof, it is difficult to see how they would not have had a precisely contrary effect from that of paving the way to a more complete imposition upon the credulity of the people. Upon our hypothesis, it may be easily shown, not only how he could fully have believed these assertions himself, but, also, have given them a deep significance to the minds of his disciples.

Let us see. We will consider, for example, his assumption of the character of Phoebus at the Olympic games. Let us suppose that Pythagoras, animated with a desire of alluring to the study of his philosophy a choice and enthusiastic number out of that host who, along all the radii of the civilized world, had come up to the solemn festival at Elis, had, by the talisman of hasheesh, called to his aid the magic of a preternatural eloquence; that, while he addressed the throng whoin he had charmed into breathless attention by the weird brilliancy of his eyes, the unearthly imagery of his style, and the oracular insight of his thought, the grand impression flashed upon him from the very honor he was receiving, that he was the incarnation of some sublime deity. What wonder that he burst into the acknowledgment of his godship as a secret too majestic to be hoarded up; what wonder that this sudden revelation of himself, darting forth in burning words and amid such colossal surroundings, wend down with the accessories of time and place along the stream of perpetual tradition?

If I may illustrate great things by small, I well remember many hallucinations of my own which would be exactly parallel to such a fancy in the mind of Pythagoras. There is no impression more deeply stamped upon my past life than one of a walk along the brook which had frequently witnessed my wrestlings with the hasheesh-afreet, and which now beheld me, the immortal Zeus, descended among men to grant them the sublime benediction of renovated life. For this cause I had abandoned the serene seats of Olympus, the convocation of the gods, and the glory of an immortal kingship, while, by my side, Hermes trod the earth with radiant feet, the companion and dispenser of the beneficence of deity. Across lakes and seas, from continent to continent, we strode; the snows of Hæimus and the Himmalehs crunched beneath our sandals; our foreheads were bathed with the upper light, our breasts glowed with the exultant inspiration of the golden ether. Now resting on Chimborazo, I poured forth a majestic blessing upon all my creatures, and in an instant, with one omniscient glance, I beheld every human dwelling-place on the whole sphere irradiated with an unspeakable joy.

I saw the king rule more wisely, the laborer return from his toil to a happier home, the park grow green with an intenser culture, the harvest-field groan under the sheaves of a more prudent and prosperous husbandry; adown blue slopes came new and more populous flocks, led by unvexed and gladsome shepherds, a thousand healthy vineyards sprang up above their new-raised sunny terraces, every smallest heart glowed with an added thrill of exaltation, and the universal rebound of joy came pouring up into my own spirit with an intensity that lit my deity with rapture.

And this was only a poor hasheesh-eater, who, with his friend, walked out into the fields to enjoy his delirium among the beauties of a clear summer afternoon! What, then, of Pythagoras?

The tendency of the hasheesh-hallucination is almost always toward the supernatural or the sublimest forms of the natural. As the millennial Christ, I have put an end to all the jars of the world; by a word I have bound all humanity in etern alligaments of brotherhood; from the depths of the grand untrodden forest I have called the tiger, and with bloodless jaws he came mildly forth to fawn upon his king, a partaker in the universal amnesty. As Rienzi hurling fiery invective against the usurpations of Colonna, I have seen the broad space below the tribune grow populous with a multitude of intense faces, and within myself felt a sense of towering into sublimity, with the consciousness that it was my eloquence which swayed that great host with a storm of indignation, like the sirocco passing over reeds. Or, uplifted mightily by an irresistible impulse, I have risen through the ethereal infinitudes till I stood on the very cope of heaven, with the spheres below me. Suddenly, by an instantaneous revealing, I became aware of a mighty harp, which lay athwart the celestial hemisphere, and filled the whole sweep of vision before me. The lambent flame of myriad stars was burning in the azure spaces between its string, and glorious suns gemmed with unimaginable lustre all its colossal frame-work. While I stood overwhelmed by the visions, a voice spoke clearly from the depths of the surrounding ether, "Behold the harp of the universe!" Again I realized the typefaction of the same grand harmony of creation, which glorified the former vision to which I have referred; for every influence, from that which nerves the wing of Ithuriel down to the humblest force of growth, had there its beautiful and peculiar representative string. As yet the music slept, when the voice spake to me again -- "Stretch forth thine hand and wake the harmonies!" Trembling yet daring, I swept the harp, and in an instant all heaven thrilled with an unutterable music. My arm strangely lengthened, I grew bolder, and my hand took a wider range. The symphony grew more intense; overpowered, I ceased, and heard tremendous echoes coming back from the infinitudes. Again I smote the chords; but, unable to endure the sublimity of the sound, I sank into an ecstatic trance, and was thus borne off unconsciously to the portals of some new vision.

But, if I found the supernatural an element of happiness, I also found it many times an agent of most bitter pain. If I once exulted in the thought that I was the millennial Christ, so, also, through a long agony, have I felt myself the crucified. In dim horror, I perceived the nails piercing my hands and feet; but it was not that which seemed the burden of my suffering. Upon my head, in a tremendous and ever-thickening cloud, came slowly down the guilt of all the ages past, and all the world to come; by a dreadful quickening, I beheld every atrocity and nameless crime coming up from all time on lines that centred in myself. The thorns clung to my brow, and bloody drops stood like dew upon my hair, yet, these were not the instruments of my agony. I was withered like a leaf in the breath of a righteous vengeance. The curtain of a lurid blackness hung between me and heaven, mercy was dumb forever, and I bore the anger of Omnipotence alone. Out of a fiery distance, demon chants of triumphant blasphemy came surging on my ear, and whispers of ferocious wickedness ruffled the leaden air about my cross. How long I bore this vicarious agony, I have never known; hours are no measure of time in hasheesh. I only know that, during the whole period, I sat perfectly awake among objects which I recognized as familiar; friends were passing and repassing before me, yet, I sat in speechless horror, convinced that to supplicate their pity, to ask their help in the tortures of my dual existence, would be a demand that men in time should reach out and grasp one in eternity, that mortality should succor immortality.

In my experience of hasheesh there has been one pervading characteristic -- the conviction that, encumbered with a mortal body, I was suffering that which the untrammeled immortal soul could alone endure. The spirit seemed to be learning its franchise and, whether in joy or pain, shook the bars of flesh mightily, as if determined to escape from its cage. Many a time, in my sublimest ecstasy, have I asked myself, "Is this experience happiness or torture?" for soul and body gave different verdicts.

Hasheesh is no thing to be played with as a bauble. At its revealing, too-dread paths of spiritual life are flung open, too tremendous views disclosed of what the soul is capable of doing, and being, and suffering, for that soul to contemplate, till, relieved of the body, it can behold them alone.

Up to the time that I read in the September number of this Magazine the paper entitled "The Hasheesh-eater," I had long walked among the visions of "the weed of insanity." The recital given there seemed written out of my own soul. In outline and detail it was the counterpart of my own suffering. From that day, I shut the book of hasheesh experience, warned with a warning for which I cannot express myself sufficiently grateful. And now, as utterly escaped, I look back upon the world of visionary yet awful realities, and see the fountains of its Elysium and the flames of its Tartarus growing dimmer and still dimmer in the mists of distance, I hold the remembrance of its apocalypse as something which I shall behold again, when the spirit, looking no longer through windows of sense, shall realize its majesty unterrified, and face to face gaze on its infinite though now unseen surroundings.

Made in the USA
Lexington, KY
20 September 2012